WOZA AFRIKA!

WOZA AFRIKA!

An Anthology of South African Plays

SELECTED & EDITED BY
Duma Ndlovu

Foreword by Wole Soyinka
Preface by Amiri Baraka

GEORGE BRAZILLER
NEW YORK

Published in the United States in 1986
by George Braziller, Inc.

Forword © 1986 by Wole Soyinka. Preface © 1986 by Amiri Baraka.
Introduction © 1986 by Duma Ndlovu. *Woza Albert!* © copyright 1982
by Percy Mtwa, Mbongeni Ngema, and Barney Simon, published in
Great Britain by Methuen London Ltd. Gangsters © 1985 Maishe
Maponya, published in Great Britain by Polypton Press. *Children of Asazi*
© 1986 Matsemela Manaka. *Born in the RSA* © 1986 by Barney
Simon, Vanessa Cooke, Melanie Dobbs, Timmy Kwebulana, Neil
McCarthy, Geina Mhlophe, Fiona Ramsay, Thoko Ntshinga, Terry
Norton. *Asinamali!* © 1986 by Mbongeni Ngema. *Bopha!* © 1986 by
Percy Mtwa. "Ridovhakunda Ridovhavhulaya" © 1977 by Duma
Ndlovu, used by permission of the author.

For information address the publisher:
George Braziller, Inc.
60 Madison Avenue
New York, New York 10010

Library of Congress Cataloging-in-Publication Data

Woza Afrika!

   Contents: Woza Albert! / Mbongeni Ngema, Percy Mtwa, and
Barney Simon—Bopha / Percy Mtwa—Children of Asazi / Matsemela
Manaka—[etc.]
   1. South African drama (English)—20th century. 2. South African
drama (English)—Black authors. 3. Blacks—South Africa—Drama. I.
Ndlovu, Duma. PR9366.6.W69 1986   822   86–20762
ISBN 0-8076-1169-7
ISBN 0-8076-1170-0 (pbk.)

Book design by Levavi & Levavi
Printed in the United States of America
Second printing

for Mankosi,
    who brought me into this world, and
for Nonkululeko, my daughter
    who keeps me going.
for Gibson Kente, (Bra Gib)
    the father of black theater in South Africa
    who still remains in the shadows, and
for Mthuli kaShezi,
    who never lived to see the fruits of the seeds
    but mostly,
for Bantu Biko (Bra Steve),
    the father of us all.

SONQOBA SIMUNYE

TABLE OF CONTENTS

FOREWORD

The torture and death of Steve Biko, the massacres of Sharpeville and Soweto, internecine wars at Crossroads ignited and fueled by a diabolical regime, death and torture in hidden cells. An entire generation of schoolchildren forced to abandon childhood, and innocence . . . and the heroic faces also, rising above the stench of evil and destruction . . . the Father Huddlestons, the Ruth Firsts, the Nelson Mandelas indomitable even in seemingly endless captivity . . . these are the images of reality that flood the mind by the mere fact of contemporary South African theater. Such is the overwhelming presence in world consciousness today of this irrational denial of humanity to millions, the willful abrogation of identity, the staggering scale of repression that every statement is constantly dwarfed by the images it provokes. The artistic effort to come to terms with any situation of tragic horror, borrowing from an environment whose future seems permanently overcast, presents the mind with that paradox born of the fact that the act of creating is firstly an act of affirmation, however stubbornly the material of existence denies it. Nowhere is this more easily remarked than in the emergence in the theater of plays such as *Sizwe Banzi Is Dead*, or the more recent *Woza Albert!* which I had the fortune to see when it was first presented in London. Two black actors on an empty stage with minimal props . . . gradually vignettes of South African urban life develop, poignant and hilarious, filling the stage with villains, heroes and clowns, understating the sheer will and defiance that makes survival possible in an inhuman cul–de–sac. *Woza Albert!* creates a "theater of poverty" at its most affirmative, a reflection of the cultural reality that brought it into being, yet transcends its stranglehold on the human spirit.

The many techniques of attempting to surmount the tyranny of reality over art in inhuman systems like Apartheid are constantly fascinating. *Born in the RSA* is another remarkable contribution in that direction. The deadly drama enacted daily in the streets and suburbs of South Africa being in itself "total theater," permitting no audience, a drama whose participants play out their roles with predictable inevitability, this theater necessarily invites deliberate distancing when the attempt is made to shift its *locus* to a "voyeuristic" context. *Born in the RSA* adopts a deceptively dispassionate, clinical approach to follow the lives of a number of individuals who, like all others in that unfortunate land, are trapped in the messy web Apartheid spins from official lies, denials and contradictions.

What gives birth to the torturer, to the accomplice or collaborator? What circumstances produce the traitor? We know of course that it is precisely the same situation that produces the victim, the same circumstances that produce the heroic resister. Psychological explanations are too imprecise to be of help and the socioeconomic facts of life are often the same for opposing role–players. The "docu–drama" technique chooses therefore to confront us with the constant—the situation itself, its monstrosity, leaving us to be appalled anew by its capacity to destroy, to corrupt and defile human relationships. The torturer in *Gangsters* is the same as we encounter in *Born in the RSA*, dutiful men carrying out their tasks in the defense of "the law." The collaborators easily mouth the compulsion of economic realities; the realities of resistance constitute an alien terrain which menaces them and justifies even acts outside the law to protect the law.

"Hanged himself from his cell-window . . . fell to his death from a seventh–story floor trying to escape interrogation . . . banged his head forcefully against the wall and suffered brain damage" . . . the road to each individual Calvary is covered in such cynical, official formulas. The poet Rasecheba in *Gangsters* finds that he cannot provide even his own epitaph; the final word is the torturer's, the murderer's, the state's.

But only for now. For if there is one truth in common to the statements provided by these plays, it is the fact that the security which is sought by the rampages of the bulldozer, the raids of the "hippo," and the electric button of the torturer is contradicted by the very methods by which that security is sought. This truth becomes abundantly manifest by the fatal drama of the shantytowns, the white streets of Johannesburg, the mines and shopping centers. Much sooner than later, the last word will revert to the people, and the Rasechebas of the struggle will inscribe the epitaph of Apartheid.

Wole Soyinka

PREFACE

In his heavy work *Marxism and Poetry* George Thomson says that drama is a form that rises to its most effective expression during periods of sharp social transformation.

In the U.S. there are two particularly productive periods of African–American drama: the Harlem Renaissance of the 1920s, reflecting the rising tide of Black national consciousness and open political struggle (Marcus Garvey, African Blood Brotherhood, W.E.B. DuBois), which produced a great playwright like Langston Hughes; and the Black Theater Movement, part of the Black Arts Movement during the Civil Rights–Black Liberation '60s and '70s. Lorraine Hansberry, James Baldwin, Milner, Bullins, and myself come out of that.

Today, the most universally significant struggle for social transformation is focused in South Africa. So significant because it is here that the last vestiges of open colonialism still exist. The continuation of South African white supremacy–based fascism ties the people of the world and our societies internationally to an all but vanished primitive and monstrous form of social deviation, racial slavery.

This is the reason the plays in *Woza Afrika!* exist as they do, in both form and content. They issue from a blood–filled society staggering toward revolution and social transformation.

Up to now, for the most part, we have had no broad presentation of the art of the Black South African majority. Instead we have been steadily exposed to the voices of white liberal South African authors in literature and the theater.

But in the last year, as the intensity of black mass struggle against the fascists has sharpened and they in turn have responded with their emergency and super double–emergency emergency decrees, we have reached a point where not only has the whole world grown painfully more aware of what is happening in South Africa, but the day-to-day coverage of the struggles between oppressed and oppressor have served to demonstrate the real meaning of the words "civilized" and "uncivilized."

This, in essence, is what the plays in this book do, make us see more clearly, clarify and redefine. The struggle's intensification made it necessary to unveil the people themselves, their own voices and the tearful accents of their personal tragedies—brought together to make national and international tragedy.

The lives that *Bopha!* or *Gangsters* or *Woza Albert!* speak to cannot really be stated directly by the well–meaning white South African authors. The fact that their's has been heretofore the only voice out of South Africa points to the deep continuity of western chauvinism, even while ostensibly fighting racial chauvinism!

As the American slave narratives told of the underside of a prosperous slave society, revealed the evil sick oppressive social relations of the whole system in their descriptions of slavery, so does this group of plays, based much on improvisation and broad mimicry of facts that are infinitely more terrifying, expose the tragic hell of white supremacist colonialism. South Africa as a world of jails and racist madness, as with some vanished civilization or some futuristic one. It is the world as the slaves live in it. Through their eyes and from their mouths. Rooted in the living lives of South African people.

These plays carry a contemporary style, spare, symbolic, ironic, sharp and bitterly funny. At times Apartheid *is* bizarre, we find out—*is* funny or makes you laugh out loud that we are still faced with such a "civilization."

Yet there is also a genuine *comedy*, a hatchet–edged satire, the development of characters out of the regime, apartheid specimens (black and white) whose humor is painful only because it is true.

Bopha! (Arrest!) is like some rhythmic catch phrase of a

horrible game! The foghorn of consequences so brutal, to speak of it without this distance is to rage and seek to kill the thing that maintains it. Yet it can be danced to and sung. "Fun" can be made of it! At the same time not only is there always carried with these concerns the deep rumble of a real and tragic world but a pit of human despair so dark and filled with sickness, loss, frustration, unregenerate animalism, that even what passes as light–hearted is by its own accent and implications not light at all.

Maponya's *Gangsters* is actually "tender" in the sense of its raising of idealism as a foil for opportunism, but its echo of the concerns of *Bopha!* is even deeper, its "humor" like a blue sky with breathless white clouds, yet it is an "illusion," we see space and water vapor.

We are also made aware of the cultural structure of the aesthetic. There must be song, dance, "Boot Dance," Zulu Dance, the newer township forms and music. There is a broad use of mime and multiple characterizations.

It is the kind of spirited improvisation of revolutionary periods. As Percy Mtwa has said, "We don't have to make up stories." Yet realism to be *critical* must assess as well as reflect, be both an analysis of society and a reflection of its multi forms and class caste stock characters—villains and fools and poets and revolutionaries and a whole battery of living images of the masses of people in their terrifying crazy absolutely *jive* enslavement.

Barney Simon's *Born in the RSA*, which echoes Bruce Springsteen's populist declaration, is the result of improvisation in the RSA's only integrated theater. It speaks of the greys between the black and white, what is happening in the world of "meanwhile."

But in spite of the poignance and purposeful self-evaluation that the works carry, they also reveal the joy of bearing witness. We are always *touched* and forced to face humanity. Listening to Manaka speak recently at New York University, one could hear the pain and intelligence, and above all the will to live. To triumph, despite a world controlled by actual monsters.

Most of the plays here come out of black township oriented theater companies—Committed Artists, Earth Players, Soyikwa Cultural Theater, Bahumutsi. The playwrights are young and write with the quick precision of bards striding purposefully through flames. *Woza Afrika!* introduces a new group of playwrights and their important works. It also introduces, for many people, perhaps the foremost human tragedy in our comtemporary world. Reality sets the works aflame, the writers (some of whom are also the actors) bear their torches, which give heat as well as light.

Amiri Baraka
Newark, August 1986

ACKNOWLEDGEMENTS:

The plays in this anthology, with the exception of *WOZA ALBERT!*, were performed at the WOZA AFRIKA! Festival at Lincoln Center Theater in New York September–October 1986.

I have had great pleasure in working with the plays. I have to take responsibility for whatever misrepresentation or misinterpretation has occurred. I want to say also that if any exists, none was intended.

In attempting to interpret certain words, I found it impossible, at times, to attach literal translations and resorted to contextual meanings. The help of Letticia Diescho, a Capetonian presently furthering her medical studies at Columbia University, was enlisted for the more complicated Afrikaans terms. To her I am forever grateful.

There were certain key players in the creation of both the festival and this anthology. There were those in the forefront and those whose contributions were in silent ways. I want to thank them all.

Matsemela Manaka thought I would be the perfect person to do this. I hope I did not disappoint him and want to thank him first and foremost. Mbongeni Ngema has been very supportive throughout and has been a friend and a brother, thanx Zuluboy. I want to thank all of the playwrights for trusting me with their plays, especially since I had to use, in most cases, scripts that were either incomplete or were non–existent. I hope I have handled their precious work well. Rick Menell and Miles Rubin have spent sleepless nights working to support the arts in South Africa. Well done guys, this is only the beginning! Mannie Manim and his staff at the Market Theatre helped to bring most of the material to the United States. Victor Palmieri, Bernard Gersten, Gregory Mosher and the staff at Lincoln Center were extremely supportive. Thank you folks. Wole Soyinka and Amiri Baraka agreed, at very short notice, to contribute to this effort. Thank you brothers! I thank Jill Pilgrim for most of the legal work and Barbara Janowitz for being there. I want to thank my U.S. mother, Ida Wood, for her continued support over the years, and Makhosazana for keeping up with my crazy work schedule. But above all, I wish to thank my ancestors for their guidance and protection. AZANIA WILL BE FREE!

—SONQOBA SIMUNYE—

INTRODUCTION

In years to come, this period will be credited with the emergence of Black South African theater, not because there has not been any such theater before, but because it is only recently that it has had the opportunity to be seen and to receive the international attention that it has always deserved.

Long before Athol Fugard brought to America his passionate plays, which deal largely with whites' reactions to South Africa's racial problems, there had been fiery theater taking place in the townships. Long before the musical epic *King Kong* introduced Mirriam Makeba to international audiences, there had been lively theater in the townships. For as long as there had been Black townships in South Africa, this theater existed as an extension of the oral tradition that is so much a part of the African way of life. Transported to the cities when the men had migrated to the "gold spots," looking for work, just like the slaves had transported their culture in their forced sojourns to the other side of the seas, this theater maintained its most basic African elements. It would be enhanced later when the women followed the men to the cities and new societies were created. In the city dwellers' minds there remained vivid images of grandmothers and grandfathers telling their stories to families by the fireside. This was theater at its most natural, its most creative. This is the trend that has influenced our drama and has set it apart from western theater.

In his well–researched book *Theater and Cultural Struggle*

in South Africa, Robert Kavanagh rightfully traces township theater to the early twenties, to Esau Mthethwa and his Lucky Stars performing troupe. He goes back a little further, although not far back enough (lack of documented data, he says), and links this theater to the story–telling tradition of the early African village communities before the coming of the whites into South Africa—so much for the notion of the Europeans having brought theater (and civilization) to the African continent.

Perhaps one strong reason why this theater never made a significant impact outside its own communities was that its participants never really looked at it as an activity that had monetary value, to be peddled and sold. Theater was more community–oriented and therefore not regarded as a totally separate and commercial entity. It was a way of passing on information from one generation to another, or, in the case of township theater, a way of trying to forget the frustrations of life in South Africa. Therefore, of necessity, it was only after whites had shown interest in commercializing this theater, after they had "discovered" a potential for overseas markets, that there was a need for a new approach.

In the late fifties some musicians and other performers were brought together by a group of impresarios and the musical *King Kong* was born; the play later toured England and the United States. Back in South Africa, efforts to duplicate the "success" of *King Kong* were attempted. Athol Fugard collaborated with a few black intellectuals on *No Good Friday*. A barrage of plays either written by white producers or co–written with some of the black artists of the time followed. But these productions were aimed largely at the fairly liberal English–speaking white audiences who were "discovering" the beauty of African music and wanted to explore their "discoveries" a little further in theatrical ventures.

Gibson Kente, now widely regarded as the "father of theater in South Africa," emerged during this period. His first musical, *Manana the Jazz Prophet*, had all the makings of township theater and was written for that audience. There was, therefore, no attempt to glamorize any aspect of township life. The dance rhythms and movements in the play were not meaningless gyrations that formed the producer's image of what African dance was about, they sprang from the actors' own experiences and were something that both actors and audience could relate to.

Kente's play was performed in the townships and became very successful. In addition, the Black music scene was bubbling with talent at that time, a lot of groups were coming out of the townships, and the play provided an outlet for those performers. A subsequent Kente musical became even more successful. *Sikalo* took a sharp look at the gangster movement in that period, known to many South Africans as the "Msomi era" after a notorious gang–leader and his followers. Rival gangs, influenced by American Mafia-movies, were rampant in black townships, hard hit by unemployment and the ills that descended upon peri–ghettoes. Athol Fugard (in the plays *Nongogo* and *No Good Friday*), Alan Paton (in *Sponono* and *Mkhumbane*), and other white writers had also attempted to document this era, but with little success. Even though these plays were written in collaboration with black actors and other black writers, they were not reaching the townships, the very audience they sought to portray. In contrast, Kente's *Sikalo* took all the realities of township living and brought them to the people in a comedic fashion that attracted large audiences. By the end of the sixties, with plays like *Lifa*, *Zwi*, *Sikalo Two*, and *Too Late*, Kente had demonstrated beyond argument that he was the biggest force in the country's theater, and he had achieved his success without having to patronize the white theater audience in the cities. The trend had been set and most of the productions that mushroomed all over the country tried to combine the Kente ingredients, making them clones of the Kente theater, albeit none as successful.

But in the seventies, the birth of the Black Consciousness Movement brought new demands to cultural expression. Mthuli kaShezi, one of the founders of the movement and its cultural "ambassador," started the People's Experimental Theater and through it spread the notion that any cultural expression should reflect a people's conditions. Kente and other playwrights came under heavy attack for their "light–hearted" and comedy–filled plays.

In 1973 Kente responded to this criticism with the political epic *How Long?* The play depicted the abhorrent pass laws and the havoc they created in the Black family and community. At a time when a new kind of consciousness was defining a new way of life, this play enjoyed great success. Kente attempted to make a film version and had raised most of the money from the Black community. In June 1976, the film was almost finished when the government banned *How Long?* and Kente was detained. He was kept in prison under the country's security laws and released six months later without being charged for any crime. The detention seems to have slowed him down considerably—after that, while at the same time talking about the problems within the townships, he wrote only apolitical musicals that made an effort not to offend the government.

In Port Elizabeth (Ebhayi) in 1974, members of the Serpent Players collaborated with Athol Fugard and created two important plays, *Sizwe Bansi Is Dead* and *The Island*, performed largely in white theaters where they received critical acclaim. Since the white theater–going audience had missed all the Kente plays (in South Africa most whites are oblivious to what goes on in the townships) this was for them an introduction to "Black theater." But the sad irony for John Kani and Winston Ntshona, the co–creators and the two actors in both plays, was that their efforts were confined to the cities and they remained virtually unknown in the townships. They went on to present their work in the United States on Broadway, where in 1976 they won Tony awards for Best Featured Actors in a play. The presentational style of the two plays was striking and unique. Using mime and the story–telling tradition so common in most African theater, they had introduced to the white world a different kind of theater. Here were two black men, on an almost–bare stage, with scant costumes, bringing to life a whole world of images devised from their experiences as victims of a government that made them foreigners in their own land. Their plays were highly political, but the fact that they performed largely in white theaters, which the government seldom invaded, gave them a protection they would not have had if they had based their works in the townships. They did run into problems when they attempted to perform their plays in Ciskei, one of the "homelands" not very far from their hometown, where they were promptly arrested and thrown behind bars. They were released after an international outcry protesting their detention.

It is doubtful that Kani and Ntshona had much impact in the townships with their two—man plays in the early seventies. Their plays introduced agitprop to South African audiences who looked to theater for musical entertainment. Most township theater—goers were families who went to the theater to share in an event, music, laughter, joy, exuberance, and sorrow. Kente's milder plays provided all these things in one evening with huge casts that included dancers, singers, and "township characters" that brought his audience to tears with laughter and sadness. Neither Kani nor Ntshona wrote another play after *Sizwe Bansi Is Dead* and *The Island*, and this has limited their influence in Black theater circles to a very small clique. Kente continued to blaze the township trails with new plays, but the impact that *How Long?* had made was hard to duplicate. The press was forever critical of his new pieces which "lacked the depth and strength" that had been evident in *How Long?* But in terms of developing and providing work for new actors, "Bra Gib," as Kente is affectionately called in the townships, was still the "biggest game" in town.

In 1979, the actors Mbongeni Ngema and Percy Mtwa were touring with a Kente production, *Mama and the Load*, when they decided to collaborate on a play of their own. "We were on a bus travelling to a show when we suddenly got into a discussion about the 'second coming of Jesus'," Mbongeni has said. "What if Jesus decided to come back to South Africa, with its present political confusion?" asked Mtwa. They decided to provide their own answers in the stage production *Woza Albert!* They left Kente and spent a year writing and rehearsing in kitchens, bedrooms, cars, buses, trains, backyards, wherever they found convenient. They lived in other people's homes without money to feed themselves, let alone finance the production, a common story with township theater. It was only after they approached the Market Theater in Johannesburg, a multi—racial group, and enlisted the help of Barney Simon as director that they found a financial pipeline that supported the final stages in the creation of their work. Simon suggested key inclusions (and exclusions) in Ngema and Mtwa's "rough work" and then became a co-writer. *Woza Albert!* went on to become the biggest theatrical event in South Africa, Black or white. It embarked on a five–year overseas tour and achieved unprecedented success. In New York Ngema and Mtwa performed in Harlem and off–Broadway and won the prestigious Obie Award. But most importantly, they performed in the townships of South Africa, as well as the cities, whenever they were in the country and were thus accessible to a much wider audience.

Woza Albert! introduced a new kind of theater, not only in its popularity but also because the play fused excellent theatrical skills with an urgent political message. Here again the oral tradition was being elevated into a higher art form. But there were new elements as well: abundant energy and a rhythm that gave the play a strong musical feeling, something that Kani and Ntshona had lacked. *Woza Albert!* had been created *for* the townships. As part of the Kente school, Ngema and Mtwa understood the demands of township audiences, who became noisy or walked out during a performance if they were not impressed. But by this time the country was more prepared for their kind of agitprop. The formation of the Medupe Writers Association and similar cultural groups encouraged new, younger writers to move away from big musicals and write plays with fewer characters. The political tide in the country also provided a larger audience for more direct and forceful political messages. The uprisings of 1976, in which hundreds of people were killed in Soweto, had had a lasting effect. Ngema and Mtwa had written their stories not to inform outsiders about the goings–on in the townships, but to document and share a history, as the Africans of old had done. Kente's influence was still felt, but there was also the strong presence of "Black consciousness," reflecting the prevalent trend in the townships.

After *Woza Albert!*, Ngema wrote a new play, *Asinamali!* Mtwa created *Bopha!* Both plays indicate how the two had grown and developed since their collaborative piece. *Asinamali!* was written for Ngema's Committed Artists, a company he formed after coming back from a U.S. tour where he had been exposed to Louis Valdez' El Teatro Campesino and was greatly moved. Ngema used a pot-pourri of ideas, as well as his own theatrical techniques and brought together more than thirty youngsters with a love for culture and the arts. A rent strike in Lamontville township in 1983, not far from Ngema's home in Umlazi, Durban, provided the idea for the play. The strike leader, Msizi Dube, was killed and the slogan he had devised and led the people with echoed all over the townships: "ASINIMALI!"—"we have no money and cannot afford high rents." Ngema selected five members of the Committed Artists and developed them into "human machines," assuming a variety of strenuous and unusual positions. Their performances and portrayals were extremely strong and reflected Ngema's ability to train and develop actors.

Mtwa, whose father had been a policeman, had always been intrigued by the idea of Black policemen arresting their own people. His play *Bopha!* concerns a policeman whose life revolves around his work, a son who is a radical student, and a brother who is not qualified to be in Johannesburg because his passbook is not "in order." "Brother or no brother, BOPHA!"—"ARREST HIM!"—says a white police officer when brother confronts brother in the rough township streets. *Bopha!* was written for The Earth Players, founded by Ngema and Mtwa when they were creating *Woza Albert!* The company had been overshadowed by the Market Theater after the Market had assumed production of *Woza Albert!*, and they received little recognition. Mtwa returned to his hometown of Daveyton, recruited new actors, and continued with the company name.

Bopha! and *Asinamali!* draw strongly on the life of the townships in present–day South Africa at a time when soldiers roam the streets. The two plays illustrate different dimensions of black life yet both offer a vision of hope. This is a key difference from work that comes from white South African writers, work which has a tendency to "throw its arms up in the air" and sound a note of hopelessness. These plays give direction, ask questions, provide answers, and tell us, yes, there will be change in the country, sooner than most people think. The exuberance of *Asinamali!*, as names of heroes past and present are intoned in a "roll-call" fashion at the end of the play, is in itself judgment that these heroes did not die or languish in jails in vain. The voice of the young man from behind prison bars at the end of *Bopha!*, imploring his father to "change before it is too late," warning him of the tide that is sweeping the townships, tells us that the young are not only bent on destroying those who stand between them and their goal of achieving freedom for their country, they are the bearers of light into a situation which is in desperate need.

Matsemela Manaka and Maishe Maponya, represented here by *Gangsters* and *Children of Asazi*, come out of a different tradition. Both playwrights began writing after the 1976 uprisings in Soweto and were part of the youth cultural movement that swelled all over the country, infused with a new sense of purpose. They had never belonged to the Kente "school," and in fact had been critical of Kente's "soft" plays.

Matsemela Manaka wrote his first play, *The Horn*, in 1977. A year later, he wrote the play that brought him both national and international attention. *Egoli–The City of Gold* was the story of a family broken by the migrant labor system. The three-character play traces the life of a rural family in which the father moves to the city of gold, Eboli (Johannesburg), to work to support his family. He never returns, or even writes, and his son soon follows, leaving behind a lone woman to fend for herself in a desolate land. The play examines the lives of Black men as they labor in the mines and ends with chained workers breaking free and declaring imminent independence. The play went on a limited tour of Europe and was voted Play of the Year in London. Manaka's subsequent plays outline a similar story, starting with a united family in the rural areas, the men then leaving to seek the means to support their families and being swallowed up by the big city. Manaka won the Edinburgh Festival Fringe First Award in 1983 with two one-act plays, *Pula* and *Imbumba*. Back in the townships, Manaka had the usual problems producing his plays, but his pride and politics prevented him from seeking refuge in theater companies in the city. He founded the Soyikwa Institute of African Theater to encourage theater in the townships, and his work at the Funda Arts Center, an arts education institution in Soweto, has given him a base and a place to rehearse and develop new works.

Maishe Maponya's first play, *Peace and Forgive*, premiered in Soweto in 1977. *Hungry Earth*, a largely experimental piece that documents the destruction of the land by industrialization and the coming of the white man, written in 1978, won him significant recognition both in and outside of South Africa. *Umongikazi* followed in 1982 and *Dirty Work* and *Gangsters* (the latter included here) were written in 1984. Maponya is one of the few township playwrights who often does not use music in his plays, and with *Dirty Work* and *Gangsters* he became the first Black playwright of note to write parts for and direct white characters. Until then, as is still usually the case, Black playwrights use Black actors, and all sorts of props, to portray white roles. Both plays examine the inside of a police institution. In *Dirty Work*, the lone white policeman tries to convince his invisible audience that the country's situation is stable. In *Gangsters*, a Black policeman, at the instruction of his white superior, tortures a Black poet to death. The play is an eerie glimpse of what goes on in the darkness of the prison cells where detainees have been killed at the hands of the police. The two plays are slow-paced but effective.

Born in the RSA is the only play in this volume to come from a theatrical institution (a home with four walls). The Market Theater, in the heart of Johannesburg, was founded in 1976 by artistic director Barney Simon and executive director Mannie Manim. The two men, both of whom had worked extensively with black as well as white theater groups, opened their theater to mixed audiences and presented multiracial casts at a time when such a practice was illegal. (The government has since made a number of concessions that make it possible for certain institutions to have mixed audiences, but these changes are dismissed by the black population.) The Market continues to encourage work in defiance of the laws of South Africa, and Simon, in some cases collaborating with the casts, developed a number of plays that make anti-apartheid statements in a manner slightly different from the township theater. *Born in the RSA* grew out of that climate. Because of the less limited resources, in comparison with Black theater groups, it took the seven-member cast of *RSA* a little over a month to research and rehearse the material that became the play, which is presented in a "docu-drama" fashion. The political nature of the play sets it apart from most theater that comes out of the cities, created by white directors for white audiences.

   These works underline part of the history of South African theater. It is unfortunate that ours is a country where one can never seem to escape describing work, art, theater, dance, religion, any aspect of life in black and white. But maybe this tension is the very reason that South African art is as dynamic as it is. The five playwrights in this volume, all of whom are an important part of the "new theater" in South Africa, merit serious attention. But much more research could be done—there are many different facets of South African theater and scores of playwrights who struggle every day to make ends meet. Most of them will never be able to complete their work because of a lack of resources and only a few will manage to stage their plays. I hope that this volume will inspire and encourage not only these artists but also greater interest in this extremely vital theater.

—SINQOBA SIMUNYE—

Dumakude kaNdlovu
New York, August 1986

WOZA
ALBERT!

Percy Mtwa, Mbongeni Ngema,
Barney Simon

In 1979, while touring with one of Gibson Kente's plays, Percy Mtwa, the lead singer and dancer in the play, and Mbongeni Ngema, the lead actor, conceived an idea for a new play of their own. They were talking about the "second coming of Jesus." As they related the idea to South Africa and its racial problems, the two actors wondered what would happen if Jesus returned and "landed" in South Africa today. How would blacks receive him? What would their expectations be? What questions and deeds would they ask of him? How would the white government react? The idea of putting these questions into a stage production and presenting them in a dramatic form resulted in their award–winning play, *Woza Albert!*

Kente's production, *Mama and the Load*, in which Mtwa and Ngema were touring, had been very successful. It had provided the two men with security and assured them of employment until the tour was over—in the case of Kente's plays, two years at the very least. Their decision to leave Kente and work on a new play when they had neither financial support nor professional production experience, was a big risk, but their dedication and confidence in their work carried them through.

The initial rehearsals took them to the Transkei, hundreds of miles from their homes, where a group of black business-people had promised to support their venture. The Transkei is one of the areas that the South African government has granted nominal "independence" to, although no other country recognizes these "sovereign nations" and the majority of the black population inside them rejects them. The actors had been in rehearsal for three months when the "government" of the Transkei pounced on them, detained them, and kept them in solitary confinement for thirty days. Ngema and Mtwa had lost their support in the Transkei, and upon their release, under a deportation order, they returned to Soweto.

In Soweto, they carried on with the development of their piece, staying in other people's homes. "We were not just rehearsing a piece of work that would be ready after a few months," Ngema explains. "We were creating something different, we needed all that time to work on it until we were satisfied." They continued their efforts until ultimately Vusi Magudulela, another Black businessman, came to their rescue, offering to pay them thirty South African rands a week (about ten U.S. dollars) while they rehearsed. "This was very gracious of him and it came in handy," Mtwa says. "But we still needed a lot of things—to produce the play the way we wanted to we needed a lot of money and had no idea how we were going to raise it."

After a year of rehearsals, the two invited a group of black and white directors to see a run–through of the play. Barney Simon, of the Market Theater in Johannesburg, was greatly impressed and he came on board as the director. He worked with the two actors on what he called a "rough and raw idea" and when it was decided that the play was ready, Ngema and Mtwa agreed to share the writing credit with Simon. The Market Theater provided the play with the much–needed financial support and *Woza Albert!* opened at the Market to critical acclaim. *Woza Albert!* was taken on a tour of Europe and the United States and became, over a stretch of time, the most successful play to come out of South Africa. The play won the Edinburgh Fringe First Award in 1982 and the actors presented the award to Vusi Magudulela, who had supported their efforts in Soweto, as a gesture of appreciation. *Woza Albert!* has won more than twenty awards worldwide.

Woza Albert!, written by Percy Mtwa, Mbongeni Ngema, and Barney Simon, was first performed in Johannesburg in 1980.

WOZA ALBERT!
Percy Mtwa, Mbongeni Ngema, Barney Simon

CHARACTERS

PERCY MTWA
MBONGENI NGEMA

> *The stage is lit by the house-lights. The set consists of two up-ended tea-chests side by side about center stage. Further upstage an old wooden plank, about ten feet long, is suspended horizontally on old ropes. From nails in the plank hang the ragged clothes that the actors will use for their transformations. The actors wear grey track-suit bottoms and running shoes. They are bare-chested. Around each actor's neck is a piece of elastic, tied to which is half a squash ball painted pink —a clown's nose, to be placed over his own nose when he plays a white man.*

SCENE ONE

> *The actors enter and take their positions quickly, simply. Mbongeni sits on the tea-chests at the point they meet in the middle. Percy squats between his legs. As they create their totem, the house-lights dim to blackout.*

> *On the first note of their music, overhead lights come on, sculpting them. They become an instrumental jazz band, using only their bodies and their mouths — double bass, saxophone, flute, drums, bongos, trumpet etc. At the climax of their performance, they transform into audience, applauding wildly.*

Percy stands, disappears behind the clothes rail. Mbongeni goes on applauding. Percy reappears wearing his pink nose and a policeman's cap. He is applauding patronisingly. Mbongeni stares at him, stops applauding.

PERCY: Hey! Beautiful audience, hey? Beautiful musician, né? Okay, now let us see how beautiful his pass book is! (*To appalled Mbongeni:*) Your pass!

MBONGENI (*playing for time*): Excuse my boss, excuse? What?

PERCY (*smugly, to audience with his back to Mbongeni*): Okay, I'll start again. You know you're a black man, don't you?

MBONGENI: Yes, my boss.

PERCY: And you live here in South Africa?

MBONGENI (*attempting to sidle off-stage behind Percy's back*): Yes, my boss.

PERCY: So you know that you must always carry your pass.

MBONGENI: Yes, my boss.

PERCY: Okay, now what happens if you don't have your pass?

MBONGENI: I go to jail, my boss.

PERCY: And what happens if your pass is not in order?

MBONGENI (*nearly off-stage*): I go to jail, my boss.

PERCY (*wheels on Mbongeni*): H-E-E-EY! Your pass!!!

MBONGENI (*effusively*): OOOOhhh, my pass, my constable! (*Moves to Percy, holding out his pass.*) Here's my pass my lieutenant.

PERCY: Okay, now let's have a look. (*Examines the pass.*) Where do you work?

MBONGENI: I work here, my Captain.

PERCY: You work here? If you worked here your passbook would be written 'Market Theatre, Johannesburg'. But

look, it is written 'Kentucky Southern Fried'. Is this
Kentucky Southern Fried? And look at the date. It tells
me you haven't worked in four years. This is vagrancy,
you're unemployed. (*To audience:*) Ja, this is what I
call 'loafer-skap!'

MBONGENI: No, my Colonel, I am a guitarist, I've been
playing music for five years, my boss.

PERCY: Hey, you lie, you fuckin' entertainer!

MBONGENI: It's true, it's true, my boss.

PERCY: Can you show me where it is written 'musician'?
Hey? Where's a guitar? Where's a guitar? Where's a
guitar?

MBONGENI: Ag, nee—my Brigadier, I am self-employed!

PERCY: Self-employed? (*Chuckling collusively to audience:*)
Hell, but these kaffirs can lie, hey?

MBONGENI: Maar, dis die waarheid, but it is true—my
General!

PERCY: You know where you should be?

MBONGENI: No, my boss.

PERCY: You should be in prison!

MBONGENI: No, my boss.

PERCY: And when you come out of prison, do you know
where you should go?

MBONGENI: No, my boss.

PERCY: Back to the bush with the baboons. That's where
you belong! Kom hierso! Section 29. (*To audience,
pleasantly:*) Do you know about Section 29? That's a
nice little law specially made for loafers like him. And
I've got a nice little place waiting for him in Modder-B
Prison. Kom jong! (*Pulls Mbongeni by his track-suit.*)

MBONGENI (*aside*): Shit!

PERCY (*threatening*): What did you say? Wat het jy gesê?

MBONGENI: Nothing—my President!

The policeman (Percy) chases the musician (Mbongeni) behind the clothes-rail.

SCENE TWO

Enter both actors with prison blankets wrapped around their shoulders. Both are singing a prison song, a prisoner's fantasy of his woman's longing for him:

SONG :   Ha-ja-ka-rumba
            Ha-ja-karumba
(*Solo*)   Bath'uyeza—uyez'uyezana?
            Bath'uyeza—uyez'uyezana?
            Kuthima ngizule kodwa mangicabanga
            Yini s'thandwa sithando sami ye—

(*Chorus*) Hajakarumba—hajakarumba.
            Hajakarumba—hajakarumba.
            [They say he is coming. Is he really coming?
            I am mad when I think of it.
            Come back my love, oh my love.]

Under the song, Mbongeni gives orders:

MBONGENI: Modder-B Prison . . . prisoners—line up! Body Inspection. Hey wena cell number 16. Inspection cell number 16. Awusafuni na? Awusafunukuvula vula hey wena wendoda. Vul'ingqwza sisbone. [Hey you, cell number 16. Inspection cell number 16. Are you hiding anything? Don't you want to show what is hidden— come on you men—show me your arses!] Prisoners inspection!

BOTH (*doing 'Towsa' dance, revealing empty orifices and armpits*): Ready for body inspection, my Basie! Blankets clear, my Basie! No tobacco! No money! No watch! My Basie! Mouth clear! Ears clear! (*Open mouths wide:*) Hooo! Hooo! (*Pull ear-lobes:*) Haaa! Haaa! My Basie!

PERCY: Hands up!

BOTH (*raise arms*): Arms clear, my Basie! (*Raise legs:*) Everything clear, my Basie! Also arse, my Basie!

MBONGENI: Inspection! (*They pull down their trousers, display bare backsides.*) See nothing hidden, my Basie! Prisoners! Lights out! (*Lights dim.*)

BOTH (*lying on the floor covering themselves with blankets*): Goodnight, Basie, goodnight. Dankie Baba, dankie. Beautiful arse, my Baba. Nothing hidden, my Basie.

Lights dim on sleeping figures.

SCENE THREE

PERCY (*singing in his sleep*): Morena walks with me all the way / Watching over me all the day / When the night time comes he's there with me / Watching over, loving me.

MBONGENI (*restless, stirring from sleep*): Hey man uyangxola man—uyangxola man. [Hey man, you making noise man.]

The singing continues.

MBONGENI: Hey! Hey, hey! Stop singing your bloody hymns man, you're singing in your bladdy sleep again! Morena! Morena hoo-hoo, there's no Morena here!

PERCY (*dazed*): I'm sorry. (*Silence. He begins to hum again.*)

MBONGENI (*kicks Percy, who jumps up, is chased*): Hayi man—isejele la. [This is prison man.]

PERCY (*cowering*): Morena, the saviour, is watching over you too, my friend.

MBONGENI: Morena, the saviour, here in Modder-B Prison? BULLSHIT!

Lights up bright. Work yard. Actors holding picks.

MBONGENI: Prisoners! Work yard!

BOTH (*working and singing a work-song*):
Siboshiwe siboshel'wa mahala
Wen'utha senzenjani
Siboshiwe siboshel'wa mahala
Wen'utha senzenjani
[They arrested us for nothing
So what can we do?]

Mbongeni hurts his hand, nurses it.

MBONGENI: It's this bladdy hard labour!

PERCY (*attempting comfort*): Don't worry my friend.
Morena is over there, he's watching over us.

MBONGENI: Morena. Here in prison?

PERCY: He's watching over you too.

MBONGENI (*kicking at him, chasing him*) : Morena here??
BULLSHIT!!

SCENE FOUR

MBONGENI: Prisoners! Supper!

BOTH (*running*) : Supper! Supper! Supper!

*Transforms to supper-time. Prisoners racing around in
a circle, carrying plates, handing them in for food.
Mbongeni bullies Percy out of the way.*

PERCY: Thank you, soup, Baba. Thank you, Baba.

MBONGENI: Soup, Baba. Thank you soup, Baba, thank you
Baba.

PERCY: Porridge, Baba. Little bit of sugar, Baba.

MBONGENI: Porridge, Baba! Porridge. A little bit of sugar,
Baba. A little bit of sugar, Baba. Thank you, Baba.

PERCY: A little bit sugar, Baba. Please, little bit, Baba.
Thank you, Baba. Thank you, Baba, too much sugar,
Baba.

MBONGENI: Sugar . . . (*Reaches for Percy's food. Percy points to a guard, stopping Mbongeni who smiles to the guard.*) No complaints, my boss. Geen klagte nie.

PERCY: No complaints, Baba.

Mbongeni eats in growing disgust; Percy with relish.

MBONGENI (*spits on the floor*): Ukudla kwemi godoyi lokhu [This is food for a dog]—No, a dog wouldn't even piss on this food. Ikhabishi, amazambane, ushukela, ipapa, utamatisi endishini eyodwa—ini leyo? [Cabbage, potatoes, sugar, porridge, tomatoes in one dish—what is this?]

PERCY (*eating unconcerned*): Thank you Morena for the food that you have given me. Amen.

MBONGENI (*turns on him, furious*): Hey uthini Amen? [What do you say Amen for?]—For this shit? Thank you Morena for this shit?

Percy crawls away. Mbongeni beckons him back.

MBONGENI: Woza la! [Come here!]

Percy hesitates.

MBONGENI (*moves threateningly; points to the ground at his feet*): Woza *la!*

Percy crawls over reluctantly.

MBONGENI: On your knees!

Percy, terrified, gets down on his knees.

MBONGENI: Pray! Mr Bullshit, I'm getting out of here tomorrow. Pray to your Morena, tell him thanks for me. I'll never listen to your voice again!

Mbongeni pushes Percy forward on to the floor. Percy goes down with a scream that becomes a siren.

Blackout.

SCENE FIVE

The siren transforms into train sounds. Lights up. Both men are sitting back-to-back on boxes, rocking as in a train. Mbongeni is reading a newspaper, Percy a Bible. Mbongeni spits out of the window, sits again.

PERCY (*evangelically*): Blessed are those that are persecuted for righteousness' sake, for theirs is the Kingdom of Heaven. Blesséd are ye when men shall revile ye and persecute ye and shall send all manner of evil against ye falsely, for thy sake. Rejoice, and be exceedingly glad for great is the reward of heaven. For so persecuted they —

MBONGENI (*turns on him, hits him on the head with newspaper*): Hey! Persecuted? Prosecuted! Voetsak! Voetsak! (*Recognises his former fellow prisoner:*) Hey, brother Bullshit! When did you come out of prison? They promised me they would keep you in for life!

PERCY: Be careful, my friend, of the anger in your heart. For Morena will return and bear witness to our lives on earth and there will be no place to hide. He will point his holy finger and there will be those who rise to heaven and those who burn in hell. Hallelujah! I hope you're not one of them!

MBONGENI: Rise to heaven? Where is heaven?

PERCY: It is the Kingdom of God.

MBONGENI: Up there? Neil Armstrong has been there.

PERCY: Neil Armstrong?

MBONGENI: Hallelujah! He's been right up to the moon and he found a desert, no god!

PERCY: My brother, I don't care what you or your friend on the moon say, because I know that he will return to his father's kingdom on earth, even as I know that his father has heard your blasphemies and forgiven you!

MBONGENI: Where does his father live? In Jerusalem?

PERCY: The Lord, our father, is everywhere.

MBONGENI: And Morena, the saviour, is coming to South Africa?

PERCY: Hallelujah!

MBONGENI: How is he coming to South Africa? By South African Airways jumbo jet? (*He transforms into a photographer photographing the audience.*) And everybody will be waiting in Johannesburg at Jan Smuts airport. Pressmen, radiomen, South African television, international television, ABC, NBC, CBS, BBC, and they will all gather around — (*He turns to Percy, who has transformed into the Prime Minister with pink nose and spectacles.*) — our honourable Prime Minister!

SCENE SIX

PERCY (*moving forward ingratiatingly into spotlight*):
Thank you very much, thank you very much. My people, Morena is back and South Africa has got him! I hope that the free world will sit up and notice whose bread is buttered and where! Let them keep their boycotts, their boxers, rugby players, and tennis racketeers. Stay home Larry Holmes! Stay home John McEnroe! We have got Morena! But there is already rumours going around that this is not the real Morena, but some cheap impostor. And to those that spread such vicious rumours I can only say, 'Tough luck friends! He chose us!' (*Raises his hands in V-signs, laughs.*)

Blackout.

SCENE SEVEN

Lights up on Mbongeni wearing a Cuban army cap and smoking a fat cigar.

PERCY (*as announcer*): And now ladies and gentlemen, on the hotline straight from Havana — the comrade from Cuba — Fidel Castro! Sir, have you got any comment to make on the impending visit of Morena to South Africa?

MBONGENI (*laughing*): Morena in South Africa? Who's playing the part? Ronald Reagan?

Blackout.

SCENE EIGHT

Lights up on Percy playing cool bongo on boxes.

MBONGENI (*dancing flashily*): And now for you to see on Black TV—the face of Black South Africa! (*Enjoying the bongo, dancing up to the player.*) Beautiful music my brother, cool sound, man, cool! Real cool! Beautiful music, oh yeah, oh yeah. Now tell me, my brother—what would you say—if Morena—walks in —right through that door?

PERCY (*making a rude finger-sign*): Aay, fok off man!

Blackout.

SCENE NINE

Lights up bright on Percy, now a young street meat-vendor. The boxes are his stall. He is swatting flies with a newspaper held in one hand. His other hand holds a second newspaper as shade against the sun.

MBONGENI (*enters, singing, as a labourer-customer*):

(*Song*): Siyitshil'igusha sayigqiba
Siyitshil'igusha sayigqiba
Muhla sitsh'igusha.
Wena wendoda wawuphina
Wena wendoda wawuphina
Muhla sitsh'igusha.
[We ate and finished a big sheep the other day.
Where were you when we blessed ourselves with a sheep?]

MBONGENI: Hullo, my boy.

PERCY: Hello, Baba.

MBONGENI (*not tempted by the display*): Ehhh, what meat can you sell me today?

PERCY: I've got mutton, chicken, and nice sausages. (*Swats a fly on the sausages.*)

MBONGENI: Oh yeah . . . the chicken does not smell nice, hey? Must get some cover, some shade from the sun, hey? (*Deliberating.*) Ehhh, how much are those chops?

PERCY: It's two rand fifty, Baba.

MBONGENI: Two rand fifty? Are they mutton chops?

PERCY: Ehhh, it's mutton.

MBONGENI: No pork?

PERCY: No pork, Baba. I don't like pork.

MBONGENI: Okay my boy, give me mutton chops. Two rand fifty, hey? Where's your mother, my boy?

PERCY: She's at work.

MBONGENI: She's at work? Tell her I said 'tooka-tooka' on her nose. (*Tickles the boy's nose.*) She must visit me at the men's hostel, okay? Dube hostel, room number 126, block 'B', okay? Bye-bye, my boy. 'B', don't forget. (*About to leave, he turns astonished at sight of —invisible— TV interviewer.*)

PERCY (*awed by TV interviewer*): Hello, Skulu. I'm fine, thanks. And you? (*Listens.*) Morena? Here in South Africa? What shall I ask from Morena if he comes to South Africa? Baba, I want him to bring me good luck. So that the people that come will buy all this meat. And then? I want him to take me to school. Sub-A, uh huh. (*Watching the interviewer leave.*) Thank you, Baba. Inkos'ibusise [God bless]. Yeah, Baba . . . Au! TV!

Blackout.

SCENE TEN

Lights up, dim, on Mbongeni as Auntie Dudu, an old woman, wearing a white dust-coat as a shawl. She is searching a garbage bin (upturned box). She eats some food, chases flies, then notices the interviewer. She speaks very shyly.

MBONGENI: Hey? My name is Auntie Dudu. No work my boy, I'm too old. Eh? (*Listens.*) If Morena comes to South Africa? That would be very good. Because everybody will be happy and there will be lots and lots of parties. And we'll find lots of food here — (*Indicates bin.*) — cabbages, tomatoes, chicken, hot-dogs, all the nice things white people eat. Huh? (*Receives tip.*) Oh, thank you, my boy. Thank you, Baba. Inkos'ibusise. [God bless.] God bless you. Bye bye, bye bye . . .

A fly buzzes close. She chases it.

Fade.

SCENE ELEVEN

Lights up bright on a barber's open-air stall. Percy — the barber — is sitting on a box, Mbongeni — the customer — between his knees. Auntie Dudu's shawl is now the barber's sheet.

PERCY: Ehh, French cut? German cut? Cheese cut?

MBONGENI: Cheese cut.

PERCY: Cheese cut — all off!

MBONGENI (*settling*): That's nice . . . How much is a cheese cut?

PERCY: Seventy-five cents.

MBONGENI: Aaay! Last week my cousin was here and it was fifty cents.

PERCY: Hey, you've got very big hair my friend. (*He begins cutting hair.*)

MBONGENI (*squirming nervously during the — mimed — clipping, relaxing at the end of a run*): That's nice. What machine is this?

PERCY: Oh, it's number ten . . .

MBONGENI: Number ten? Ohhh.

PERCY: Though it's a very old clipper.

MBONGENI: That's nice. (*More cutting, more squirming.*) That's nice. Where's your daughter now?

PERCY: Ohh, she's in university.

MBONGENI: University? That's nice. What standard is she doing in university?

PERCY: (*clipping*). Ohhh, she's doing LLLLLB. I don't know, it's some very high standard.

MBONGENI: Oh yeah, LLB.

PERCY (*confirming with pleasure*): Uh huh, LLB.

MBONGENI: That's nice! I remember my school principal failed seven times LLB!

PERCY: Ohhh, I see! I understand it's a very high standard.

MBONGENI: Tell me my friend, but why don't you apply for a barbershop? Why do you work in the open air where everyone is looking?

PERCY (*continuing clipping*): Aaahh, don't ask me nonsense. I had a barbershop. But the police came with the bulldozers during the Soweto riots.

MBONGENI: Ooohh, 1976?

PERCY: Uh huh. During the times of black power. Everything was upside down . . . (*To the invisible interviewer as he enters:*) Oh, hello, Skulu. I'm fine, thanks. And you? (*Listens.*) Morena? Here, in South Africa?

MBONGENI: That's nice.

PERCY (*clipping, talking excitedly*): Well now, I want him

to build me a barbershop in a very big shopping center in Johannesburg city, with white tiles, mirrors all over the walls, and customers with big hair! (*The clipper gets caught in Mbongeni's hair. He struggles.*)

MBONGENI: EEEEeeeeiiiiii!

Blackout.

SCENE TWELVE

Lights up. Percy and Mbongeni are coal-vendors, soot-stained sacks on their heads. They are climbing onto boxes—a coal lorry—taking off.

PERCY & MBONGENI: Hey! Firewood for sale! Coal for sale! Smokeless coal for sale! Firewood for sale! (*They make the sound of the lorry's engine revving. The lorry moves off.*)

PERCY: *Coal for sale!* Hey wena, Auntie Ma-Dlamini, phum'endlini. [Hey, you, Aunt Dlamini, come out of your house.] (*He spies a young girl, gestures.*) Dudlu—mayemaye, the sugar the pumpkin. [Hallo there, hi hi, you are the sugar, the pumpkin.]

MBONGENI: Red light! Hey wena! [Hey you!] Driver—awuboni irobbot? [Can't you see the red light?]

PERCY: Don't you see the red light?

MBONGENI: Awuboni la uyakhona? [Don't you see where you're going?]

PERCY: He hasn't got a license.

Noise of the lorry revving. They discover the invisible interviewer below, turn to him impatiently.

PERCY: What? Morena here in South Africa? You're talking rubbish! (*Lorry sounds again. It jerks forward.*) Smokeless coal for sale! Firewood for sale! (*Looks back.*) Putsho putshu ikaka kwedini. You're talking shit, boy.

MBONGENI: Inkanda leyo-kwedini-iyashisa he? [Your prick is hot, boy—heh?]

Percy looks back contemptuously and makes a rude sign with his finger as the lorry drives off.

Fade.

SCENE THIRTEEN

Lights up on Mbongeni entering as a fragile, toothless old man. He sings throughout the following action. He settles on the boxes, attempts to thread a needle. His hands tremble but he perseveres. He succeeds on the third, laborious attempt and begins to sew a button on his coat.

MBONGENI (*humming*):
Bamqalokandaba bayimpi
Heya we-bayimpi izwelonke
Ngonyama ye zizwe
Ohlab'izitha
UNdaba bamgwazizwe lonke okazulu
Amambuka nkosi

[The soldiers of our enemies have come to attack the king
They are coming from the four corners of the world to attack the Lion
We must kill the enemies
They are attacking him from all over the world, the son of Zulu
These strangers from another place attack our King.]

Mbongeni becomes aware of the (invisible) interviewer. Laughs knowingly.

MBONGENI (*speaking*).: Eh? What would happen to Morena if he comes to South Africa? What would happen to Morena is what happened to Piet Retief! Do you know Piet Retief? The big leader of the white men long ago, the leader of the Afrikaners! Ja! He visited Dingane, the great king of the Zulus! When Piet Retief came to Dingane, Dingane was sitting in his camp with all his men. And he thought, 'Hey, these white men with their guns are wizards. They are dangerous!' But he welcomed them with a big smile. He said, he said, 'Hello. Just leave your guns outside and come inside and eat meat and drink beer.' Eeeeii! That is what will happen to Morena today! The Prime Minister will say, just leave your angels outside and the power of your father outside and come inside and enjoy the fruits of apartheid. And then, what will happen to Morena is what happened to Piet Retief when he got inside. Dingane was sitting with all his men in his camp, when Piet Retief came inside. All the Zulus were singing and dancing ... Bamqalokandaba bayimpi ... (*Repeats snatches of the song.*) And all the time Dingane's men were singing and dancing, (*Proudly*) they were waiting for the signal from their king. And Dingane just stood up ... He spit on the ground. He hit his beshu and he shouted, "Bulalan'abathakathi. Kill the wizards! Kill the wizards! Kill the wizards!" And Dingane's men came with all their spears. (*Mimes throat-slitting, throwing of bodies.*) Suka! That is what will happen to Morena here in South Africa. Morena here? (*Disgusted.*) Eeii! Suka!

Blackout.

SCENE FOURTEEN

Lights flash on, Percy, an airport announcer, is standing on a box, calling out.

PERCY: Attention, please! Attention, please! Now this is a great moment for South Africa! The Lord Morena has arrived! The jumbo jet from Jerusalem has landed! Now lay down your blankets, sing hosanna, hosanna, lay down your presents. Hey, you over there, move away from the tarmac! (*More urgently.*) Move away from the runway! Move away!

MBONGENI (*rushing in as a photographer*): Hosanna! Hosanna! Son of God! 'Hosanna nyana ka thixo!' ['Son of God'.] Hey, what will you say if Morena comes to you? (*To a member of the audience:*) Smile, smile! (*He turns to Percy then back to the camera crew.*) Sound! Rolling! Slate! Scene twenty-seven, take one. And action . . .

SCENE FIFTEEN

Percy, wearing his pink nose and flash sunglasses, alights from the plane (box).

MBONGENI (*approaching him with a mimed microphone*): Happy landings, sir.

PERCY (*flattered by this attention*): Oh, thank you. Thank you.

MBONGENI: Well sir, you've just landed from a jumbo jet!

PERCY: Eh, yes.

MBONGENI: Any comments, sir?

PERCY: I beg your pardon?

MBONGENI (*arch interviewer*): Would you not say that a jumbo jet is faster than a donkey, sir?

PERCY: Eh, yes.

MBONGENI: Aaahh. Now tell me, sir, where have you been all this time?

PERCY: Around and about.

MBONGENI: And how is it up there in the heavens?

PERCY: Oh, it's very cool.

MBONGENI: Cool! (*laughs artificially loud*) So, I'm to understand that you've been studying our slang, too!

PERCY: Right on!

They laugh together.

MBONGENI: Now tell me, sir, in the face of alI boycotting moves, why did you choose South Africa for your grand return?

PERCY: I beg your pardon?

MBONGENI: I mean, uuuh, why did you come here, sir?

PERCY: To visit my Great-aunt Matilda.

MBONGENI: Excuse me, sir?

PERCY: Yes?

MBONGENI: Your name, sir?

PERCY: Patrick Alexander Smith.

MBONGENI: You mean you're not Morena, sir?

PERCY: Who?

MBONGENI: Morena.

PERCY: Morena?

MBONGENI: Are you not Morena? (*To film-makers:*) Cut!!! Morena! Where is Morena? (*Percy minces off, insulted. Stage dim, Mbongeni wanders across stage, calling disconsolately.*) Morena! Morena! Morena! M-o-o-o-r-e-e-e-n-a-a-a! . . .

Lights dim. Percy begins to join the call, alternating, from behind the clothes rail. He emerges calling and addressing a high and distant Morena. As he talks, the lights come up.

SCENE SIXTEEN

PERCY: Morena! Morena-a-a! Where are you? Come to Albert Street! Come to the Pass Office! We need you here Morena! Ja, Morena, this is the most terrible street in the whole of Johannesburg! Ja, Morena, this is the street where we Black men must come and stand and wait and wait and wait just to get a permit to work in Johannesburg! And if you're lucky enough to get the permit, what happens? You wait and wait and wait again for the white bosses to come in their cars to give you work. (*Turns back to Mbongeni.*) But I'm lucky! I've got six months special! (*Shows his pass-book.*) Qualified to work in Johannesburg for six months!

MBONGENI: How many months? Eh?

PERCY: Six months!

MBONGENI: Six months? Congratulations. (*Laughs, slaps Percy's back, shakes his hand.*) Eh! Six month special!

PERCY: Three weeks in a queue!

MBONGENI: But you're still their dog! (*Moves upstage to urinate, with his back to the audience.*)

PERCY: Aaahh, jealous! You jealous!

MBONGENI: Have you got a job? Have you got school fees for your children? Have you got money for rent? Have you got bus fare to come to the Pass Office? Oh, come on man, we've all got specials but we're still their dogs!

Car sounds.

PERCY (*leaps up*): Hey! There's a car! A white man! (*Moves to the car at the front edge of the stage, follows it as it moves across.*) Are you looking for workers, my boss? Ya, I've got six month special, qualified to work in Johannesburg.

Mbongeni moves forward trying frantically to distract the driver. Car sounds continue, actors alternating.

MBONGENI: Boss, I've got fourteen day special. This is my last chance. This is my last chance. Take two boys, my boss, two!

PERCY: Messenger boy, tea boy, my boss. One! I make nice tea for the Madam, my boss. Bush tea, China tea, English tea! Please, Baba. Lots of experience, Baba. Very good education; my boss. Please my boss. Stand-ard three, very good English, Baba.

Mbongeni's sound of a departing car transforms into a mocking laugh.

MBONGENI: I told you, you're still their dog! (*Laughs, mocks.*) Standard three, bush tea, China tea — where do you get China tea in Soweto?

PERCY: Aah voetsak! I've got six months special!

MBONGENI (*shows Percy his pass book*): Hey, look at my picture. I look beautiful, heh?

PERCY (*laughs bitterly*): How can you look beautiful in your pass book?

Car sounds again. Mbongeni rushes forward to the stage edge, follows the car, Percy behind him.

MBONGENI: One! One, my boss! Everything! Sweeper, anything, everything, my boss! Give me anything. Carwash? Yeah, always smiling, my boss. Ag, have you got work for me, my boss? I'm a very good nanny. I look after small white children. I make them tomato sandwich. I take them to school, my boss. Please, my boss. Please.

Car leaves. Mbongeni wanders disconsolately upstage. Percy watches him.

PERCY (*laughing*): Ja! Who's a dog? Don't talk like that! This is South Africa! This is Albert Street. (*Laughs.*) Nanny, nanny, tomato sandwich!

Car sounds again.

BOTH ACTORS (*confusion of requests from each*): Six month special, my boss. Fourteen day special, Baba. This is my last chance. Hey man, this is my corner! Very strong, Baas. Ek donder die kaffers op die plaas. [I beat up the kaffirs on the farm.] One, my boss. Two, my boss. Anything, my boss. Have you got anything for me, Baba?

PERCY: Basie, he's a thief, this one.

MBONGENI: He can't talk Afrikaans, this one, my boss.

PERCY: He's lying, Basie. Hy lieg, my baas!

The third car pulls away.

PERCY (*confronting Mbongeni angrily*): Hey, this is my corner, these are my cars. I've got six months special.

MBONGENI: Hey! Fuck off! I stand where I like, man.

PERCY: You've got fourteen day special. There's your corner.

MBONGENI: Hey! You don't tell me where to stand!

PERCY: You've got fourteen day special. You're not even qualified to be on Albert Street.

MBONGENI: Qualified? Qualified? Wenzani uthath'a ma shansi hey uthatha ma shansi. [What are you trying to do? You taking chances Hey? You taking chances.]

Mbongeni kicks Percy. Percy turns on him.

PERCY: Baas Piet! Baas Piet! I'll tell Baas Piet you got forgery.

MBONGENI (*mimes picking up stone*).: Okay, okay. Call your white boss! I've got friends too!

PERCY: Baas Piet!

MBONGENI (*beckons his friends, wildly picking up stones*): Hey Joe! We Joe! Zwakala—sigunu mfwethu. (*To Percy:*) Angihlali eZola mina—angihlali eMdeni mina —Joe zwakala simenze njalo. [Joe come here—It's happening. (*To Percy:*) I don't live in Zola—I'm not from Mdeni—Joe come here let's work on him.]

Mbongeni quietens, struck by something in the audience.

PERCY (*muttering sulkily*): These are my cars, man. I've got six month special, these are mine. This is my corner— That's the temporal corner! I'll tell Baas Piet!

MBONGENI (*now totally stunned by what he is watching*): Heeey, heeey! Ssh man, ssh.

PERCY (*cautious*): What?

MBONGENI (*indicating the audience*): Morena . . .

PERCY: Aaay, fok off!

MBONGENI: It's Morena—that one there with the white shirt.

PERCY (*doubtfully*): Morena? Ay, nonsense . . . Is it Morena?

MBONGENI: It's him—I saw him in the *Sunday Times* with Bishop Tutu. It's him!

He sidles forward to the edge of the stage. Percy shyly eggs him on.

PERCY: Hey, speak to him.

MBONGENI (*nods with the invisible Morena*): Excuse. Are you not Morena? Yiiiii! Hosanna! Morena!

The actors embrace joyously. Then follow Morena, frantically showing their passes and pleading.

BOTH ACTORS: Morena, look at my pass book!

PERCY: I've got six month special but I can't find work.

MBONGENI: I've been looking here two months, no work. Take us to heaven, Morena, it's terrible here.

Mbongeni follows Morena. Percy falls behind.

PERCY: Temporary or permanent is okay Morena! (*Silence as Mbongeni converses with Morena. He comes back exhilarated.*) Hey, what does he say?

MBONGENI: He says let us throw away our passes and follow him to Soweto!

PERCY: Hey! He's right! Morena! Morena!

BOTH ACTORS (*sing, exhorting the audience*):
Woza giya nansi inkonyane ye ndlovu—
Aph'amadoda sibabambe sebephelele.
Wozani madoda niyesaba na?

[Come on join this child of an elephant
Where are the men? Let us face them!
Come men, are you afraid?]

PERCY (*under the song*): Morena says throw away your passes and follow him to Soweto.

MBONGENI: We are not pieces of paper, man! We are men!

PERCY: Ja! Let them know our faces as Morena knows our faces!

MBONGENI: Morena says no more passes!

PERCY: Ja!

MBONGENI: We don't have numbers any more!

PERCY: Ja!

MBONGENI: Let them look at our faces to know that we are men.

PERCY: Ja! When we follow Morena we walk as one!

The actors throw away their passes and their song transforms into train sounds.

SCENE SEVENTEEN

The actors mime standing beside each other at a train window. They wave to people outside.

PERCY: Hey madoda! Sanibona madoda! May God bless them! Ja, you've got a very good imagination. I really like your stories. But you must go to church sometimes —Hey, there's a train coming! (*Looks to one side.*)

Flurry of their faces and noises as they mime watching adjoining train pass. Then they pull their windows up. Siren. Mbongeni moves downstage. Percy stands on a box, begins Regina Mundi Song:

Somlandela—somlandela u Morena
Somlandela yonke indawo
Somlandela—somlandela u Morena
Lapho eyakhona somlandela.

[We shall follow—we shall follow Morena
We shall follow him everywhere
We shall follow—we shall follow Morena
Where-ever he leads—we shall follow.]

While the song continues:

MBONGENI (*joyous siren*): Ja, madoda, hundreds of thousands will gather at the Regina Mundi Church in the heart of Soweto. And people will sing and dance. There will be bread for all. And wine for all. Our people will be left in peace, because there will be too many of us and the whole world will be watching. And people will go home to their beds. (*He joins in the song for a few phrases.*) These will be days of joy. Auntie Dudu will find chicken legs in her rubbish bin, and whole cabbages. And amadoda—our men—will be offered work at the Pass Office. The barber will be surrounded by white tiles. The young meat-seller will wear a nice new uniform and go to school, and we will all go to Morena for our blessings. (*Song subsides. Percy lies on boxes as sleeping woman. Lights dim.*) And then . . . the government will begin to take courage again . . . The police and the army will assemble from all parts of the country . . . And one night, police dogs will move in as they have done before. There will be shouts at night and bangings on the door . . .

PERCY (*banging on a box*): Hey! Open up, it's the police! Maak die deur oop! Polisie!

MBONGENI (*ducking down by the boxes as if hiding beside a bed*): . . . There will be sounds of police vans and the crying of women and their babies.

PERCY (*turns over on the boxes as an old woman waking in bed, starts crying and calling in Zulu*): We Jabulani, hayi-bo-hey-hey-we-Nonoza, akenivule bo nanka amaphoyisa esesihlasele, we Thoko akenivule bo. Auw-Nkosi-Yami, ezingane ze-Black Power! [Hey, Jabulani, Hey no, hey-hey, Nonoza, open the door can't you hear the police are here. They've come to attack us. Thoko, please open the door. Oh my God, these children of Black Power!]

He goes to open the door. Throughout Mbongeni tries to stop him.

MBONGENI: Sssh Mama! Tula Mama! Mama! Mama! Leave the door! (*Mbongeni gives up, stands silent, transfixed, hiding.*) They'll start surrounding our homes at night. And some of our friends will be caught by stray bullets. There will be roadblocks at every entrance to Soweto, and Regina Mundi Church will be full of tear-gas smoke! Then life will go on as before.

He throws his arms up in the air in disgust, cries out.

SCENE EIGHTEEN

Lights flash on. Bright daylight. Coronation Brickyard. Mbongeni, as Zuluboy, is singing:

MBONGENI (*singing*):
Akuntombi lokhu kwabulala ubhuti ngesibumbu kuyamsondeza. [This is no woman. She killed my brother with a fuck and she never lets him go.]

(*He calls out towards the street*): Hey Angelina — sweetheart! Why are you walking down the street? Come here to Coronation Brickyard! Zuluboy is waiting for you with a nice present! (*Points to his genitals, laughing*).

PERCY (*enters as Bobbejaan — Baboon — Zuluboy's fellow brickyard worker*): Hey! Zuluboy, forget about women. Start the machine!

Mbongeni sings on.

PERCY: Hey! The white man is watching us. Boss Kom is standing by the window! Start the machine.

He makes machine sounds as he attempts to start it. He pulls the starter cord abortively, flies backwards across the yard.

MBONGENI (*laughs*): Hey Bobbejaan! Start the machine!

PERCY: You laugh and I must do all this work! I'll tell Baas Kom. Baas Kom! Basie! Baas Kom!

MBONGENI: Ssshhhhhh! Bobbejaan! Bobbejaan . . . ssh — I want to tell you a secret.

PERCY: What secret?

MBONGENI (*whispers*): We don't have to work so hard any more. Because Morena, the saviour, is coming here.

PERCY: Huh? Morena here? Hau! Baas Kom!

MBONGENI: Hau, no Bobbejaan! Listen—I was there on Thursday by the Jan Smuts Airport. We were delivering bricks. People were coming with taxis, bikes, trains, trucks, others on foot. There were many people, Bobbejaan. They were singing and crying and laughing and dancing and sweating and this other woman was shouting: Morena, give me bread for my baby. The other woman was shouting: Morena, my son is in detention. The other man: Morena, give me a special permit to work in Johannesburg city. The little girl, standing next to me: Morena, give me a lollipop. The big fat Zulu—the driver from Zola Hostel—Morena, give me a Chevrolet Impala! And me—I was there too —

PERCY: What did you say?

MBONGENI: Morena, come to Coronation Brickyard tomorrow morning! And he's coming here.

PERCY: To Coronation Brickyard? Morena?

MBONGENI: Hau—Bobbejaan, at the wedding, long ago— ten thousand years ago—he take a bucket of water, he make wine.

PERCY (*smugly*): Ja, everybody knows that!

MBONGENI: He take one fish, he make fish for everybody! Fried fish!

PERCY Hau!

MBONGENI: He take one loaf of brown bread, he make the whole bakery! Here at Coronation Brickyard, you will see wonders. He will take one brick, number one brick, and throw it up in the air. And it will fall down on our heads, a million bricks like manna from heaven!

PERCY: Hey! You're talking nonsense. Morena? Here at Coronation Bricks? Start the machine. I'll tell Baas Kom!

*Percy goes off. Mbongeni begins rolling a cigarette,
singing his Zuluboy's song. Percy, as Baas Kom with
pink nose and white dust-coat, enters quietly from
behind the clothes rail and creeps up on him.
Mbongeni spits, just missing Percy who leaps back.*

MBONGENI: Oh, sorry, Boss. Sorry, sorry . . . (*He runs to
start the machine.*)

PERCY: Sis! Where were you brought up?

MBONGENI: Sorry Boss!

PERCY: Ja Zuluboy! And what are you sitting around for?

MBONGENI: Sorry, Boss. Sorry.

PERCY: Are you waiting for Morena?

MBONGENI: No, Boss. No.

PERCY: Ja, I've been listening. I've been watching. You're
waiting for Morena. Ja. Did you not listen to the Prime
Minister on the radio today?

MBONGENI: I don't have a radio, Boss.

PERCY: We don't like Morena anymore. And everybody
who's waiting for Morena is getting fired.

MBONGENI: Oh, very good, Boss. Me? I'm Zuluboy — ten
thousand bricks in one day!

PERCY: Ja. Where's Bobbejaan?

MBONGENI (*attempting to start the machine*): He's gone to
the toilet.

PERCY: Call him. Call him, quickly!

MBONGENI: Hey! Bobbejaan! (*He makes motor sounds as
the machine kicks over but does not fire.*) Bobbejaan!

PERCY (*still as Baas Kom, with Mbongeni watching over
his shoulder*): Now listen. I want two thousand bricks
for Boss Koekemoer. Two thousand bricks for Baas
Pretorius. Two thousand bricks for Mrs Dawson.
(*Mbongeni indicates his pleasure in Mrs Dawson. Percy
cautions him:*) Zuluboy! Six thousand bricks for Boss

Van der Westhuizen. Two thousand bricks for Boss Koekemoer. Two thousand bricks for Baas Pretorius. Two thousand bricks for Mrs Dawson.

MBONGENI: Baas, sorry, I'm confused.

PERCY: What confused? What confused? You're bloody lazy, man! See to these orders and push the truck. (*He indicates the truck on the side of the stage.*)

MBONGENI: Hey! This truck is too heavy, Baas!

PERCY: Get other people!

MBONGENI: People have gone to lunch.

PERCY: Get Bobbejaan!

MBONGENI: Ten thousand bricks, Boss!

PERCY: Hey! Get Bobbejaan!

MBONGENI: Bobbejaan! Uyahamba laphe khaya. [They'll fire you.] Bobbejaan! (*Mumbling:*) Two thousand bricks Mrs Dawson . . . Hau! (*Laughs with pleasure.*) Mrs Dawson! Ten thousand brick Baas van Des-des-destuizen . . . Too much! (*He starts the engine. Engine fires. Mbongeni shouts:*) Bobbejaan!

PERCY (*off-stage, as Bobbejaan*): I'm coming, man! (*He enters.*) Hey, hey. Where's Morena?

MBONGENI: No, Morena. Hey, shovel the sand. Baas Kom is firing everybody that's waiting for Morena.

PERCY (*laughing*): Ja! I've been telling you! Hey, bring down the pot. (*They alternate shovel and motor sounds, as they mime shovelling. Mbongeni begins to sing and dance his Zuluboy song.*) Hey, stop dancing. Stop dancing!

MBONGENI: Hey! I am boss-boy here!

Mbongeni switches off the machine.

PERCY: Lunch time!

MBONGENI: No Bobbejaan. First push the truck.

PERCY: Hau! Ten thousand bricks! Hau! Lunch time!

MBONGENI: Baas Kom said, push the truck! Get Bobbejaan, push the truck. PUSH!

Percy joins him reluctantly. They start to chant while they mime pushing the heavy truck.

BOTH (*chanting*):
Woza kanye-kanye! [Come together!]
Abelungu oswayini! [Whites are swines!]
Basibiza ngo-damn! [They call us damns!]

Woza kanye-kanye! [Come together!]
Abelungu oswayini! [Whites are swines!]
Basibiza ngo-damn! [They call us damns!]

They finally stop, exhausted.

PERCY (*holding his back, moaning*): Oh, oh, oh, yii, yii! Lunch time! Hayi ndiva kuthi qhu. [My back is breaking.]

MBONGENI: Hayi suka unamanga. [Hey you lie.] (*He squats to examine the truck.*) It has gone too far. Reverse!

PERCY: Reverse?! Reverse?

Muttering, he joins Mbongeni. They pull the truck back again, chanting.

BOTH (*chanting*):
Woza emuva! [Come reverse!]
Phenduka ayi. [Change now.]
Abelungu oswayini! [Whites are swines!]
Basibiza ngo-damn! [They call us damns!]

PERCY: Hayi. (*Percy goes off.*)

MBONGENI: Bobbejaan, come back, it stuck in ditch.

PERCY (*off-stage*): Hayi, xelel'ubaas Kom ukuba sifuna i-increase. [Tell Baas Kom we want increase.]

MBONGENI: We . . . kuyintekentekana lokhu okuwu-Bobbejaan. [Hey man, Bobbejaan is too weak.] Come back, Bobbejaan! Uyahamba laphe khaya. [They'll fire you.] Where's my cigarette? (*Mimes lighting a cigarette. Talks to himself. Starts praise-chant.*)

PERCY (*enters as Baas Kom*): And now? And now? (*Mocking praise-chant:*) Aaay, hakela, hakela. What the bloody hell is that? Huh? Push the truck! Come!

MBONGENI: Having rest, baas. Still smoking.

PERCY: Do you think I pay you for smoking? (*Glances at the truck.*) Hey, push the truck!

MBONGENI: We pushed the truck! Ten thousand bricks! Boss, there's too much work for two people. Me and Bobbejaan start the engine. Me and Bobbejaan shovel the sand. Me and Bobbejaan load the bricks. Me and Bobbejaan push the truck! Aaay suka! We need other people!

PERCY: There's no jobs!

MBONGENI: There *is* jobs!!! Ten thousand bricks! This morning there were many people at the gates standing there looking for work. And you chased them away!

PERCY: Zuluboy, you're getting cheeky, huh?

MBONGENI: I'm not getting cheeky. It's true.

PERCY: Ja! I'm cutting down your salary. I think you're getting too much. Ja! Ja!

MBONGENI: The boss can't cut salary.

PERCY: Ek gaan dit doen! [I'm going to do it.]

MBONGENI: That's not showing sympathy for another man. The cost of living is too high. There is too much inflation.

PERCY: Zuluboy! Zuluboy! You sit around waiting for Morena and then you come and tell me about the cost of living? You talk about inflation? What do you know about inflation? I've got you here, just here. One more mistake, once more cheeky, and you're fired!

MBONGENI: Okay. All right boss. Let's talk business like two people.

PERCY (*bangs on the box*): He-ey! Push the truck, man!

MBONGENI (*furious, bangs on the box. Percy retreats towards his office space*): Hey! You must listen nice when another man talks!

PERCY: Okay. Talk, talk. (*Mbongeni advances.*) No—talk over there, talk over there!

MBONGENI (*backs away*): All right. Okay, okay. The people want increase. Where's the money for the people?

PERCY: Increase?

MBONGENI: Increase!

PERCY: Don't I give you free food? Free boarding and lodging?

MBONGENI: The people don't like your free food! They want money. There is too big families to support. Too may children.

PERCY: I don't give a damn about your too many children. Don't you know about family planning?

MBONGENI: Family planning? What is that?

PERCY: Don't you know that you must not have too many children? You must have two, three, and stop your fuck-fuck nonsense! Too many pic-a-ninnies! Too many black kaffir babies all over the country. (*Sharing this with the audience:*) Their kaffir babies cry 'Waaaaa! Waaaaa!' Just like too many piccaninny dogs!

MBONGENI (*threatening*): Hey!

PERCY: Zuluboy!

MBONGENI: Whose children cry 'Waaa, waaa!'?

PERCY: Zuluboy!

MBONGENI: Whose children is piccaninny dogs?

PERCY: Bring your pass-book!

MBONGENI: Why?

PERCY: You're fired! Bring your pass-book. I'm signing you off.

MBONGENI: You can't sign me off!

PERCY: I'm calling the police! I'm calling the government buses and I'm sending you back to your homelands. Ek stuur julle na julle fokken verdomde, donorse, bliksemse plase toe! [I'm sending you to your fucking, cursed, useless farms.] You don't like my work? You don't like my food! Go back to your bladdy farms! Go starve on your bladdy farms!

MBONGENI: I must starve?

PERCY: Ja!

MBONGENI: My children must starve?

PERCY: Ja!

MBONGENI: Go on strike!!!

PERCY: Hey! Bring your pass-book!

MBONGENI (*pulls out his knobkerrie from behind the box*): Here's my pass-book!

PERCY: Zuluboy!

MBONGENI (*advancing*): Here's my pass-book.

PERCY (*ducking behind the rack of clothes at the back of the stage*): Bobbejaan!

MBONGENI: Here's my pass-book! Stay away—hlala phansi wena ngane ka Ngema. Hlala wena ngane ka Madlokovu—hlala. Wena dlula bedlana inkunzi engena mona, hlala phansi mfana—Hlala!! Pho—kuhlala ba. [Stay away—sit down you son of Ngema. Sit down son of Madlokovu. Sit. You fuck and you never feel jealous. Sit down great son. Sit. So who am I—the greatest!] (*Mutters to himself:*) Stay away. Go on strike. My children cry 'Waa waa'. (*Suddenly he sees Morena approaching. He wipes the sweat from his eyes, shakes his head in disbelief. Falls to his knees.*) Hey. Hey! Morena! So you've come to Coronation Bricks! Come, Morena. Did you listen to the radio today? Everybody's waiting for you, and everybody is fired. Come, sit down here, Morena. (*Offers a box.*) Sit down. Sit down Morena. (*Calls out:*) Bobbejaan!

PERCY (*entering as Bobbejaan, angrily*): Hau! One minute 'Bobbejaan!' One minute 'Bobbejaan!' (*He sees Morena, stops complaining and turns away shyly.*)

MBONGENI (*laughs*): Bobbejaan, who is this? Who is this!!!

PERCY (*backs away smiling shyly*): Hey. I don't know him. Who is it?

MBONGENI: Who is this? I win the bet. Give ten rands.

PERCY: Who is he?

MBONGENI: Give ten rands!

PERCY: Who is he?

MBONGENI: Morena!

PERCY: Hey! Morena?!

MBONGENI: He's from heaven. He has come now. He landed at Jan Smuts Airport on Thursday by the airline from Jerusalem.

PERCY: Hey Morena! (*Clapping hands.*) I saw your picture in the paper. Morena, I could not believe you're coming. I thought you're coming back by the clouds. (*He sits on the floor.*)

MBONGENI: The clouds are too hot now. It's summer. He flies air-conditioned. Excuse, Morena, this is Bobbejaan. Bobbejaan, shake hands with Morena. (*Percy stands, embarrassed, backs away.*) Shake hands with the Son of God! Shake hands, Bobbejaan! (*Percy ducks behind the Zuluboy on the box. Zuluboy laughs.*) Bobbejaan is shy! We are working together here, Morena. When I say, 'Morena, come to Coronation Brickyard', I mean you must make bricks like you make bread and wine long ago. I mean you must make bricks to fall down like manna from heaven—

PERCY: Like you made fried fish!

MBONGENI: Ja! But now, I say no! Stay away! No! You must not make bricks for Coronation Brickyard! You must go on strike like me and Bobbejaan! Angithi

Bobbejaan? [Isn't it so, Bobbejaan?] We work hard here. We sweat. Sweating for one man!

PERCY: Boss Koekemoer!

MBONGENI: Every Friday, Boss Koekemoer, seven thousand bricks —

PERCY: Boss Pretorius!

MBONGENI: Boss Pretorius ten thousand bricks!

PERCY: Van de Westhuizen!

MBONGENI: Boss Van-des-destuizen, eleven thousand bricks! Where do we stay?

PERCY: In a tin!

MBONGENI: In a tin! Like sardine fish!

PERCY: In a tin, Morena!

MBONGENI: Where do the bricks go to!? The bricks go to make a big house, six rooms, for two people. A white man and his wife! Angithi Bobbejaan? [Isn't it so, Bobbejaan?] Our fingers are breaking Morena! Is nie good kanjalo man. [That's not good like that, man.]

PERCY: Ten thousand bricks!

MBONGENI: Ten thousand bricks! Me and Bobbejaan must push the truck. Aaay suka! Stay away! No bricks for Coronation Bricks! (*He puts out his cigarette and clears his nose — to Percy's embarrassment.*) Are you hungry, Morena? Are you hungry? I've got nice food for you. I've got a packet of chips. (*Mimes.*) It's very good, this one. There's lots of vinegar and salt — I bought them from the shop just around the corner.

PERCY: That's potatoes, Morena.

MBONGENI: I've got half-brown bread. Whole-wheat. You made this long ago, huh? I've been telling Bobbejaan, you made plenty in the wedding — He's got power, this one! (*Mimes.*) This is Coca-cola, Morena.

PERCY: It's cold drink.

MBONGENI: For quenching thirst.

PERCY: Ha, Morena, there's no Coca-cola in heaven?

MBONGENI: What do you drink up there?

They listen, then laugh uproariously.

PERCY: These two!

MBONGENI: You and your father! Skelm! [Mischief-makers!]

He mimes opening a cola bottle.

PERCY (*looks upstage, then calls in Baas Kom's voice, as if from offstage*): Bobbejaan! (*Then as Bobbejaan again:*) Baas Kom! Morena, I must go! One minute 'Bobbejaan!' One minute 'Bobbejaan!' (*Going off:*) Hey Zuluboy, I want my chips!

MBONGENI (*drinks from the mimed cola bottle, burps, offers it to Morena*): Yabhodla ingane yenZule ukuba okungu—MSuthu ngabe kudala kuzinyele. [There burps the son of a Zulu; if it was a Sotho he would be shitting.] Did you hear that man who was shouting 'Bobbejaan'? That's our white boss. Boss Kom. He's not good. But don't worry . . .

PERCY (*offstage in Baas Kom's voice*): Bobbejaan!

MBONGENI: Lots of vinegar . . .

PERCY (*enters as Baas Kom, stops at sight of Morena*): En nou! En nou? Who is this? Who is sitting around eating lunch with my kaffirs? That's why you're getting cheeky, hey? Ja, you sit around and have lunch with terrorists!

MBONGENI: Hau! He's not a terrorist, Baas! He's a big man from heaven!

PERCY: This man is a communist, jong! Ek het va jou nonsense gehoor. Die hele land praat van jou. [I've heard of your nonsense. The whole country is talking about you.]

MBONGENI: Excuse. He cannot understand Afrikaans.

PERCY: What? Cannot understand Afrikaans?

MBONGENI: Right.

PERCY: Cannot understand Afrikaans? Stay where you are! (*Retreats to his office behind the clothes.*) I'm calling the police. Fuckin' agitator!

MBONGENI: Aay suka!! Don't worry, Morena, don't worry. (*He proffers the cola bottle.*) He does not know who you are. He does not know who your father is.

PERCY (*as Baas Kom, offstage*): Hello? Hello? Lieutenant Venter? Ja! Now listen here. There's a terrorist here who's making trouble with my kaffirs. Ek sê daar's'n uitlander hier wat kak maak met my kaffirs. [I say there's a foreigner here who's making shit with my kaffirs.] Ja. Hello? Hello? Ag die fuckin' telephone! Bobbejaan! (*As Bobbejaan:*) Ja, Basie? (*As Baas Kom:*) Kom, kom, kom. (*As Bobbejaan:*) Ja, Basie? (*As Baas Kom:*) You see that man eating with Zuluboy? (*As Bobbejaan:*) Ja, Basie. (*As Baas Kom:*) He's a terrorist! (*As Bobbejaan:*) A terrorist, Basie? That's Morena! (*As Baas Kom:*) It's not Morena—Now listen here. Listen carefully. I'm writing down this message. You take this message to the police station and I'm going to give you a very nice present. A ten rand increase, okay? (*As Bobbejaan:*) Ja, thank you Basie, thank you Basie. (*As Baas Kom:*) Ja, go straight to the police station and don't tell Zuluboy. (*As Bobbejaan:*) Ja Basie, ja. (*As Baas Kom:*) Go to the police station and you get the ten rand increase!

MBONGENI: Did you hear that, Morena? (*He listens.*) What? Forgive a man seventy times seventy-seven? Aikhona Morena! This is South Africa. We fight! Bobbejaan is very dangerous. (*Listens to Morena.*) Okay, you win. Wait and see, Morena.

PERCY (*enters as Bobbejaan, putting on his shirt*): Morena, I'm going to the shop, just around the corner.

MBONGENI: Bobbejaan, your chips are here.

PERCY: Give them to Morena.

MBONGENI: Morena is not hungry.

PERCY: Eat them yourself.

MBONGENI: I'm not hungry either. Where are you going, Bobbejaan?

PERCY: To the shop!

MBONGENI: Why, Bobbejaan?

PERCY: I'm going to buy hot-dogs for Baas Kom.

MBONGENI: Where's the money?

PERCY: I've got it here.

MBONGENI: Show it to me.

PERCY: Why?

MBONGENI: Ja. You Judas, Bobbejaan!

PERCY: What are you talking about?

MBONGENI: You betray Morena, Bobbejaan.

PERCY: Haw! Morena, do you hear that?

MBONGENI: Bobbejaan, you betray Morena, Bobbejaan! You Judas, Bobbejaan!

PERCY: I'm going to buy hot-dogs for Baas Kom!

MBONGENI: You . . . you . . . you take a message to the police. And you get ten rands increase Bobbejaan!

PERCY: Aay Morena. Morena, do you hear that?

MBONGENI: Morena, shhh. Keep quiet. This is South Africa. Ten rands increase (*He reaches for the knobkerrie.*)

PERCY: Baas Kom! (*He runs off.*)

MBONGENI (*mimes his knobkerrie being grabbed by Morena*): Morena, leave it! Leave it! Morena! Morena, leave it! Morena! He has run away now. Bobbejaan, sodibana nawe wena. [Bobbejaan, you and I will meet again.] A man hits this cheek you give him the other. Aikhona, Morena! They're calling the police to arrest you now! Okay, come. Let me hide you there by the trees — Quickly — (*Siren sounds. He stops.*) There's one, two, three . . . there's thirteen police cars. Huh? Forgive them, they do not know what they are doing? Aikhona, Morena! They know! They know! (*He sings and performs a Zulu war dance, which ends with him thrusting his knobkerrie again and again at the audience in attack.*)

Qobolela njomane kandaba heya-he
soze sibajahe abelungu he ya he.

[Be ready you horses of the black warriors
Time will come when we'll chase these whites away.]

SCENE NINETEEN

The lights come up on the actors wearing military hats and pink noses. Percy has a bloody bandage under his hat.

MBONGENI: Address! Ssshhhooo! Attention!

They drill in unison.

PERCY (*saluting*): Reporting sir! John Vorster Squad, sir!

MBONGENI: What have you to report, Sergeant?

PERCY: Operation Coronation, sir!

MBONGENI: Meaning, Sergeant?

PERCY: We have finally captured Morena, sir!

MBONGENI: You've what? Attention! One-two-three-one-two-three-one! (*They march to each other, shake hands.*) Excellent, Sergeant! Excellent!

PERCY: Thank you, sir.

MBONGENI: And now, what's happened to your head, Sergeant?

PERCY: A mad Zulu, sir.

MBONGENI: A mad Zulu?

PERCY: Yes sir. He struck me with the branch of a tree, sir.

MBONGENI: A branch of a tree?

PERCY: They call it a knobkerrie, sir.

MBONGENI: Ah! When, Sergeant?

PERCY: During Operation Coronation, sir.

MBONGENI: You mean Morena was with a bunch of mad Zulus?

PERCY: No, sir.

MBONGENI: What does he mean, this stupid Sergeant?

PERCY: He was with one mad Zulu, sir!

MBONGENI: One mad Zulu?

PERCY: Yes, sir!

MBONGENI: And how many men did you have, Sergeant?

PERCY: Thirty, sir!

MBONGENI: And where are they now, Sergeant?

PERCY: In hospital, sir!

MBONGENI: And the mad Zulu?

PERCY: He got away, sir!

MBONGENI: God! Wat gaan aan?! [God! What's going on?!] Where is Morena now, Sergeant?

PERCY (*pointing proudly above the audience*): He's upstairs, above us, sir. On the tenth floor of John Vorster Square Prison, sir!

MBONGENI: Aaaahhh! (*Looking up.*) And you've provided ample guard, Sergeant?

PERCY: Yes, sir. One hundred and twenty, sir.

MBONGENI (*moving forward, watching the tenth floor, mesmerised*): Are you sure he's on the tenth floor, Sergeant?

PERCY (*following his gaze nervously*): Yes, sir.

MBONGENI: Then what is that I see?

PERCY (*moving behind him, also mesmerised, both eye-lines travelling above the audience*): I'm sorry sir.

MBONGENI: Why are you sorry, Sergeant?

PERCY: I see two men floating, sir.

MBONGENI: Then why are you sorry, Sergeant?

PERCY: I'm afraid one of them is Morena, sir.

MBONGENI (*moving in, nose-to-nose, menacingly*): Precisely, Sergeant! And-who-is-the-other?

PERCY: The Angel Gabriel, sir.

MBONGENI (*despairing*): Ha! Gabriel!

PERCY: I'm sorry, sir. I never thought of air flight, sir.

MBONGENI: Eeeeeiiiii! One-two-three-four-one-four! Attention! Dismissed, Sergeant!

SCENE TWENTY

Lights find both actors travelling beside each other on a train.

MBONGENI (*laughing*): Jaaa. And where do we go from there? After a miracle like flying men, I'm telling you the government will be real nervous. And they won't start nonsense with him for a long time. In fact, they will try very hard to please Morena. He will be taken to all the nice places in the country. Like the game reserve where he can lie down with a leopard and a lamb. (*They cuddle.*) And then—(*They mime a high-speed lift.*)—they will take him right up to the high spots of Johannesburg City—Panorama Wimpy Bar, Carlton Centre, fiftieth floor! And then, on a Thursday they will take him down—(*They mime going down, pink noses on their foreheads like miners' lamps.*)—the gold mines to watch. (*They mime deafening drills.*) And then, on a Sunday the mine dancers. (*They perform a short dance routine.*) And—(*Hand to ear.*)—aah, the government gardens in Pretoria. (*Doves cooing.*) And then, they will take him on a trip to SUN CITY— (*Stage radiantly light.*)—THE LAS VEGAS OF SOUTH AFRICA, where they will build him a holy suite and President Lucas Mangope, the puppet, will offer him the key to the homeland of Bophutatswana! And then, what will happen? They will take him past the good-time girls. (*Standing on a box, Percy mimes.*) And the gambling machines. (*Percy transforms into a one-armed bandit, Mbongeni works him, wins triumphantly.*) And when television cameras turn on him, will he be smiling? Will he be joyous? No. He'll be crying. And when all the people shout—

BOTH: Speech! Morena, speech!

MBONGENI: —Morena will say, 'No.'

PERCY (*miming holding a mike*): No, speak up.

MBONGENI: No! Morena will say, what key is this? What place is this? This place where old people weep over the graves of children? How has it happened? How has it been permitted? I've passed people with burning mouths. People buying water in a rusty piece of tin, and beside them I see people swimming in a lake that they have made from water that is here!

PERCY: Be careful, there are police spies here.

MBONGENI: What spies? Morena will say, I pass people who sit in dust and beg for work that will buy them bread. And on the other side I see people who are living in gold and glass and whose rubbish bins are loaded with food for a thousand mouths.

PERCY: Hey! That's not your business. There are security police, man.

MBONGENI: What security police? Morena will say, I see families torn apart, I see mothers without sons, children without fathers, and wives who have no men! Where are the men? Aph'amadoda madoda? [Where are the men?] And people will say, Ja, Morena, it's this bladdy apartheid. It's those puppets, u Mangope! u

Matanzima! u Sebe! Together with their white Pretoria masters. They separate us from our wives, from our sons and daughters! And women will say, Morena there's no work in the homelands. There's no food. They divide us from our husbands and they pack them into hostels like men with no names, men with no lives! And Morena will say, come to me, you who are divided from your families. Let us go to the cities where your husbands work. We will find houses where you can live together and we will talk to those who you fear! What country is this? (*Spits on ground.*)

Percy starts to sing and march on the spot. Mbongeni joins him. They mime carrying a banner.

BOTH ACTORS (*sing a Zulu song and march*):
Oyini oyini madoda
Oyini oyini madoda
Sibona ntoni uma sibon'u Mangope
Siboni sell-out uma sibon'u Mangope
Sibona ntoni uma sibon'u Gatsha
Siboni puppet uma sibon'u Gatsha
Khulula khulula Morena
Khulula khulula Morena
Sibona ntoni nang'u Matanzima
Sibon'u mbulali nang'u Matanzima

[What is this, what is this men
What is this, what is this men
What do we see when we see Mangope
We see a sell-out when we see Mangope
What do we see when we see Gatsha
We see a puppet when we see Gatsha
Help us — Help us Morena
Help us — Help us Morena
What do we see — there is Matanzima
We see a killer when we see Matanzima.]

PERCY (*interrupted*): Hey! Tear gas!

They struggle, continuing the song, throwing stones, sounding sirens, dogs barking. Lights go down as they are subdued.

BOTH.: Morena-a-a-a! Morena-a-a-a!

SCENE TWENTY-ONE

Spotlight finds Percy as Prime Minister, pink nose, spectacles.

PERCY: My people, as your Prime Minister I must warn you that we stand alone in the face of total onslaught. Our enemies will stop at nothing, even to the extent of sending a cheap communist magician to pose as the Morena, and undermine the security of our nation. But let me assure you that this cheap impostor is safely behind bars, from which he cannot fly. Peace and security have returned to our lovely land.

SCENE TWENTY-TWO

Lights come up on Mbongeni squatting on a box, wrapped in a prisoner's blanket.

MBONGENI (*knocking*): Cell number six! Morena! (*Knocking.*) Cell number six! Morena! Bad luck, hey! I hear they got you again. They tell me you're in solitary confinement just like us. From Sun City to Robben Island! (*Laughs ruefully.*) You've made us famous, Morena. The whole world is talking about us. Hey bayasiteya labedana bamabhunu man! [Hey they are riding us these white boys.] Morena, I sit here just like you with this one light bulb and only the Bible to read! Ja! And the New Testament tells me about you, and your family, and your thoughts. But why do they give us your book to read, Morena? They must be bladdy mad, Morena. This book only proves how mad they are. Listen. (*Knocking.*) Cell number six! For people like us, to be locked here like this is just rubbish. So what do you want here? What does your father know? What does he say? Come on Morena, man! (*Knocking.*) Cell number six! You've got all the power! How can you let these things happen? How can you just sit there like that, Morena? Okay, okay, I know you don't like miracles, but these are bladdy hard times, Morena. Morena, I must tell you, now that I've gone into your book, I really like you, Morena. But I'm getting bladdy disappointed. How long must we wait for you to do something? Morena, I must tell you, I'm among those who have stopped waiting. One day we'll have to help you! Pamberi ne hondo! [Power to the people!] Can you hear me Morena? Cell number six!! (*'Sarie Marais' being whistled offstage. Knocking more cautiously:*) Cell number six!! Morena! Morena . . . Cell number six . . .

SCENE TWENTY-THREE

Percy enters whistling 'Sarie Marais'. He is a soldier, pink nose, camouflage hat. Mimes carrying rifle.

MBONGENI (*enters similarly dressed*): Two three! Morning Corporal!

PERCY: Morning Sergeant!

MBONGENI: How are things going, Corporal? (*He rests on a box.*)

PERCY: I'm tired, Sergeant.

MBONGENI: Oh, God. To be a guard on bladdy Robben Island!

PERCY: Ja, ever since they brought Morena out here to Robben Island everything has been upside down.

MBONGENI: All those bladdy interviews, that's what's killing us!

PERCY: I'm sick of having my photograph taken.

MBONGENI: I know. The next photographer I see, I shoot to kill!

PERCY: Daily News.

MBONGENI: Sunday Times.

PERCY: Time Life.

MBONGENI: Pravda.

PERCY: London Observer.

MBONGENI: New York Times.

PERCY: All those bladdy communists!

MBONGENI: You know, I got a letter from a woman in Sweden. She saw my photograph in her newspaper. And my wife was chasing me with a frying pan! I told her I never knew the woman, but she didn't believe me.

PERCY: I wish they had kept him in John Vorster Square or Pretoria Central.

MBONGENI: Come on, Corporal. You know what happened at John Vorster Square. Gabriel got him out of there in ten seconds flat! Only Robben lsland has got the right kind of AA missiles.

PERCY: AA? What is that?

MBONGENI: Anti-Angel.

PERCY: Anti-Angel? I never heard of that!

MBONGENI: He'll never get away from Robben Island!

PERCY (*distracted, points into the audience*): Hey! Sergeant! What's that you said? Just look over there! Just look over there!!!

MBONGENI (*moves lazily toward him singing 'Sarie Marais'*): My Sarie Marais is so ver van my hart . . . (*Suddenly he looks into the audience, horrified.*) God! Hey! Fire! Fire!

They riddle the audience with machine-gun fire.

PERCY: Call helicopter control, quick!!!

MBONGENI: Hello? Hello? Radio 1254 CB? Over. Hello? Radio 1254 . . .

SCENE TWENTY-FOUR

Lights reduce to spot-light the boxes. Actors turn their hat brims up. Mbongeni spins his hand above his head. Helicopter sounds. They are in a helicopter, looking down.

PERCY (*mimes radio*): Radio 1254 CB receiving, over.

What? That's impossible! Are you sure? Okay, over and out. Hey, what do you see down below?

MBONGENI (*miming binoculars*): Oh, it's a beautiful day down below. Birds are flying, swimmers are swimming, waves are waving. Hey! Morena's walking on water to Cape Town! Ag shame! His feet must be freezing! Hey, I wish I had my camera here!

PERCY: This must be the miracle of the decade!

MBONGENI: Ag, I always forget my camera!

PERCY: Down! Down! Radio 1254 CB receiving, over. Yes, we've got him. Yeah, what? Torpedo? Oh no, have a heart! He's not even disturbing the waves! Ja, I wish you could see him, he looks amazing!

MBONGENI (*nodding frenetically into mike*): Ja jong, ja! [Yes man, yes!]

PERCY: What? Bomb Morena? Haven't you heard what they say? You start with Morena and it's worse than an atom bomb! Over and out! Hey, this is a shit bladdy job! You pull the chain.

MBONGENI: No, you!

PERCY: No! You pull the chain!

MBONGENI: No, man!

PERCY: This man is mos' happy, why blow him up?

MBONGENI: No come on, come on. Fair deal! Eenie, meenie, minie moe. Vang a kaffir by the toe. As hy shrik, let him go. Eenie, meenie, minie, moe! It's you!

PERCY: Okay! This is the last straw! I think I'm resigning tomorrow!

MBONGENI: Ready . . . target centre below . . . release depth charges . . . bombs . . . torpedoes . . . go!

They watch. The bombs fall. A moment of silence and then a terrible explosion. They separate, come together detonating each other. Light reduces to stark overhead shaft.

BOTH: Momeeeee! Aunti-i-i-eee! He-e-e-l-l-p!

Blackout.

SCENE TWENTY-FIVE

South African television news theme is proclaimed in darkness.

MBONGENI: News!

Lights on.

PERCY (*in pink nose, proudly holds a cardboard TV screen shape around his face*): Good evening. The United Nations Security Council is still waiting further information on the explosion which completely destroyed Cape Town and its famous Table Mountain. (*Bland smile.*) United Nations nuclear sensors have recorded distinct signs of nuclear disturbance in the Southern African sector. Investigators have suggested a strong possibility of a mishap to a SAA Military Helicopter carrying a nuclear missile over the bay. However, Mrs Fatima Mossop, domestic servant, Sea Point, a freak survivor of the calamity, insisted that the explosion emanated from a human figure walking across the bay from the Island, supporting the superstition that the nuclear-type explosion was an inevitable result of a bomb attack on Morena. The Prime Minister himself continues to deny any relationship between Morena and the agitator imprisoned on the Island. Mrs Fatima Mossop is still under observation by the state psychiatrists. Well, that is all for tonight. Goodnight. (*Fade on fixed smile.*)

SCENE TWENTY-SIX

The graveyard. Mbongeni in a hat and dust-coat is weeding and singing Zuluboy's song from Scene Eighteen. Percy is sleeping on the boxes. Mbongeni sees him, rouses him.

MBONGENI: Hey! Hey! Hey! This is not a park bench. It's a tombstone. This is a cemetery, it's not Joubert Park.

PERCY (*groggy*): I'm sorry, I should know better.

MBONGENI: You want Joubert Park? You want Joubert Park? You catch the number fifty-four bus. Or you want Zola Park? You catch a Zola taxi. Or you want to have a look at the ducks? Go to the Zoo Lake. But don't sit on my tombstones. Please.

PERCY: Okay, I'm sorry about that. Can I have a look around?

MBONGENI: Oh, well if you want to have a look around, look around, but don't sit around! The dead are having a hard enough time. These tombstones are bladdy heavy!

PERCY: Aaahh, tell me, do you keep your tombstones in alphabetical order?

MBONGENI: Yeah. What do you want?

PERCY: Where's 'L'?

MBONGENI: You want 'L'?

PERCY: Ja.

MBONGENI: Serious? Okay. Right there. That whole line is 'L'. By that big tombstone. See? Livingstone . . . Lamele . . . Lusiti . . . Lizi . . .

PERCY: Have you got any Lazarus here?

MBONGENI: Lazarus? Lazarus? Oh, Israel Lazarus! That was a very good man! You mean that one? American Half-Price Dealers? That was a very good man, I used to work for him in 1962. But he's not dead yet! Why are you looking for his grave here?

PERCY: I'm just looking for something to do.

MBONGENI: But this face I know. Are you his son?

PERCY: No, not his.

MBONGENI: Then who are you?

PERCY: Morena.

MBONGENI: You? Morena? Aaay suka! They killed him. That is his tombstone.

PERCY: Oh no, Baba. Have you forgotten? I will always come back after three days, bombs or no bombs.

MBONGENI: Hay! Morena! Aawu nkulunkulu wami! [Oh my God!]

PERCY: Ssssshhhh! Please, don't shout my name.

MBONGENI: Do you remember me?

PERCY: Who are you?

MBONGENI: Zuluboy from Coronation Brickyard!

PERCY: Hey! Zuluboy! (*They embrace.*) What are you doing here?

MBONGENI: I'm working here at the cemetery. I'm disguised from the police! Lazarus . . . Lazarus . . . aaaahhh! Now I understand! Morena, you're looking for people to raise!

PERCY: Ja!

MBONGENI: But why didn't you ask me?

PERCY: How would I know?

MBONGENI: I know exactly who my people want! Come, let us look at these tombstones.

Mbongeni leads Percy in a dance around the cemetery, singing. Mbongeni stops, Percy beside him. He points to a corner of the audience.

MBONGENI: Morena! Here's our 'L' — ALBERT LUTHULI — the Father of our Nation! Raise him Morena!

PERCY: Woza Albert! [Rise up Albert!]

Mbongeni falls over, stunned then ecstatic.

BOTH (*singing*):
    Yamemeza inkosi yethu
    Yathi ma thambo hlanganani
    Uyawa vusa amaqhawe amnyama
    Wathi kuwo

[Our Lord is calling.
He's calling for the bones of the dead to join together.
He's raising up the black heroes.
He calls to them]

MBONGENI (*addressing the risen but invisible Albert
    Luthuli*): Hey, Luthuli uyangibona mina? U Zulu boy.
    Ngakhula phansi kwakho e-Stanger. [Hey, Luthuli, do
    you remember me? I'm Zuluboy. I grew up in Stanger.]

They dance on, repeating the song.

BOTH (*singing*):
    Yamemeza inkosi yethu
    Yathi ma thambo hlanganani
    Uyawa vusa amaqhawe amnyama
    Wathi kuwo

[Our Lord is calling.
He's calling for the bones of the dead to join together.
He's raising up the black heroes.
He calls to them]

Mbongeni stops, Percy beside him.

MBONGENI: Morena! Robert Sobukwe! He taught us Black
    Power! Raise him!

PERCY: Woza Robert!

MBONGENI (*ecstatic*): Hau Mangaliso! Mangaliso!

They dance on.

BOTH (*singing*):
    Yamemeza inkosi yethu
    Yathi ma thambo hlanganani
    Uyawa vusa amaqhawe amnyama
    Wathi kuwo

[Our Lord is calling.
He's calling for the bones of the dead to join together.
He's raising up the black heroes.
He calls to them]

MBONGENI: Lilian Ngoyi! She taught our mothers about freedom. Raise her!

PERCY: Woza Lilian!

MBONGENI (*spins with joy*): Woza Lilian!—Hey Lilian, uya mbona uMorena? Uvuswe uMorena. [Come Lilian— hey Lilian, do you see Morena? It's Morena who raised you.]

They dance on.

BOTH (*singing*):
Yamemeza inkosi yethu
Yathi ma thambo hlanganani
Uyawa vusa amaqhawe amnyama
Wathi kuwo

[Our Lord is calling.
He's calling for the bones of the dead to join together.
He's raising up the black heroes.
He calls to them]

MBONGENI: Steve Biko! The hero of our children! Please Morena— Please raise him!

PERCY: Woza Steve!

MBONGENI: Steve! Steve! Uyangikhumbula ngikulandela e Kingwilliams-town? [Steve, do you remember me, following you in Kingswilliamstown?]

BOTH (*dancing*): Woza Bram Fischer! . . . Woza Ruth First! . . . Woza Griffith Mxenge . . . Woza Hector Peterson . . . (*They stop, arms raised triumphantly.*) WOZA ALBERT!!!

Blackout.

SONQOBA SIMUNYE

GANGSTERS

Maishe Maponya

Steve Biko is perhaps the most famous detainee to die at the hands of the South African police. His death dramatized the plight of countless men and women who disappear into the prisons never to be heard from again. In *Gangsters,* Maishe Maponya takes us into a prison cell where a lone poet hangs from a cross, a victim of police brutality.

In South Africa, where the laws protect police activity, no one really knows what happens in those cells except the detainees and their interrogators. Maponya's play brings us much closer to the action, to witness with our own eyes the mentality that leads to people being killed in prison. In this instance the culprit is a black policeman, Jonathan, who executes orders from "his master's voice" with mechanical precision. The white security officer, Captain Whitebeard, is there to reassure the state that the "terrorists" are dealt with properly and to make sure that the black officer follows orders.

Through flashbacks, the play juxtaposes the interrogation, where the white officer tries to persuade the poet Masechaba to tone down his poetry, with the aftermath, where the two policemen try to concoct a reason for the poet's brutal death.

The play deals with an issue that is still very much of a problem in South Africa: even after numerous inquests and the unveiling of the most contrived police cover-ups, those who killed Steve Biko have never been brought to trial.

GANGSTERS
Maishe Maponya

CHARACTERS

MAJOR WHITEBEARD — a white Security Police Officer
JONATHAN — a black Security Policeman
RASECHABA — a poet

> *The stage is divided into two acting areas, stage left*
> *and stage right, by lighting or other means. Stage Right*
> *is a security cell; Stage Left represents various settings.*
> *Additional lighting needed is a Blue Cover (for the re-*
> *citing of poems) and a Special used at two points only.*
> *The Transitions between these states are marked in the*
> *text.*

Props. *Cross (red) on a platform; table; two chairs; cell*
window bars; rope (two metres); two tape recorders; two
Bibles; a briefcase; books; papers; two photos; a gun and a
holster; handcuffs. Uniforms for Jonathan and Whitebeard;
churchgoing clothes for Jonathan and Rasechaba; street
clothes and pyjamas for Rasechaba; a black gown with
hood.
Sound. *A hymn; Rasechaba's voice (both on tape).*

OPENING — THE CELL

Black-out both stage areas. Lights come up instantly on stage right. Rasechaba dressed in black with hood on head is balanced on the cross-structure. Dead. The major is standing on the left of the structure with Jonathan in the same position on the right. They pace round and round contemplating Rasechaba, ending up in the same positions as before.

WHITEBEARD: So, this is what you did?

JONATHAN: Yes my lord.

WHITEBEARD: How long has he been like this?

JONATHAN: My lord knows.

WHITEBEARD: I forget!

JONATHAN: One week!

WHITEBEARD: So, so! (*pause*) This is serious! I'll have to see what I can do. Why the structure?

JONATHAN: So that you can see him well!

WHITEBEARD: Why the gown?

JONATHAN: To have him all black!

WHITEBEARD: Why the hood?

JONATHAN: To help hide the head!

WHITEBEARD: What?

JONATHAN: It is common practice my lord that when detainees are in this state, we dress them in black.

WHITEBEARD: He wasn't dressed in black when I first saw him!

BLACKOUT. PAUSE. TRANSITION to FIRST EN-COUNTER.

Whitebeard is seated on a chair and reading a newspaper, while Jonathan is standing somewhere at the back —idle.

WHITEBEARD: Jonathan!

JONATHAN: Yes Sir.

WHITEBEARD: Has somebody gone to fetch the poet?

JONATHAN: Yes sir; Sergeant Ngobese's gone to fetch him.

WHITEBEARD: Alright (*pause*) I see Kaizer Chiefs are playing Orlando Pirates on Saturday—who do you think is going to win?

JONATHAN: (*excited*) Of course it goes without saying; it will be Orlando Pirates all the way—it's like I see it happening again. Exactly what happened in nineteen-seventy-three when they collected all the titles. They are the darlings of our soccer in black and white. (*mimics*) Nang'u Rhee! Nang'u Jomo Sono! Wa libamba umfana wa li khahela—laduma! (*kicks with one leg*) [Here comes Rhee, passes to Jomo who scores!]

WHITEBEARD: (*interrupting*): Jonathan!

JONATHAN: (*freezes, leg still in the air*) Yes sir.

WHITEBEARD: Fetch the poet.

JONATHAN: Yes sir. (*opens door for Rasechaba to come in*)

Rasechaba walks in slowly, noting the tape recorder on the major's desk. He stops.

WHITEBEARD: (*folds the newspaper and stands up*) Mr Rasechaba? (*mispronounces*)

RASECHABA: (*correcting*) Rasechaba is my name.

WHITEBEARD: Oh I'm sorry Mr Rasechaba—major Whitebeard is my name—security. (*producing an identification document*)

RASECHABA: Yes, what can I do for you?

WHITEBEARD: Mr Rasechaba, we in the branch are a little worried about your poetry. We feel it's inflammatory.

RASECHABA: Can you explain yourself? What do you mean?

WHITEBEARD: I don't have to explain myself. All I have to do is to play one of the cassettes that we've got of you reciting those poems—particularly the one called—(*recalling*) 'The spirit of the Nation.' All I have to do is play one of the video tapes that we've made of you reciting your poetry at Regina Mundi commemorative services, that's explanation enough of what I mean. Oh, I'm forgetting my manners, please sit down. (*offers him a seat*) Let me just get one thing clear for myself; do you write as well as perform these poems?

RASECHABA: Yes I do.

WHITEBEARD: Don't you feel that they are inflammatory?

RASECHABA: They're not

WHITEBEARD: They're not inflammatory?

RASECHABA: No.

WHITEBEARD: So Mr Rasechaba, when you stand in front of a hall full of people and you've just recited one of your poems and the people start screaming and waving their fists in the air—you don't feel it's your poetry that's caused them to react like that?

RASECHABA: No.

WHITEBEARD: That interests me. It interests me... (*sees Jonathan in the room*) I don't think we need you any longer Jonathan. Why don't you go out and get yourself a cup of coffee. (*Jonathan leaves. Major switches off tape*)

RASECHABA: So, you have been taping all this?

WHITEBEARD: Regulations, I'm afraid, that's why I got rid of Jonathan. I wanted to have an off-the-record chat with you and I didn't want him to report me upstairs for breaking the rules. But Mr Rasechaba — it really interests me that a man as obviously intelligent and sensitive as you can actually believe that your poetry and the reaction it evokes are unrelated? How does the whole thing work?

RASECHABA: You see major, the manner in which I write my poetry is decided by the situation and inspiration at a given time. Major, when a poet pens anything on paper and the spirit of nature moves within him, he will write about nature. If the spirit of the nation moves within him, he will write about the nation. He will talk about man, he'll talk about pain and he'll talk about that which moves the people. If his people live in happiness, this happiness will be seen in his works; and that will be evidence to the world of how marvelous the lives of his people are. If I don't feel anything, I don't write anything.

WHITEBEARD: Very interesting Mr Rasechaba, very informative but that doesn't explain the militant style that you've chosen.

RASECHABA: Major, a poet sees things not in the manner that you and your colleagues see them. You may regard their world as fantasy, but it is in that abstract frame of mind that things start to take a certain shape and form and that shape is influenced by the material that inspires the poet; hence the manner that I express myself in my poetry.

WHITEBEARD: Very good and very informative. (*sighing*) But unfortunately, as you yourself put it, my colleagues and I see things differently from you and your people. We live in a different world, far from your abstract frames of mind — so what interests us is not so much the creative process as the effect that your poetry has on ordinary people, people who don't have the insight and understanding that you and I have, and there can be no doubt Mr Rasechaba that your poems have made a lot of people feel very angry, even violent, and it is my job to put a stop to that sort of thing and so I called you in to have a friendly chat and to warn you.

RASECHABA: But you talk about violence! I think it's your frame of mind. It is guilt.

WHITEBEARD: But your poetry is responsible for the creation of a violent frame of mind in the people who hear it.

RASECHABA: I am not responsible for the creation of the squatters. I am not responsible for the starvation of millions of children because their parents have been forced into arid lands. I did not create the humiliating laws—and I never created the racial barriers in this land. Who do you expect me to blame when life becomes unfair to black soul.

(No response. Lights fade down leaving Rasechaba covered by blue light for poem)

When life becomes unfair to a black soul?
Who is to blame?
When a child leaves home for school never to come
    back,
When a mother hides the cracks on her face created by
    tears of crying,
When a brother dashes in fear to seek refuge in the
    wilderness—
We are all taken by surprise!
When life becomes unfair to a black soul
Who is to blame?
When a child throws a stone in anger and dies!
When a family takes a brazier into a shack and dies!
When a young girl—walks into the path of a stray
    bullet and dies!
We are all taken by surprise
But God is not at all taken by surprise!

(Blue light fades as general lights come up. Rasechaba turns challengingly to the major) Who do you expect me to blame?

WHITEBEARD: O.K. Mr Rasechaba, for the purpose of this discussion I will agree that things are not perfect with your people, and this government is doing everything within realistic terms to improve their situation. But you as a poet have a responsibility to your people. I don't know why you choose to depress them by concentrating on the negative aspects of their life. Why don't you cheer them up by talking about the good things that surround them — by telling them of the natural beauty that surrounds them — I'm no expert of course but I had to learn one poem at school which has stuck in my mind. It goes something like this:

(he recites any Afrikaans poem about flowers or nature)

Now that sort of poem Mr Rasechaba has a beautiful melody to it and it makes me feel good inside not violent and angry...

RASECHABA: Of course I said I could write about flowers. But where are the flowers in Winterveld for me to write about? What kind of flowers will ever grow in Crossroads? If that poet of yours lived in Alexandra, he would write about the stagnant pools of water and the smell of shit filtering through the streets at night because there is no drainage system. He would write about the buckets of feces placed in the streets at night as if families are bragging which family eats more to shit more.

WHITEBEARD: I don't think we need that kind of language Mr Rasechaba!

RASECHABA: And my people that kind of life Major Whitebeard. *(there is tension as they look each other in the eye)*

WHITEBEARD: Alright. Let's get back to your poetry. Can't you see that you are inciting the people to violence with your poetry. When you use lines like "the barbed wire mentality of a good-looking Afrikaaner" you are insulting the Afrikaaner people. When you write about the "trigger-happy fingers" it shouldn't surprise you when the people respond and raise their fist into the air and shout "Amandla Ngawethu!"

RASECHABA: But you having to direct your...

WHITEBEARD: Yes Mr Rasechaba! (*points to the chair for Rasechaba to sit*) It's been a very interesting discussion. But the fact remains that I have a job to do and that job is to warn you. (*walks to behind the chair on which Rasechaba is seated*) You are playing with fire. And remember my friend that people who play with fire must expect to get burned. If you want to continue playing with fire, don't blame anyone when you get those poetry-writing fingers of yours burned. Well thank you very much for coming to this chat with me. You may go. (*there is tension as Rasechaba stands to leave the room*)

WHITEBEARD: (*calling out*) Jonathan!

JONATHAN: (*comes in*) Yes sir.

WHITEBEARD: I want you to keep an eye on Rasechaba. This means, Jonathan, that you do not go to Ellis Park, to watch the soccer match on Saturday. I want you to do a good job. Do you hear me Jonathan?

JONATHAN: Yes sir.

BLACKOUT. TRANSITION to CELL.

WHITEBEARD: How's the head?

JONATHAN: You've seen it.

WHITEBEARD: I forget! (*Jonathan moves towards Rasechaba to show his head*) Say it! (*Jonathan stops*)

JONATHAN: Bald. Septic.

WHITEBEARD: Colour?

JONATHAN: Red and pink.

WHITEBEARD: Put calamine lotion on head.

JONATHAN: Okay my lord, I make a note. (*takes out pad and pen, notes down*) Calamine lotion on head.

WHITEBEARD: And why the long sleeves?

JONATHAN: To help have him all black.

WHITEBEARD: No! The court won't take it!

JONATHAN: I make a note. (*takes out pad and pen, writes*) Hands exposed. (*slowly with a sad look on his face*) Hands exposed.

WHITEBEARD: What is wrong now Jonathan?

JONATHAN: I have seen those hands many a times in church.

WHITEBEARD: Remember, you had a job to do.

JONATHAN: Yes my lord.

> BLACKOUT. TRANSITION to CHURCH—*flashback to meeting between Rasechaba and Jonathan. Hymn backstage; Rasechaba enters, Bible in hand, closely followed by Jonathan, also carrying a Bible.*

RASECHABA: (*stands still without looking at him*) Jonathan, is there anywhere where one can go without you following him?

JONATHAN: (*jokes*) Yes. Toilet.

RASECHABA: No Jonathan this is serious. I am getting irritated at the manner in which you keep following me. What is it that you want from me?

JONATHAN: (*amused*) You must be exaggerating. What makes you such an expert on the special branch? Anyway what would I find to do here besides attending the church service?

RASECHABA: You should be ashamed of yourself coming to church every Sunday and knowing that your job is to help the white man preserve an ungodly Status Quo.

JONATHAN: Remember Rasechaba that I'm doing a job like any other person who wakes up in the morning to go to town for a white man. On Friday when that person gets his salary, I also get my salary.

RASECHABA: But the difference is that your salary is dirty. It is enveloped with the blood of your own brothers!

JONATHAN: How many children die of malnutrition because their parents cannot find jobs? (*Rasechaba makes move to go away but Jonathan pulls him by the hand*) I have mouths to feed. (*makes sure that he is not heard by other congregants*) I have my children's school fees to attend to. Do you know that since I took up this job, things have changed for the better for me. I'm also convinced that we must stand aloof from politics. We are servants of God, and God does not wish for us to enter the political arena.

RASECHABA: I've had enough of this senseless talk. The sermon delivered by the priest in church was enough. I'm not going to listen to a sell-out sermon from you. Jonathan, you are a blood-sucker. You have no conscience. You are dead inside.

JONATHAN: What do you mean I'm dead? I'm alive. I've the same feelings as you.

RASECHABA: (*moving away from him*) I knew you wouldn't understand me. By dead—(*blue light comes up, simultaneously general light fades down*) I mean the smile you put on when the enemy grins at you. Death is when the colour of your skin turns against you and you don't know where you stand as others decide your fate.
Death is when your mouth can utter no cry.
Death is when your eyes cannot see light beyond the darkness.
Death is when your ears cannot hear the call filtering through the noise.
Death is when your feet can no longer carry you through the distance.
Death is when you stop to be you!
And above all,
(*general lights come up whilst the blue fades down*)
Death, is when you start to hate to be black!

JONATHAN: Rasechaba you are too hasty to condemn me before you understand my situation better. Maybe we are not so different after all.

RASECHABA: Ag fuck off you are a sell-out! (*moves away*)

JONATHAN: (*humiliated*) Hey Rasechaba you ridicule me in the presence of all these people—that is nice for you. (*Rasechaba leaves—calls after him*) But one day you'll know who I am. Then you'll know what death is. Mnqundu wakho! Lenkwenkwe iyandigezela, masimb'akho! shit! [Bloody arse, the uncircumsized bastard thinks I'm a fool. Bloody shit.] Bastard! (*realises that he's got the Bible in his hand*) O! I'm sorry Lord!

BLACKOUT. TRANSITION to CELL. *The mood has changed.*

JONATHAN: (*apologetic*) I'll say he threw himself out of the window in an attempt to escape.

WHITEBEARD: No good. The interrogation room is on the ground floor!

JONATHAN: No no, it's simple. We called him to have breakfast with us—he was so hungry that he ate his food so fast that it choked him.

WHITEBEARD: Not so convincing. We never have breakfast with detainees in our rooms.

JONATHAN: (*Tries again*): Alright, I'll say he was on hunger strike since we took him in.

WHITEBEARD: No! Jonathan when last did you check your record book? We gave that excuse some time ago!

JONATHAN: (*still panicking*) How about saying he hanged himself with his own trousers—that's right, suicide!

WHITEBEARD: Not convincing. There's nothing in the cell to hang himself from!

JONATHAN: (*a bit hopeless but tries*) Seems like nothing is convincing. I'll try one more time—he slipped on a piece of soap . . .

WHITEBEARD: You can't fool the public with that one again.

JONATHAN: (*defeated*) My lord knows all.

WHITEBEARD: Maybe we should look back at our history with him. Maybe that will give us a clue.

JONATHAN: Yes my lord maybe that will give us an idea.

TRANSITION to SECOND ENCOUNTER. At table, the major is sorting through papers.

WHITEBEARD: Jonathan, where are those poems of Rasechaba's that the Soweto Business Association is complaining about?

JONATHAN: Which ones are those sir?

WHITEBEARD: The ones that I gave you to photostat.

JONATHAN: (*going through his bag, to himself*) My driver's licence, my insurance contract. O, sir look my daughter turned two years yesterday. This is her picture taken last week.

WHITEBEARD: (*business-like*) Later Jonathan. Bring me poems. (*Jonathan gives him the poems*) Now call the poet inside.

JONATHAN: Rasechaba!

Rasechaba walks in and stops.

WHITEBEARD: Mr Rasechaba, you disappoint me. When I had you in here the last time I thought we'd come to some understanding. But when I read these poems I'm not sure. Sit down please — and listen objectively to these poems of yours. I'm going to read them the way that you do . . .

RASECHABA: No. If they have to be read I'll read them for you — I wrote them.

WHITEBEARD: No! I want you to hear the way they sound.

Rasechaba stands to take the page from the major but quickly Jonathan steps in, his hand nearly at the ready for his gun. Rasechaba stops, realises the risk and sits down.

Look deep into the ghetto
And see into the ghetto
And see the modernized graves
Manacled with chains
So as not to resist.
Look deep into the ghetto
And see streets dividing the graves
Streets with pavements
Dyed with blood
Blood of the innocent.

Look deep into the ghetto
And see yourself silenced
By a ninety-nine year lease
Thus creating a class-struggle
Within a struggle for survival

Look the ghetto over
You will see smog hover
And dust choking the lifeless living-dead
Can you hear the beast hell
And creatures evil
Howling and brawling
As they rush to devour you
and suck the last drop of blood
From your emaciated corpse . . .

RASECHABA: That is not the way tha . . .

WHITEBEARD: I haven't finished yet. (*pause*) Now 'class
struggle' that is Marxist talk. It is dangerous talk Mr
Rasechaba. Don't you feel that Marxism and Afri-
canism are contradictory?

RASECHABA: No. They are not contradictory.

WHITEBEARD: Oh, so you admit that you are a Marxist.

RASECHABA: I didn't say that.

WHITEBEARD: I'm glad you didn't say that. Because if you
had, you wouldn't be here with me. Mr Rasechaba
you're fortunate that you're here with me tonight
because some of my colleagues would have dealt with

you firmly. (*slight pause*) You puzzle me Mr Rasechaba. You claim to be an Africanist and yet when one of your people goes out to improve his or her living condition and when some of them participate in the political organs that are available to them you attack them. Can't you see that places like Crossroads and Mogopa are a health hazard? Can't you see that the proliferation of shacks and shanties in the townships are a drawback to those blacks who want to live a better life? What is your Black Consciousness motto 'Blackman—you are on your own.' Why then do you try and belittle the black men who are trying to go on their own by owning businesses and improve the lives of their people—it seems you in your poetry attack them.

RASECHABA: I am not attacking those who are caught in the capitalists' spider's web.

WHITEBEARD: Who do you attack then? Who do you attack? (*no response*) I asked you a question, who do you attack? (*general lights fade, blue comes up*)

RASECHABA: (*standing on chair*):
On the wings of the storm of liberation
Waving black tickets in their hands
Degrees hanging like monuments
In their glass houses,
Sit the cheese and wine
Drinkers of our struggle.

others are undegreed
Unread, underpaid
And deprived of the right to quench
Their education thirst.
Pity, they too are caught in the web.

The motto reads thus!
Divide and rule
A new dispensation
Is the name of the game.

The ghetto is fast becoming a suburb,
Beverley Hills
Selection Park
Prestige Park
Monument Park
"Who cares
It's my sweat
It's my money
You're just wasting your time.
Damn it, I'm going out
To have a swim."

Hats off for the Master's plan
We salute you Soweto Homemakers' Festival
Thank you Urban Foundation
Thank you Gough Cooper
Voertsek. You have messed up our struggle!

(general lights come up, blue fades)

WHITEBEARD: I asked you a question—whom do you attack?

RASECHABA: *(seated and uncaring)* The cheese and wine-drinkers of our struggle.

WHITEBEARD: Always a poet. That rings a bell—here in this poem you write 'silenced by a ninety-nine year lease . . . Selection Park, Monument Park . . . ' It seems to me Mr Rasechaba that these people who go and live in these better suburbs are worthy of your contempt?

RASECHABA: Everything I feel is in the poem and the poem says it all.

WHITEBEARD: *(immediately)* Would I be correct in assuming that organizations like, for example, the Soweto Business Association are targets of your attack?

RASECHABA: You can make up your mind on that.

WHITEBEARD: *(tension as their eyes lock; pause)* I'll do that! You may go. *(before Rasechaba reaches the door)* One more thing before you go—*(Rasechaba stops)* It might interest you Mr Rasechaba to know that a lot of people give us information. Normally we don't want to share it but sometimes we do — every Thursday night, for the past four weeks — you've been going to these rent boycott meetings and reciting your poetry in support of those leaders of yours who've been saying to the people "Don't go and live in Selection Park, don't go to that petit-bourgeois place" — It might interest you to know that those very same people have applied for bigger and better houses in Beverley Hills and Prestige Park — would you like to see their names? (*Rasechaba is silent*) I thought not. What about your black consciousness, Africa for the Africans leaders of yours who send their children secretly to white schools to get a white education — would you like to see their names?

RASECHABA: Every struggle has its betrayers. My leader is the people.

WHITEBEARD: The people — (*disappointed*) I'll try and remember that. (*gesturing with finger for Rasechaba to go, and then*) O, just before you go! I have a poem of yours which seems to be written in some ethnic language; would you tell me what it means? It's called 'Ridovhakunda Ridovhavhulaya.'

RASECHABA: Ridovhakunda Ridovhavhulaya
When we meet them at the hilltop
Before sunset
Ridovhakunda Ridovhavhulaya
We shall leave no stone unturned

Ridovhakunda Ridovhavhulaya!
For godsake
We shall do it
Be it morning, Be it night
Ridovhakunda Ridovhavhulaya!

Ridovhafara ngamilen'e
Ridovhakunda ngamatsheloni
Ridovhavhulaya ngamadegwana —
It does not matter

Victory is our aim
And conquest our goal.
Ridovhakunda Ridovhavhulaya
That is the theme of our struggle!

Kharitangana nabone Thoho-ya-Ndou
We shall sort them out!
And sort them out, I said!
We will chase them down Tshipinga Road
Ridovhadiya!
Ndizone Ridovhavhulaya!

Boda hafano and claimed
They found nobody in the land
Our forefathers so loved and adored
Ridovhakunda my God!
Ridovhavhulaya!

(Blue light fades, general comes up)

WHITEBEARD: It's called Ridovhakunda Ridovhavhulaya.
Would you care to tell me what it means?

RASECHABA: *(immediately)* No! I'm sure you have
translators in here who'd be happy to do it for you.
(angrily moves)

WHITEBEARD: *(with same anger)* Rasechaba!! *(points to a
chair. Rasechaba sits down).* Jonathan, it seems you are
going to get a chance to read this after all. *(hands him
a written page)* Read clauses four, five and six out
loud.

JONATHAN: Clause four: You are to report at your nearest
police station daily before eight o'clock every evening.
Clause five: You are not to attend any gathering and
note that talking to more than one person at a time
will be a contravention of your banning order. Clause
six: This banning order is imposed on you for the next
three years.

WHITEBEARD: I warned you and you chose to ignore my
friendly advice. You asked for it. Jonathan explain the
full implications of that document to our Soweto poet
laureate. *(makes a move for the door)*

RASECHABA: (*immediately*) Just before you go major! (*the major returns and stands facing Rasechaba—obviously irritated. A pause*) Mr William Shakespeare wrote some very wonderful lines about you—which go;
'Man proud man,
Dressed in a little brief authority
Plays such fantastic tricks before high heaven
As makes the angels weep.'

WHITEBEARD: (*chuckling first*) You really amuse me. What did you expect me to answer? Who is this Shakespeare? What political organization does he belong to? (*softer*) We are not as stupid as you might think. (*leaves*)

JONATHAN: Ja Rasechaba, poet of the people. How far did you think you'd get to? Where are all the people you were preaching your poetry to? Do you think the people will eat your poetry when they starve? Let me tell you something, I can't be led by a bastard like you! I know your kind. Showing off all the time with your name in the front pages of newspapers. All you know is jet-setting. From time to time, screwing white women and then come and think you can fool us with your petty politics. Ha! You think we are impressed by your behavior—putting on a tie and a suit—carrying an executive bag when you go and talk to the same white people that you criticize. Ah! but when you read your poetry; you put on dirty trousers—leave your hair uncombed and then you think you can fool everybody. (*laughs*) Mr Bigmouth I'm talking to you—talk! you've just earned yourself a banning order!

RASECHABA: (*grabbing the banning order, crumpling and throwing it away*) This is just a piece of paper—I'm still myself. My conscience is clear. The people out there are waiting for me—Rasechaba the father of the nation. Not you! They will scorn you, they'll reject you!

JONATHAN: C'mon enjoy yourself for this is your last poetry session.

RASECHABA: Yes, they can ban me here but they won't ban the spirit of the nation. For as long as those millions of people are still thirsty — the march will continue. I respect the convictions of my people and they respect my beliefs. I will help them carry the cross . . .

JONATHAN: Don't give me this shit about your people. I know your kind.

RASECHABA: You don't know for you have no conscience.

JONATHAN: It's easy for you because you get your money from the World Council of Churches. You have nothing to lose, because you have no mouths to feed . . .

RASECHABA: And so, that is what makes you sell your people out. Why don't you stand up and pull up your pants and tell the whiteman it's enough — your face against his; tell him you've had enough . . .

JONATHAN: You are dreaming for the whiteman is in power — can't you see?

RASECHABA: (*changes mood*) Jonathan, you don't understand. You are black and I'm black . . .

JONATHAN: And then?

RASECHABA: In the beginning it was you and me — the land belonged to us. We tilled it. We shared everything equally. Then came the whiteman with his own thoughts. He put us asunder; put us against each other and while this was going on, he fenced us around and then moved about freely declaring our land his land — no man's land. Have you not seen those boards along the road as you came from home this morning saying: 'In front of you, behind you and all around you is a Rand Mines Property?' Have you bothered to ask yourself 'where did Rand Mines get our land from?' He stole it from us. Do you know what the whiteman is doing today? He is sharing every little bit of our soil equally with his own brother. (*Jonathan is torn apart*) The system is so planned that we don't realize these tricks easily. (*voice building up*) Why should we let the whiteman decide our fate? Are you not matured to know and understand the world around us? (*holding him by the palm*) the whiteman is aware that your clenched fist together with mine is the dawning of a new era. And when that dawn comes—no amount of machinery will put us apart. This is the spirit of the nation! and this is what moves the people today!

WHITEBEARD: (*bursts in*) Rasechaba, you have overstayed your welcome! (*picks up the crumpled banning order and puts it into Rasechaba's pocket. Rasechaba exits*)

JONATHAN: (*guilty*) Major, what he was saying to me—there is sense in his talk.

WHITEBEARD: Do you think he makes sense?

JONATHAN: I—I—

WHITEBEARD: Let me make some sense to you. How many children have you got?

JONATHAN: Four major.

WHITEBEARD: Where are they being educated?

JONATHAN: Waterford, in Swaziland.

WHITEBEARD: And who pays for their education?

JONATHAN: You do it sir, as a benefit for me.

WHITEBEARD: Am I making sense Jonathan—am I making sense?

JONATHAN: (*ashamed*) Yes sir!

WHITEBEARD: Now, I'm detaching you from normal duties. I want you to organise a team of four men to follow him wherever he goes. I want to know who he meets. I want his telephone tapped and mail screened—and I have a suspicion that since the bastard is banned he's going to pursue his activities underground. I want you to do a good job—hear me Jonathan!

JONATHAN: Yes sir. (*slight pause*) By the way major, you promised that I could take the blue Mercedes Benz home for the weekend.

WHITEBEARD: Yes. The keys are in the key-box.

JONATHAN: (*excited*) Thank you sir!

BLACKOUT. TRANSITION to CELL.

JONATHAN: (*apologetic*): when do you think the pathologist will see him?

WHITEBEARD: (*authoritative*) Confidential to the party. Be here on Sunday. Eight o'clock—write your statement in full.

JONATHAN: Should I make up anything?

WHITEBEARD: No! That's important. He has to know what direction to channel his finding. Let him know it. What happened. Where. When it happened and who was present.

JONATHAN: I'll remember. I make a note. (*louder*) Details of torture in full.

WHITEBEARD: Shhh! Even walls have ears. Now let's take a closer look at him.

JONATHAN: Why my lord?

WHITEBEARD: Don't be stupid, the court will order it.

JONATHAN: Fine. Orders taken.

WHITEBEARD: Remove the hood. Now the gown—snap it! I have a meeting! (*Rasechaba now in pyjamas*)

JONATHAN: Like him better without?

WHITEBEARD: No. This looks horrible—calamine back of neck.

JONATHAN: I make a note. Calamine back of neck.

WHITEBEARD: The pyjamas and cap—where did he get them from?

JONATHAN: They are his—he refused to change into different clothes when we picked him up.

BLACKOUT. SPECIAL LIGHT comes up on Rasechaba's face behind bars.

RASECHABA:
  They broke one window first
  then on all windows played sounds
  Made by the drums of wars.
  Both doors joined the chorus
  The front emitting quick soprano notes
  The back a slow dub-dub-dub.
  It all happened in minutes
  The vocalists shouted
  The notes one after the other
  Like they'd never rehearsed before
  Vula! Vula! Bulang man!
  [Open! Open! Open!]
  Open! The lyrics went
  The timing was bad.

  This is the music
  That has become notorious
  It plays at the first hour of the day
  When your name rings
  To be registered in the books
  Of those messengers of darkness
  You jump to your feet
  Try to say something you think makes sense —
  You take all poems.
  Hide all manuscripts
  Throw some into the stove
  To destroy the creation
  rather than see it defiled by them
  With their dirty hands.

  If you're the poet's sister —
  'Don't open they are thugs!'
  And then the poet will follow
  'We won't open you are thugs!'
  To give himself time to destroy
  everything and quickly relay messages
  to the family

But then the door has to be opened—
Delaying tactics won't last forever
You saw it in Zimbabwe.
The back door is kicked open
While you open the front
within seconds
the musicians spit their songs into every room
while others guard the doors for escapers.
Torches flashing all over!
And the poet is TAKEN.

TRANSITION to INTERROGATION ROOM. Rasechaba is thrown in.

RASECHABA: (*exhausted and handcuffed*)
I could not say no to them—
Does the impala say no the lion?
Could the star of David say no to the jackboot?
I could not say no.

(*The major bursts in. He switches on the tape. Tension*)

RASECHABA: And why all this to me . . .

WHITEBEARD: Shut up! If I want you to talk I'll pull your beard. Mr Rasechaba spirit of the nation, poet, word merchant—what is the protector of the state? (*no response*) I asked you a question, what is the protector of the state? Jonathan, will you tell Mr Rasechaba what the protector of the state is?

JONATHAN: Yes. The law.

WHITEBEARD: And you Mr Rasechaba have chosen to break that law . . .

RASECHABA: I have not . . .

WHITEBEARD: (*interrupts*) Shut up! Six months ago, I had you in my office, I talked to you man-to-man. One intelligence to what I thought was another intelligence. I said to you, Mr Rasechaba, your poetry is inciting the people, please—I said to you—you are a man of reason, stop this! You are treading on a dangerous path. You wouldn't listen to me. Three months later, I bring you in here again — I say to you, I'm sorry justice has to prevail everywhere. I don't want to do this to you — I respect you — but the law has decided — here is your banning order — for your own protection. Now that's not good enough for Mr Rasechaba.

RASECHABA: (*interjects*)

WHITEBEARD: Shut up! Mr Rasechaba has to ignore the provisions of his banning order. He has to go out into the halls and he has to say to the people — 'you see my banning order! this is what I do to my banning order!' (*he spits on it*) I could live with that Mr Rasechaba — I could just live with it. But then yesterday something happened. I have a press release which is going out to the press this afternoon. (*reads from a piece of paper*) 'Yesterday evening patrol police spotted four men who they suspected were part of the fifty cadres that crossed the border into the country and when the terrorists realized they were being followed, they opened fire on the police who responded by killing all four men. None of the police was injured. Large quantities of arms and ammunitions and literature were captured.' Now Mr Rasechaba, amongst the AK47s and limpet mines, among the T5s and T7s, amongst those instruments of terror that were going to sow discord and violence to your people as well as mine — among them was a book of your poetry with the inscription inside (*produces book to read*) 'To L.M.A. — Solidarity and strength my comrades — Rasechaba!'

RASECHABA: (*responding*) I have signed lots of autographs of my poetry book when people bring them to me to sign — what do I do? do I refuse? As for L.MA. I do not know who he is —

WHITEBEARD: (*immediately*) Who is L.M.A.?

RASECHABA: I said I do not know.

WHITEBEARD: (*going closer to him and punching him in the stomach*) I asked you a question, who is L.M.A.?

RASECHABA: (*writhing with pain*) How must I talk to

convince you that I do not know? Are you ever going to understand my language?

WHITEBEARD: (*making as if to punch him again*) I have no desire to understand your language. (*sarcastic assurance*) You don't need to be scared of me—remember we are friends. (*rushes to table*) I have a confession to make to a friend. Yes Mr Rasechaba you have been followed night and day. Yes you have been watched. (*indicating from a list in his hands*) This is a known terrorist hide-out. That is a known terrorist hide-out. That is a shebeen where terrorists are known to congregate—is it coincidence that you visited these places on your poetic pilgrimage? What organization do you belong to?

RASECHABA: I do not belong to any organization.

WHITEBEARD: Isn't the African Poets of Azania an organization? Isn't that an organization?

RASECHABA: It is a cultural body. It's a traditional African ensemble . . .

WHITEBEARD: (*interrupts*) Is it not an organization?

RASECHABA: Yes it is.

WHITEBEARD: Are you not their member?

RASECHABA: Yes I am.

Whitebeard presses the tape to play back Rasechaba's denials: 'I do not belong to any organization'

WHITEBEARD: Now you tell me you do. Do you know what that means Mr Rasechaba—that means my friend that you lied to me and I don't like that. You've just told me one lie—how do I know how many other lies you told me. I think I must give you a chance to decide whether you want to continue lying to me. (*pulls him by the handcuffs*) Jonathan—let's assist Mr Rasechaba to a position that will aid his thinking.

(*They tie him to a rope which has been concealed above.*) That will give you some time to think properly.

(Black-out for fifteen seconds and then lights come up. Whitebeard comes back followed by Jonathan.)

WHITEBEARD: Poor Mr Rasechaba has been treated so badly, please release him Jonathan. *(Jonathan does so. Rasechaba falls down and Whitebeard offers him a chair: when he tries to sit Whitebeard pulls it away so that Rasechaba falls again to the ground.)* Weren't you taught manners kaffir that when you're in the presence of the whiteman that you must stand up. *(kicks him)* Up! Up! I can't talk to a grown man on the floor. Up! *(Rasechaba stands)* Now who is L.M.A.?

RASECHABA: I said I do not know.

WHITEBEARD: *(with some paper in his hands)* These are all the names and addresses of people you communicated with regularly—have you anything to say?

RASECHABA: I have communicated with lots of friends in the past—some of them are fellow writers—Do you expect me to live in isolation? I'm human.

WHITEBEARD: There you are again agreeing that you have something in common with the people on our lists.

RASECHABA: Whatever my friends do because of their beliefs has nothing to do with me. I'm a simple poet.

WHITEBEARD: I have here photographs of two of your best friends who've skipped the country and received training in Moscow and in Africa. How do you respond to your friends doing that?

RASECHABA: This government sells diamonds to Moscow. It is known to be getting arms from Bulgaria. How do you respond to your friends doing that?

WHITEBEARD: Did you hear that Jonathan? Our poet friend fancies himself as a foreign policy analyst. Now you listen to me very carefully. You see these hands—they are clean, unsoiled and they look friendly. Every day when these hands get home, they lift up a one-year old bundle called David and they throw him into the air and they catch him—they tickle him and hold him steady as he threatens to fall over with pure enjoyment. But Rasechaba in order to protect that little boy from you and your Marxist friends, to stop your violence and terror from changing that little boy's joy to tears, these hands will do anything (*claps him with both hands*) anything—and the blood will wash off very easily. Do you understand me? I asked you a question, do you understand me? Well my friend, seeing that you don't understand my words maybe you'll understand my actions (*kicks him between the legs and Rasechaba falls and writhes with pain. Pause*) Is there anything that you don't understand?

(*Rasechaba on his knees boldly faces Whitebeard and . . .*)

RASECHABA: So deep is my love for my land that those who fail to understand seek to destroy me. (*standing up slowly*)
Perhaps, finally at the very end
When the curtain falls
On the last act of your pillage
You will come to understand
How deeply
We loved this land
And cared for all its people.

(*upright and now facing the audience*)
White and black
Free and unfree.

(*There is silence and tension*)

WHITEBEARD: Jonathan, will you deal with Rasechaba as deemed fit and if you have to teach him that electricity has other uses than providing light you must do it!

JONATHAN: (*in a dilemma*) But sir, it seems from the look of things he does not know who this L.M.A. is. Besides he's an ordinary poet.

WHITEBEARD: (*angry*) Do I have to start wondering where your loyalties lie Jonathan!

JONATHAN: (*quickly realizing the danger*) No sir!

WHITEBEARD: Then do it!

(Whitebeard exits leaving the two behind. A little later Jonathan takes off his jacket to start the torture of Rasechaba as lights fade to BLACKOUT.)

TRANSITION to CELL.

WHITEBEARD: Now lift the head. *(Jonathan does as instructed)* Higher. Let's see his body.

JONATHAN: Why my lord?

WHITEBEARD: Don't be stupid, the court will order it!

JONATHAN: Fine. Orders taken.

WHITEBEARD: Bare the chest. *(Jonathan unbuttons the shirt and steps back)* Now the legs. *(he rolls the trousers' legs)* Higher. The other one. Put calamine on chest and legs.

JONATHAN: I make a note. Calamine chest and legs.

Whitebeard and Jonathan take a final look at Rasechaba as in the opening scene.

JONATHAN: What if we were to clothe him in prison attire?

WHITEBEARD: That's stupid! This is detention, he hasn't been to prison yet.

JONATHAN: *(humiliated)* My lord knows everything.

More contemplation of Rasechaba.

WHITEBEARD: That's enough for the day and remember whatever happens—DON'T PANIC! You've proved your loyalty *(puts his arm around Jonathan as they exit)* and I'll do everything to protect you.

General lights fade as Special comes up on Rasechaba's head and shoulders. Dead. Slow fade to BLACKOUT.

SONQOBA SIMUNYE

CHILDREN OF ASAZI

Matsemela Manaka

Black people in South Africa find themselves caught in a web of helplessness because of the government's unbending laws. But they never seem to give up hope or surrender to the forces of evil.

In *Children of Asazi,* the protagonist is torn between his love for his pregnant girl-friend, his filial love for his father, and his quest to find his mother who had been separated from his father many years ago. In and of itself, this would be a typical family story. But playwright Manaka uses the backdrop of a governmental attempt to forcefully remove people from Alexandra township to pit the man's love for his family against his dedication to fighting the government's efforts.

The play takes us deep into the family's problems which are not unlike those of the average black family in South Africa. At the root of their problems is the government. But the people's determination to be free is the shining point. There is a high note when a street musician brings in his saxophone and belts out the blues, township style. Through the music we hear the battle-cries.

CHILDREN OF ASAZI

Matsemela Manaka

CHARACTERS

DILIZA—a young activist who is about twenty years old
CHARMAINE—a young apolitical girl who is about
   twenty years old
NDUNA—an old jazz guitarist who is in his late fifties
GOGO—a disguised woman who is about fifty years old
MAJIKA—an older politician who is about fifty years old
MABU—an old jazz saxophonist who is about forty-five
   years old
OFFICER—an old man in his early forties
SPIRITS

PROLOGUE

*(The stage resembles a proclaimed slum in Johannes-
burg, Alexandra Township. It is a windy night. There
are three corrugated irons with windows and candle-
light burning behind each corrugated sheet of iron. We
hear people singing.)*

SONG: *Alexandra Khayalami*   [Alexandra my home]
          Alexandra Khayalami
          Alexandra Khayalami
          Alexandra Khayalami

          You may be a dark city
          but you are a home

the candle blows
the night away
like in all shelters
Alexandra Khayalami

You may be a dark city
but you are a home
the candle blows
the night away
like in all shelters
Alexandra Khayalami

Alexandra Khayalami
Alexandra Khayalami
Alexandra Khayalami
Alexandra Khayalami

(*The wind blows stronger, blows off the candlelights.*
Rain falls. Lightning strikes. They continue to hum the
song. The morning breaks. They stop singing. We hear
the sound of a bulldozer; a demolition is in progress.
We hear angry voices. Some people are moving about.
They throw their belongings out of their homes. Others
peep through the windows and sing.)

SONG: *Kwenzenjani na!*   [What could have gone
         Masiduduka   wrong
         Sigoduka   When we run helter
         Ezwenilethu   skelter
                                 Going away
                                 From the land of our
                                   birth]

         Kwenzenjani na!   [We run in circles
         Kwenzenjani na!   In this land
           Masiduduka   Running helter skelter
         Sigoduka   Going away]
         Ezwenilethu

         Thina siyajikeleza
         Ho! kulelizwe
           Ho! siduduka
           Ho! sigoduka

Thina siyajikeleza
Ho! kulelizwe
Ho! siduduka
Ho! sigoduka

Kwenzenjani na!
Masiduduka
Sigoduka
Ezwenilethu

Thina siyajikeleza
Ho! kulelizwe
Ho! siduduka
Ho sigoduka

(Then a choreographed movement with corrugated
irons. It is resistance. The sound of the bulldozer fades.
People reassemble their belongings. They sing a song of
resistance.)

SONG:

Sothutha siyephina!	[Where will we go
Kulomhlaba wobawo'mkhulu	In this, the land
Sothutha siyepdina!	of our forefathers]
Kulomhlaba wobawo'mkhulu	
Sothutha siyephina!	
Kulomhlaba wobawo'mkhulu	
Masithethe ngazwinye	[Let us speak as one and say
Sithi!	We shall not move
Asihambi	Here we will die
Sizofelala	We shall not move
Asihambi	Here we will die]
Siyofelala	

(This song leads us into the first scene)

SCENE ONE

> *(Upstage people work in song to rebuild their shacks while others join the forced exodus to Soweto. Downstage is a township street scene. There is a sound of busy traffic of cars and people. Enter Charmaine who waits impatiently downstage center. Her eyes are continuously on her wrist-watch. After a while, enter Diliza.)*

Diliza: Hallo love!

Charm: Hallo.

Diliza: I am sorry to keep you waiting.

Charm: You don't look sorry.

Diliza: Are you coming to the meeting this afternoon?

Charm: What meeting?

Diliza: The Save Alexandra Campaign Meeting.

Charm: When are you going to have time for me?

Diliza: These are tough times, Charmaine. Alexandra can't just fade away because of our love dreams. Our love must be like everything else. It must take up the fight for Alexandra. (*Pause*) What must I do to make you understand?

Charm: Give up Alexandra!

Diliza: Impossible.

Charm: Then you don't love me.

Diliza: I see.

Charm: (*After a pause*) I don't want to lose you, Diliza.

Diliza: So I get lost that easy neh? I also don't want to lose you, Charmaine. Nor do I want to give up Alexandra. The cause for Alexandra is for all of us.

Charm: If it is for all of us, why are you always in the frontline like a little dog? There can never be a meeting here in Alexandra, Tembisa or in Soweto without you

on the agenda. Are you in a beauty contest or what?
Yah! It's a competition.

Diliza: A debate is not a competition.

Charm: Still, these debates are far from the man in the
street. Diliza, your words are flowers without roots.
When are you going to sit down and think? Think with
and for the community?

Diliza: Sometimes you can talk sense.

Charm: And sometimes?

Diliza: Rubbish! (*Pause*) This conversation is all mixed up.
Some sense and some rubbish.

Charm: That's because everything about our lives is mixed
up! (*Enter Mabu*) Look at that mess.

Diliza: He is not a mess. He is part of the evidence. He
needs a home. In any case, he is like us. We are all a
mess (*Pause*) If you don't feel like coming to the
meeting, will you wait for me at Gogo's cart?

Charm: I hate this waiting business, Diliza.

Diliza: I dislike your hating it.

Charm: Whether you dislike it or not I hate waiting.

Diliza: I wonder why we must hate when God created so
much to be loved.

Charm: Stop wondering and look at me.

Diliza: I am looking.

Charm: Think of a woman.

Diliza: I am thinking.

Charm: Think of my pride as a woman.

Diliza: I am thinking.

Charm: You don't look thinking.

Diliza: For godsake, I am thinking!

Charm: Think of a woman to feed and to be fed.

Diliza: I am thinking.

Charm: (*After a pause*) Are you still thinking?

Diliza: I will not stop until my heart stops.

Charm: Something inside my stomach makes me eat a lot.

Diliza: It must be a natural appetiser.

Charm: It makes me feel like vomiting.

Diliza: Why don't you vomit? It helps to vomit.

Charm: What?

Diliza: You get rid of bad luck and all the dirt in your stomach.

Charm: My God!

Diliza: Vomiting is the best medicine.

Charm: Why don't you do it?

Diliza: I have nothing in my stomach. I don't know when last I had something to eat.

Charm: Think Diliza.

Diliza: I am thinking.

Charm: Something inside my stomach makes me love you more than the first day we met.

Diliza: Then keep it inside your stomach.

Charm: But it makes me hate knowing your mother.

Diliza: In that case I must help you to vomit it now.

Charm: Think Diliza!

Diliza: I am thinking.

Charm: Think like a man.

Diliza: Am I not a man?

Charm: Not until you think like one.

Diliza: How do I think, like a dog?

Charm: Perhaps a donkey!

Diliza: (*Pause*) Charmaine.

Charm: Hh!

Diliza: I love you.

Charm: I know that.

Diliza: Alexandra is my pride, my home.

Charm: Kiss it goodbye, Diliza. Today the bulldozer is here to clean the township. It is here to crush every brick and every piece of corrugated iron. This township is no more, Diliza. With our own eyes, we have seen roofs floating in the air like disco dancers. (*Pause*) I am a woman, Diliza. You'd better start thinking of resettlement before it is too late.

Nduna: (*Calling from upstage*) Diliza! Diliza!

Charm: Your father is calling.

Diliza: Will you wait for me at Gogo's coffee cart?

Charm: Not me.

Diliza: Then when and where do we meet?

Charm: When I bring the damage.

Diliza: What damage?

Charm: I am pregnant, Diliza.

Diliza: You are pregnant?

(*Diliza is shocked. He turns his back against Charmaine who exits without saying a word. Then Diliza approaches his angry father.*)

Nduna: Come inside (*Diliza goes inside the shack*) Where are your brains? I will stop building this shack and follow the others to Soweto. What is more important, the girl or the shack?

Diliza: I am sorry baba. (*He starts helping him to build the shack*)

Nduna: You must learn to respect priorities, my son. Bring that hammer and those nails. We must finish building this shack before it rains. (*Pause*) Look at that!

Diliza: What?

Nduna: Another home goes down.

Diliza: We build, they destroy; children die in the streets, you keep quiet; children become orphans at birth, children are born of mothers unknown to them, children . . .

Nduna: Enough!

Diliza: This is the truth baba.

Nduna: What truth?

Diliza: Children are drugged at birth. Children give birth to children. Nobody cares. Soon they'll be sending baby girls to family planning. When are you going to fight back?

Nduna: Don't point your finger at me, my son.

(*Diliza goes through his school bag and silently takes out some loose pages and reads.*)

That is all you know. We don't sleep or eat words, my son. Don't let words become your master.

Diliza: Today my voice will rise and echo right through Alexandra.

Nduna: It will echo in your bladdy stomach when the security people get hold of you.

(*Diliza goes on top of the chair and recites*)

Diliza: Peace! Peace!
　　　　Peace be with you and me
　　　　Peace be with the children in bondage
　　　　Peace be with the mothers and fathers
　　　　who saw their children
　　　　die in the whirlwind.

Peace be with the children in labour camps
and concentration camps.

Nduna: Beautiful poetry.

Diliza: Peace! Peace!
Peace be here and everywhere.
I greet you in the name of a cry for a home.

Nduna: Now that sounds like a speech.

Diliza: No matter how many bulldozers
they may bring
to crush our homes,
hope must forever burn in our hearts.
They may destroy our homes,
but not our hearts.
When I die
bury me in the stench and gutters
of this township.
When I die
bury me in the depth of my heritage.
Alexandra is here to stay.
We found her here
and we will leave her here.
The bulldozer found us here
and it will leave us here.

Nduna: (*Restless, peeping through the holes of the shack*)
Are you preparing for a meeting, or what? Don't do it.
Don't ever say a word.

Diliza: It's about . . .

Nduna: I said not a word from you!

Diliza: I was just saying . . .

Nduna: What?

Diliza: It's about to rain. (*A big storm breaks*)

Nduna: You'd better stop howling and do something.

(*They continue to build the shack. Singing "Sothutha
Siyephina!" They finish building. Nduna is tired. He
takes a nip of brandy. Diliza continues to recite his
speech.*)

Diliza: Come
Come walk the streets of Alexandra
and tell them we are not moving.
Let us all shout in one voice
NO TO RESETTLEMENT
AWAY WITH FORCED REMOVALS
People of my pain
let peace be the pulse of the heartbeat
of this land.
Let it blossom in the hearts of all
men
Perhaps those who destroy
will understand what goes with building.
Let us rebuild our lives for better
or for worse.
People of the land

Nduna: Shut-up! People of the land! People of the land!
Shut-up! You are making noise.

Diliza: The bulldozer is making the noise, not me.

Nduna: Shut-up.

Diliza: We build and they destroy. It's a tragedy.

Nduna: What do you know about tragedy.

Diliza: It has been tragic enough for me to be deprived of
the loving care of a mother.

Nduna: You what?

Diliza: I have known no mother, baba.

Nduna: Rubbish! I have mothered you.

Diliza: And you have remained baba, not mama.

Nduna: So you wanted to call me mama?

Diliza: I wanted to feel how it is to call someone mama.

Nduna: Diliza, I know how you feel about your mother. It
hurts me too.

Diliza: Why did you separate?

Nduna: Ask God.

Diliza: You never taught me to expect all the answers from God.

Nduna: It is never too late to learn.

Diliza: Then it is never too late to teach the bulldozer, baba. (*Voices shout in the distance*)

Nduna: What voices were that?

Diliza: I am late baba.

Nduna: For what?

Diliza: Can you lend me your coat?

Nduna: What?

Diliza: I am asking for your raincoat. There is a big storm coming. (*Voices again*)

Nduna: Is that a boxing tournament or is it Blackpool versus Hungry Lions?

Diliza: Where is the coat, baba?

Nduna: You won't get it until you say what is happening.

Diliza: It's a protest meeting, baba.

Nduna: What protest, Bantu Education?

Diliza: It's a protest against the demolition of Alexandra.

Nduna: Is that what you were preparing for?

Diliza: Yebo, baba.

Nduna: Don't go there my son.

Diliza: I have no choice, baba.

Nduna: I am not asking you, but telling you.

Diliza: So am I.

Nduna: What?

Diliza: The situation dictates, baba.

Nduna: Who are you to tell me what the situation dictates?

Diliza: Your son. (*Nduna is restless*) Am I getting the coat or what?

Nduna: Coat or no coat, you are not getting anywhere.

Diliza: I am getting there, baba.

Nduna: You are not.

Diliza: The bulldozer must be taught how to live with people.

Nduna: Who are you to teach the bulldozer?

Diliza: Your son.

Nduna: You are hardly a threat to a rat!

Diliza: Wait and see, baba.

Nduna: I will be waiting to buy you a coffin.

Diliza: It will be the story of the white elephant and the black ant.

Nduna: Your forefathers said it long ago.

Diliza: And what happened?

Nduna: They were buried by the war. A lost war.

(*Voices again*)

Diliza: Listen to those voices in the whirlwind. It's like the voices at the victory of Isandlwana. Those children are making a vow to stop the pain.

Nduna: I have long made my vow. I made it with your mother. We sang the blues long before you were born. Today, when you throw stones, I sing the blues. When you mix whatever you mix to make a petrol bomb, I combine some chords to sing the blues. My silence is not quiet, Diliza my son.

(*Pause*)

Diliza: I am off to the meeting, baba. (*Exit Diliza*)

Nduna: Diliza! Come back, my son!

(*Re-enter Diliza*)

Diliza: I said I am off to the meeting.

Nduna: Here is the coat, my son.

Diliza: Thank you, baba.

Nduna: Take care, child of my blood.

Diliza: I will.

(*Exit Diliza, Nduna remains singing*)

SONG:

Ngabe kwenzekanina	[What is happening
Sithi kwenzekanina	We say what is happening?]
Kwenzekanina	
It's daylight or midnight	
We are always pulling and pushing	
It's daylight or midnight	
We are always pulling and pushing	

(*The song fades into the next scene*)

SCENE TWO

(*The setting is the same as in Scene One. Mabu is still on stage. Enter Gogo pulling the cart. She stops. Inside the cart, she sings and pumps the primus stove. Enter Diliza chasing a cat—mime.*)

Gogo: What's wrong, Diliza?

Diliza: Ikati elimnyama Gogo! [A black cat granny]

Gogo: Never do that to a black cat, mtwanami [my child]. It will block your road to heaven.

Diliza: Ngiyaxolisa, Gogo. [I apologize.]

Gogo: How was the meeting?

Diliza: Bewushisa! Hotter than your coffee, Gogo.

Gogo: I can see from the sweat on your face.

Diliza: And how is your business, Gogo?

Gogo: Evergreen, mtwanami.

Diliza: Then you must take care of the snakes.

(Laughter)

Gogo: Have you heard anything about your mother?

Diliza: This morning I received a letter saying she is somewhere around this township. She says it was not her intention to separate with my father. She tried several times to be reconciled with him, but my father would not have her back. Because her letter did not give enough details of their separation, I decided to ask my father why they separated.

Gogo: What did he say?

Diliza: He said I must ask God.

(Mabu approaches Gogo and asks for coffee. Gogo offers him coffee and some fatcakes. He walks away without saying a word.)

Gogo: This man knows pain, Diliza mtwanami.

Diliza: Where's his wife?

Gogo: Wadliwa imbeleko, mtwanami. She died after giving birth to a still-born baby.

Diliza: Where?

Gogo: Inside that kombi [van].

Diliza: Hawu!

Gogo: That man knows pain, Diliza mtwanami. He is the man who knows your mother very well.

Diliza: Then he probably knows her whereabouts.

Gogo: Who knows.

Diliza: I must go and break his silence now.

Gogo: But you must never say I sent you.

Diliza: Why not?

Gogo: Never mind. Go now before he walks away.

(Diliza goes to Mabu who is sitting under the Church bell cleaning his saxophone)

Diliza: Good afternoon, Ntate Mabu. *(No response)*
Dumela, Ntate Mabu. *(No response)* My name is Diliza
Mabunu. Child of Nduna kaMabunu. I am told you
know much about my mother. You know why she lives
apart from me. You know why she lives apart from my
father. You know why she lives apart from herself.
Could you by any chance know her whereabouts?
Please help me. I have grown up with this tragedy and
I am not prepared to live it unchallenged. Today I am
a man. I want to know all about the past. Your past
and my past. Without this knowledge of the past, I am
like a dead seed in fertile soil. Please come back
to your senses and remember the past. Please try and
remember. You and my mother and father.

*(As Diliza pleads, Mabu stands up, thoughtful, takes
his tenor sax. Nduna joins him. It's a song for a home.
Diliza's mother joins them and sings. This flashback
should happen like a dream sequence. Lightning effects
can be used to enhance the mood. At the end of the
song, Mabu goes back to sit under the church bell,
Nduna and Diliza's mother exit in different directions.)*
Do you remember anything? You and I have a common
past. We know this pain. We have lived this pain. We
need each other to get rid of this pain.

(Mabu stares at Diliza without saying a word)
Your silence scares me. You look at me as if I was
mad. In your eyes I meet the eyes of my oppressors. In
your silence I hear their word: "All those who are
demonstrating against the demolition of Alexandra are
mad. A normal person wouldn't fight to live in such a
slum. Anyway, the bulldozer knows how to deal with
mad people." Yah . . . We all seem to forget that
madness is caused by madness. One evil is often the
seed of many evils. We seem to forget that the little
madness we give, the more madness we will get. It's a
give and take situation, Ntate Mabu. For every debit
there must be a credit.

It's a double entry system. Repression and resistance.
Can you beat it? The little madness you give, the more
madness you will get. Are you going to talk to me or
not?
For Chirst's sake, say something!

(*Mabu stares at him. Stands up as if he is about to say
something. Takes his tenor sax and moves off without
saying a word. Diliza is confused for awhile. Then he
goes back to Gogo.*)

Gogo: Was it fruitful? . . . How did it go, Diliza?

Diliza: Well, I spoke to him. He did not speak to me. He
never said a word.

Gogo: That's how he is. Have some coffee and you will be
okay. (*Gogo continues to sing while Diliza is eating*)

(*After awhile he sees Majika approaching*)

Diliza: Here comes Ntate Majika. The only parent who
came to our meeting. (*Enter Majika*)

Majika: Sawubona Gogo. [Greetings.]

Gogo: Sibonene.

Majika: Can I have a cup of hot coffee.

Gogo: It is never cold. E dula e tshisa! [It stays hot!]

Majika: Just like Diliza. This boy is dynamic Gogo. He is
forever hot. Keep up the heat my child.

Diliza: Let's hope this time they will feel the heat.

Majika: You have said it—"Hope must forever burn in our
hearts." Courage my child.

Diliza: Thank you, Ntate Majika.

Majika: Thanks for the coffee, Gogo. (*Exit Majika*)

Diliza: Umzwile—did you hear him? He got the message
—"Hope must forever burn in our hearts." Gogo, aphi
amadoda? [Where are the men?] Men like Ntate
Majika. Men who can let their knobkieries dance in the

air. Gogo, sifuna amadoda — We need men like Ntate Majika.

Gogo: Some angels are devils and some devils are angels, mtwanami. Who knows I am an angel with a bag full of evils?

Diliza: Awuchaze Gogo, explain. What does that have to do with Ntate Majika?

Gogo: Diliza, mtwanami, when I see Ntate Majika, my eyes bleed.

Diliza: Why?

Gogo: It pains me to think of how he bought Ntate Mabu out of his house.

Diliza: What?

Gogo: Let me tell you how it happened.

> (*Flashback. Inside an Administration Office. There is an officer and a table full of papers and files. He picks up a ringing telephone. After a moment of excitement, he drops the telephone and continues to sort out his file. Enter Ntate Majika with a "dignity bag." Elegantly dressed. He puts his bag on the table. Without saying a word, they shake hands. Majika opens his bag, takes out a lump sum of money and gives it to the officer. The officer takes a receipt book out of the drawer. Writes out a receipt. Majika puts a wrapped parcel on the table. The officer unwraps the parcel. It's a bottle of whisky. Majika takes out a glass from his jacket pocket and puts it on the table. The officer pours the whisky for himself. Just when he is about to drink, Majika takes out another glass from his bag. They clink glasses before they drink. Blackout.*)

Gogo: It was "Cheers" over Ntate Mabu's house.

Diliza: Just like that?

Gogo: Bottles of whisky know why there are children who are sleeping in the streets. If you don't believe me, you can go and ask your father. Some of these "dashikis" are dangerous mtwanami. (*Enter the customer — mime*)

Diliza: Can you help this young man, Gogo?

Gogo: Ao, dumela ngwanake. [Greetings, my child]
What can I do for you, my son? Tse tala? I am sorry I
don't have the green stuff today. Try tomorrow if the
bulldozer has spared us. (*Exit the customer — mime*)
Diliza, mtwanami.

Diliza: Yebo Gogo.

Gogo: Whose hat is this?

Diliza: Esika baba-Majika. What do we do with it?

Gogo: Don't worry, he will come back for it.

Diliza: Perhaps it is time we remove the curtain and see
what is behind the curftans.

Gogo: (*Laughing*) Tomorrow it will be you, mtwanami.
Today you are like a new broom. You sweep every evil
out of your heart. Tomorrow it will be you and the
African curftans. Protection!

(*Re-enter Majika hurriedly*)

Gogo: I told you that he will come back for his protection.

Majika: Gogo, didn't you see my hat?

Gogo: Ask him (*Pointing to Diliza*).

Majika: Have you seen it, Diliza?

Diliza: Yah!

Majika: Where is it?

Diliza: I have it.

Majika: Can I have it back.

Gogo: Give him back his shelter.

Majika: Who?

Diliza: You know.

Majika: I don't know what you are talking about.

Gogo: Give him back his house before I expose you.

Majika: You don't scare me big boy. Go on. Tell the world. Tell the world that I took his house. Expose me Diliza. I thought you were a man.

Diliza: What am I?

Majika: A small boy who goes around listening to false stories. Stories that divide us.

Gogo: Majika!

Majika: Cool down Gogo.

Gogo: O seke wa batla go mpherola dibete. [Do not nauseate me.] Who lived in your house before you?

Majika: Many people. Mabu was the last owner.

Gogo: Why did they kick him out of the house?

Majika: He could not pay his rent. For your information, he had qualification problems. I was looking for a house . . .

Gogo: And they gave you his house?

Majika: Automatically.

Gogo: And you still remained the outspoken critic of the housing system in this country?

Majika: Of course, I do not approve of it.

Gogo: But you can afford buying people out of their houses?

Majika: So you are the one who has been telling Diliza all these false stories about me?

Diliza: Didn't you do it?

Majika: I never realised I was in court.

(Diliza picks up an iron and threatens to beat him. Majika is scared, retreats)

Diliza: Talk Ntate Majika. Didn't you buy his house with a bottle of whisky? So you can't talk because you can't think without your African hat. Give it to him Gogo.

Gogo: No, you must do it. Here it is mtwanami.

Diliza: Come and take your hat. Take! (*Throws it*) Put it on so that you can talk.

(Diliza threatens to hit him. Majika freezes. Everyone is silent. They sing a song. Majika is silent, and scared. Diliza is still staring at Majika.)

(Exit Majika and the spirits)

Gogo: Let him go, Diliza. Time will take care of him.

Diliza: At times, time can take a long time to deal with people like him. I feel like putting him on fire.

Gogo: Let him go!
Say thank God because I am like Jesus Christ. My colleagues would have long dealt with you accordingly. Come! Kneel down and pray. Ask for forgiveness. Get that bladdy evil out of you. Ask the ancestors to forgive you.

(Majika kneels down and prays. There is a spotlight on him. Enter two ancestoral spirits as he prays. Spotlights should also be used on both spirits.)

Majika: Oh Lord
I pray you through the spirits of our forefathers
I pray you through the ancestors of Afrika
Forgive me Lord
Give me strength so as to survive this ordeal
I don't know how the devil invaded my heart
I don't know how Satan made me do that
All the same I did what I did oh Lord
I killed a man
I did not lay my hands on him Lord
but I killed him
Because I gave him to the streets
And in the long run he was speechless,
emotionless, just a moving corpse.
Please Lord, give this young man wisdom and
patience
I need another chance in life Lord

Please Lord, ask him to give me a chance to
    change
I want to change and be accepted again
Please Lord, I beg for forgiveness.

Spirit I: Where is the money you collected in the name of
the disabled?

Majika: I am afraid, Lord, it is all spent up.
    Lord you must understand
    I did not spend the money but the devil in me did.

Spirit II: What about the money for the lawyer to defend
the residents against removals?

Majika: The money that I collected for the lawyer, I
invested it in my name Lord. Again Lord, you must
understand, I did not invest the money but the devil in
me did.
    This time the devil was in my stomach.
    I was just thinking of the future of my stomach,
    that of my wife and children.
    Oh please Lord, when the period of investment
        elapses,
    all the money will be used to defend all residents
    who were arrested in protest against removals.
    Please Lord, ask this young man to give me a
        chance.
    I want to change
    Please Lord, ask this young man to help me get rid
        of the devils in me.
    I will also pray for the devil not to visit him.
    Through the spirit of our forefathers I get for
        forgiveness Lord!

(Exit Majika and the spirits)

Gogo: That was a good ritual.

Diliza: Thanks to you Gogo.

Gogo: I never realised you are such a good healer.

Diliza: Lets hope such people do get healed. Is it not time
to go home, Gogo.

Gogo: It is my child.

Diliza: Then let's go home.

Gogo: My home is no more, mtwanami.

Diliza: When did it happen?

Gogo: Yesterday. And you know how the news come to you. Yesterday on my way to my shack, as I was going down the bridge, I was no longer pulling the cart but it was pushing me. Then I stopped right at the middle of the bridge. Dog tired! The so-called Children of Asazi saw me and came running. They were shouting, "Gogo! Gogo! Sicela amaswidi! Sicela amaswidi!" ["Please give us candy! Please give us candy!"] I gave them some sweets as usual. They helped me to pull the cart.

As we were going up the hill from the bridge, I saw my best Sunday hat, rollerskating down the donga. . . . Then I began to smell a rat. One of my little friends, a girl, noticed the hat and screamed: "Gogo! Nasi isigqoko sakho!" ["There goes your hat!"] We looked at the hat and watched her going to get it down the donga. The rest of us continued to pull the cart homeward. When she came back with the hat, she found us in tears. My home was nomore. I looked at the little children and saw citizens whose citizenship was like an ice cream under the heat of the sun. (*Pause*) Diliza mtwanami, go home. I will sleep here. I woke up right here this morning.

Diliza: That will never happen again.

Gogo: What makes you think so?

Diliza: My home is your home Gogo. Let's go.

(*Gogo starts the song, and they all sing: "Alexandra Khayalami"—Exit all of them and enter Nduna. Sits on his chair inside the shack. Re-enter Gogo still singing, followed by Diliza.*)

Nduna: Who are you to sing like my wife?

Gogo: I am Gogo. That's what the children call me.

Nduna: What brings you here?

Gogo: Your son

Diliza: Gogo's home is demolished, Baba.

Nduna: She is not an exception. We are also in transit.

Diliza: The bulldozer, not us. We are here to stay.

Nduna: Dreaming is not a sin. Go on dreaming, my son.

Diliza: Your coffee cart is still outside, Gogo.

Gogo: Here is the key, mtwanami. The lock is inside the cart.

Diliza: For what, Gogo?

Gogo: Lock the cart and leave it outside.

Diliza: Outside?

Nduna: Bring it inside, my son. Township justice will soon take place.
(*Exit Diliza*)

Gogo: But this shack is small.

Nduna: That's none of your business.

Gogo: There'll be no space left.

Nduna: Space has never been our problem, maGogo.

(*Enter Diliza pulling the cart. He exits unnoticed.*)

Nduna: There you are! It fits like a garage and two rooms in the backyards of Soweto. Look at that! It's a three room house already. Innovation! It's good you came, maGogo. Now we can afford a bit of privacy. Diliza! That will become our kitchen and your sleeping room.

Gogo: Amen!

Nduna: We grew up sleeping in the kitchen, maGogo. Thirteen of us. All children of my mother and father, living in a one-room house divided into two rooms by means of a curtain. This side where I am standing, will be our rehearsal room, our eating room, our reading room, our sitting room and our sleeping room.

MaGogo, you will see to finish in the cart. We may not be able to stretch our feet, but one day we will. Diliza! Diliza! must we ask you for coffee? Today's children are children because we call them children. Diliza! Where is this boy?

Gogo: Outside.

Nduna: Why?

Gogo: He looks worried.

Nduna: What?

Gogo: Something worries him.

Nduna: It must be the word that is flying around.

Gogo: What word?

Nduna: It is rumored the police are after him.

Gogo: My fruits and fatcakes tell me, that does not worry him.

Nduna: If they don't worry him, they will worry your fruits and fatcakes. Diliza! (*Peeps through the window*) Diliza! Diliza!

(*Nduna takes the lamp and goes outside. Inside the shack it becomes dark. Nduna is outside, calling Diliza's name. The light of the lamp can be seen but not him. There are gunshots and screams. Enter a choreographed movement with a chorus.*)

CHORUS: *It's a voice,*
              we raise our ears.
              It's a torch,
              we close our eyes.
              It's a knock,
              we shudder in fear.
              It's a gunshot,
              we run to Asazi.
              That's the pain of life
              the agony of birth.
              That's the disease of today
              the fear of mankind.

It's a voice,
we raise our ears.
It's a torch,
we close our eyes.
It's a knock,
we shudder in fear.
It's a gunshot,
we run to Asazi.

(Suddenly there is a loud bang, exit the chorus. Nduna runs back into the shack.)

Gogo: What makes you run back like a thief?

Nduna: Say thank God you were not on the spot.

Gogo: Why?

Nduna: You would have died of shock!

Gogo: Where is Diliza!

Nduna: I don't know.

Gogo: Where is the child, Nduna?

Nduna: I said I don't know! He is not a child, but a man. He will see to finish. I did not send him . . .

Gogo: You can't say that, Nduna.

Nduna: I've said it.

Gogo: If my ankle wasn't sore,

Nduna: What would you do?

Gogo: I would go and look for him until I found him.

Nduna: You would need some built-in shock absorbers, maGogo.

Gogo: Not me. I've outlived shock in my life. Me? I was not born in a house of numbers.

Gogo: My feet know thorns, I've climbed mountains with rocks as sharp as needles. Nduna, that's your child in the street.

Nduna: I did not raise him to become a thorn in my heart.

(Enter Diliza and Charmaine waits outside)

Nduna: So you are now a big man, Diliza. Who is the girl?

Gogo: You are fast becoming the Jerusalem of thorns.

Nduna: Shut up before you get your marching orders!

Gogo: Amen!

Nduna: Who is the girl outside Diliza? (*Threatening to go for her*)

Diliza: Hold your brake, baba.

Gogo: He needs some brake fluid.

Nduna: Brake fluid or no brake fluid, I will not have devils in my house. Diliza don't think this is a beer hall, where people can just walk in and out like Europe walking in and out of Africa. You walked out of that door and walked back with this tired old devil.

Gogo: Amen!

Nduna: (*Pointing the cart*) This silent devil walks in, peace walks out!

Gogo: Amen!

Nduna: Shut up! My angel will be back and I will not have you hanging around like a tired prostitute.

Gogo: Amen! (*She goes behind the cart*)

Nduna: The girl outside, is she the calabash?

Diliza: Yebo, Baba.

Nduna: I hope she is not carrying an extra parcel.

Diliza: She is.

Nduna: What?

Diliza: A suitcase and a bag.

Nduna: I didn't mean that. Anyway, let me hear her name.

Diliza: Charmaine Legadima.

Nduna: The daughter of Mr Lightning?

Diliza: Yebo, baba.

Nduna: The one who left the country?

Diliza: Yebo baba.

Nduna: That's the man who stole the little happiness I had.

Diliza: I don't understand, baba.

Nduna: He lived in adultery with your mother.

Diliza: Does that mean . . .

Nduna: Charmaine is your sister. It's a broken calabash, my son. She is the child of your mother. And God forbids the marriage of children who brushed in the same womb.

Diliza: (*After awhile*) She is expecting my baby, baba.

Nduna: Your baby?

Diliza: Yebo, baba.

Nduna: It's a sin in her stomach. She must go away. I don't want to see her.

> (*Diliza exits hurriedly. It becomes dark inside the shack. Outside, Charmaine is lying on the ground between her suitcase and bag. The wind is blowing. Enter Diliza looking for her. He finds her crying.*)

Diliza: Don't cry Charmaine. It's not our fault.

Charm: I don't care whose fault it is.

Diliza: Bring back your heart, Charmaine.

Charm: Forget it, Diliza.

Diliza: Why?

Charm: The whole thing is a flop.

Diliza: It's not a flop, Charmaine.

Charm: It is a flop, Diliza. Your father said it. It's a sin I am carrying in my stomach. Don't dream of any napkins [diapers], Diliza. I will not ask you to buy them. Don't think of those problems of support. I will not ask you to leave school and work for the baby. I will not ask you to buy SMA, Gripe Water, Nestum, Purity, Baby Powder, or Baby Soup. I will not ask you to buy anything, Diliza.

Diliza: Why?

Charm: Because there'll be no baby.

Diliza: But there is a baby in your stomach?

Charm: It's a sin in my stomach, Diliza. I must abort.

Diliza: Abortion!

Charm: What must I do? Kill myself? What must I do, not to be the child of your mother? Change my blood? (*Pause*) It's like I am dreaming.

Diliza: So am I.

Charm: I can't just think of calling you my brother.

Diliza: Nor can I think of calling you my sister.

Charm: You are the man of my dreams, Diliza.

Diliza: You are the flower of my dreams, Charmaine.

Charm: I love you, Diliza.

Diliza: I love you, Charmaine.

Charm: What if we resettle far from those who know us?

Diliza: I've long said, NO TO RESETTLEMENT.

Charm: Then I am going to abort.

Diliza: You don't have to. Please, Charmaine.

(*Nduna closes the door. It becomes bright in the shack, and dark outside. The action is inside. Gogo is still behind the cart.*)

Nduna: This boy is like castor oil in my stomach.

Gogo: (*Behind the cart*) Then your stomach must be clean.

(*Takes a sip of brandy from the bottle*)

Nduna: He makes my stomach run endlessly.

Gogo: Ijooo!

Nduna: What's wrong with you?

Gogo: It's a cat! (*She shows up from behind the cart*)

Nduna: Just like my wife, scared of cats!

Gogo: Oh is your wife scared of cats?

Nduna: Just like you.

Gogo: Where is your wife.

Nduna: Never ask that question again otherwise you will have no place to stay. Where is the damn cat?

Gogo: Stray cats are dangerous, Nduna.

Nduna: For rats not for me.

Gogo: It is inside the shack! I am scared.

Nduna: You must be a rat.

Gogo: There it is Nduna. In that corner!

Nduna: Let it come this way. Looking for rats, it will find its death.

Gogo: Please don't kill it, Nduna.

> (*Nduna pulls Gogo's cart towards him. He takes bottles from the cart and throws them at the cat. Gogo, scared and confused screams at Nduna to stop. We hear the bell ringing. Gogo and Nduna look at each other with questioning eyes. They slowly walk out. Outside they find Diliza ringing the bell. They look at him with surprised eyes. Nduna is angry.*)

Nduna: What the hell is going on up there?

Diliza: Ring the bell, child of hell, child of hell, ring the bell!

Nduna: Stop it Diliza!

Diliza: It tolls for the proclaimed sin in her stomach!

Nduna: What!

Diliza: The sin in her stomach!

Nduna: What about it?

Diliza: It tolls for it!

Nduna: Come down, Diliza! Come, lets talk like men.

Diliza: It's too late to talk. She's gone!

Nduna: What!

Diliza: She's gone to abort the baby. (*He cries*) She's gone baba. What comes must go! She came here with hopes for a better future, and you send her away in tears. Because traditional says it's a sin in her stomach, she chose to go and kill the baby.

(*A song by Gogo singing about children*)

Nduna: (*Walks downstage*) Innocent children will always suffer for the wrongs of their parents. But why must this happen to us? These children have suffered because I sent Diliza's mother away. Why? I should have taken her back. This would not have happpened. The ancestors would not have punished me. . . . I cannot forget the night he took her. The night of separation. The night I became a bachelor. The night when my soul was banished. The night of solitude. I became an Island right here in the heart of Alexandra. Legadima took her away from me. It was during a concert. I was on stage singing my song for a home. Mabu was in the same band. My wife was backstage, waiting to be called upstage. Then her turn came. She never showed up. One member of the band went backstage. She was nowhere to be found. That was the last night I saw my wife.

Five months later I received a letter from her. It did not have her address. All she said was: "*God blessed us with a baby boy. This evening our child will be strengthened.*" All I could do was to imagine the ritual of the strengthening of my child.

(Flashback. Inside a shack hideout, the ritual takes place. Figures can be seen dancing. They burn the herbs and sing the praise poem. They pray with the child exposed to the smoke of the herbs.)

That was the blood of my blood. Child of the gods. Diliza Mabunu. I could hear him cry. That very cry he is crying today. The cry for a home. In my mind I saw them strengthen my child. Protecting him against the evil spirits of the earth. This I could not understand. I could not understand how the devil, I mean the devil who took my only happiness, could protect my child against the evil spirits of this earth. How could my child be baptised by the very man who subjected him to pain and suffering? This didn't make sense in my head. Three months later, another note came from my wife: *"Expect us home soon."* I thought it was a dream when I saw them walking down the road towards me. I felt as though I was on my two legs again. Anxious to meet my son. The blood of my blood. I wanted to run towards them, but I could not run. Then I saw something I didn't like. She had two babies, one on her back and the other on her breast. A boy and a girl. That was Legadima's child. I could not forgive my wife.

Gogo: For adopting Legadima's child?

Nduna: What do you mean by adoption? That's her child with Legadima. She lived in adultery with Legadima and bore a baby girl for him. Then she came back to me because Legadima left the country. He was trying to clear his conscience by being an outspoken critic of the system. For Christ's sake, we need morality. There must be morality. Before we can fight any system, we must fight the devil in our hearts. There are too many Legadimas. Too many men who do not love their children. The love you owe your child has no price. Loving your child can teach you to be a woman.

Gogo: This little sermon does not make you more of a man.

Nduna: It makes me better than that Legadima who ran away from his child.

Gogo: He ran away from spending the rest of his life in prison.

Nduna: Why?

Gogo: He was involved in the Poqo Uprising.

Nduna: What uprising was that?

Gogo: You should know your history. It may be a painful one, but it is worth the agony.

Nduna: Diliza, my son, I don't care what this granny has to say in defence of Legadima. That is not the issue. The issue is, you can't get married to Charmaine.

Diliza: I've heard that from you already.

Nduna: She is the child of your mother.

Diliza: Now what about the sin in her stomach? (*Silence*) She's going to abort or abandon the baby at the orphanage.

Nduna: I will pray for her to abort. Why deliver the poor soul into this human misery?

Gogo: Nduna, there is something you didn't know.

Nduna: Like what?

Gogo: This girl's mother died ten days after giving birth to her.

Nduna: Rubbish! My wife is not dead.

Gogo: I mean the real mother of this girl.

Nduna: Stop this lie!

Gogo: She died when this girl was ten days old.

Diliza: But to me, Gogo, she said her mother raised her until she was eight years old.

Nduna: That could be true.

Gogo: She's never been told the truth about her mother.

Nduna: What truth?

Gogo: Her mother died on the run from the Cape. She was
together with her husband, Legadima. Then when
Legadima got to Alexandra, he burried her secretely
and got another woman to raise Charmaine. This
woman was expecting a baby at the time. She gave
birth five months later. A baby boy. And he was named
Diliza. The blood of my blood. Child of the gods.
(*Pause*) Charmaine was five months and ten days old.

Diliza: Does that mean . . .

Gogo: You are not children of the same woman.

Diliza: Baba.

Nduna: Yes my son.

Diliza: It is true.

Nduna: What?

Diliza: Charmaine is five months older than me.

Nduna: And so?

Diliza: That's impossible for her to be my blood sister. It's
not a broken calabash, baba. It's like I am dreaming.
The light is coming back to us. The day is about to
dawn. It is time we think about the children in the
streets — The so-called Children of Asazi.

(*Enter chorus the same way as the other chorus*)

CHORUS: *Yes we must all think*
Think of the empty stomach
of this township.
When we eat cheese and wine
we must think
of the burning mouths
of this township.
When we cloth and house ourselves
we must think
of the homeless and the unemployed
of this township.
Yes we must all think.

> *Think about how we can share*
> *the joys and sufferings*
> *of this earth.*
> *Yes it is time to think!*
> *Think of the children in the streets*
> *They are not the children of Asazi*
> *but the children of God.*

(Exit the chorus. Charmaine is on stage but not noticed by the others)

Diliza: Baba, you'd better start thinking now. Just make up your mind and tell me where my mother is.

Nduna: I am a slow thinker, my son. Your granny is the right person. She can think fast. She knows everything. (*Pause*) Go on maGogo. Tell him the whereabouts of the woman who gave birth to him. Go on maGogo, tell him! (*She cries*) Don't cry! Tell him!

Gogo: I happen to be that woman.

Diliza: You happen to be what, Gogo?

Gogo: You are the child of my blood, Diliza.

(Surprised as Gogo unmasks. It is an embrace of joy. They are all in a chorus)

CHORUS:　　*Devils can be angels*
　　　　　　and angels can be devils.

(Enter Majika as they repeat the same chorus)

Majika: Look at that!

Nduna: It is the whirlwind coming to take our joy and hope for peace.

Gogo: Yes the bulldozer is back in the township.

Diliza: The bulldozer's will to conquer will not crush the people's will to live in this township. We are not moving. Baba, before it is too late, I must go to Charmaine. Our child must live. If something is going to be aborted, let it be the dirty plans of the bulldozer.

(Enter Charmaine as Diliza is about to exit. They embrace each other.)

EPILOGUE

SONG: *Yes I had a dream*
          that one day
          there'll be this time

              This time of togetherness
              Yes I had a dream
          Yes I had a dream
          that one day
          there'll be this time

              This time of togetherness
              Yes I had a dream

          This is the time
          for mothers and fathers to sing together
              Let's be one
          This is the time
          for brothers and sisters to sing together
              Let's be one

          Yes I had a dream
          that one day
          there'll be this time

              Yes I had a dream

(There is resistance. They all sing "Alexandra Khaya-lami" with a fast tempo. Enter Mabu who shakes hands with Majika. Then Mabu blows the horn. Diliza joins with a recital.)

Diliza: Ring the bell and blow the horn
          Let the bell toll for the bulldozer
          Blow the hell out of the bulldozer
          Blow for Afrika
          To dance to Afrika's music

                    Curtain

              SONQOBA SIMUNYE

BORN IN THE RSA

A collaborative effort by Barney Simon and the Cast

Vanessa Cooke
Melanie Dobbs
Timmy Kwebulana
Neil McCarthy
Gcina Mhlophe
Fiona Ramsay
Thoko Ntshinga
Terry Norton

This collaborative piece, written by the director, Barney Simon and the multi-racial cast, deals with a number of inter-related themes that take us from the campuses of Witwaters-rand University in Johannesburg to the streets of Soweto. Glen, an apolitical white student, is recruited by the security police to be a campus spy. Although he is married to a woman named Nicky, Glen achieves his goal of infiltrating a multi-racial activist group by forming a liaison with Susan, a young art teacher who becomes his mistress. Subsequently, Glen betrays Nicky and succeeds in breaking the activist group and its charismatic trade unionist leader, Thenjiwe.

There are seven characters who have nothing, yet every-thing, to do with each other. There is the fast talking lawyer, Mia, to whom everybody turns when the police strike. She is called upon to go from finding detained activists to trying to locate a 10 year old black child arrested on a bogus charge of stoning police. The boy's mother is caught in the turn of events because her sister is the trade unionist pursued by security police. Zach, an unemployed musician, is an innocent by-stander also caught in the web because he happens to be the trade unionist's sub-tenant.

The conflicts of their lives, goals, frustrations, and loyalties (commitment and betrayal) and the chain of events that follow provide an accurate picture of life in South Africa. *Born In The R.S.A.* is true to life and reflective of the present day harsh realities of that country. It tells not only of the brutality of the apartheid system but reveals the resilience of the people.

BORN IN THE R S A

Barney Simon and the Cast

CHARACTERS

MIA STEIMAN
NICKY DONAHUE
SUSAN LONG
GLEN DONAHUE
ZACHARIA MELANI
SINDISWA BONA
THENJIWE BONA

11. (1) No civil or criminal proceedings shall be brought in any court of law against
     a) the state
     b) the State President
     c) any member of the Cabinet of the Republic
     d) any member of the force
     e) any person in the service of the state or acting with the direction or approval of any member or person referred to the preceding paragraphs of the above sub-regulations 1.

AND

3) if in any proceedings brought against any member or person referred to in sub-regulation 1 or the State, the question arises whether any act advised, commanded, ordered, directed or performed by him in good faith, it shall be presumed until the contrary is proved that such an act was advised, commanded, ordered, directed or performed by him in good faith.

SHOO!

How's that—off by heart too hey! OK. I know it's last year's but what the hell, the names may change but the game stays the same. Boy, I know lots more like them. Law is my language, and that. . . . that's my landscape. You know, we live in such a bloody chaos of laws that it's hard not to pass one single day without breaking one of them. My talent is understanding them, my commitment is to help those who don't.

OK! My name's MIA STEINMAN. I'm an attorney. Born in the Republic of South Africa. Both my parents were Afrikaans.

My father, Paul Le Roux, was a very active political lawyer . . . he was a colleague of Braam Fisher, Nelson Mandela. So most of my life, you could say, has been spent watching history repeat itself.

I've got very, very vague memories of the 50's treason trial and the removals from Sophiatown. More distinct ones of Sharpeville and the first State of Emergency. I remember playing with children, black and white, who stayed with us while their parents were in detention.

I watched the changing faces at our dinner table—and when I got older the extraordinary conversations that I listened to and learned from. People like Mandela, Sisula, Tambo, Ngoyi, Fisher, Mbeki, Ruth First.

Ja—it seemed so simple and inevitable then, that our country would be ruled by people like these. I watched some of them go into exile, a lot go to prison and others lose their lives.

But the one thing I learned was that the struggle would always continue, if not through their efforts, then through our government's special genius for creating activists by the thousand.

As I said, I'm a lawyer. Born to a lawyer, married to a lawyer. My husband Mike Steinman was killed in a motor accident about three years ago, and I run his practice now. I don't have kids. I've always wanted kids, but well at first Mike wouldn't and then I couldn't and in some ways, no in many ways, I'm sorry — but now my life is extraordinary — I wouldn't want it to be different. I'd like my world to be different, but not me. (*She moves across the stage. Lights come up to reveal the other actors.*)

OK. Now. I'm 5'5". A heavy smoker. Just haven't had time to stop. I haven't had a steady lover for two years. Haven't had time to look. Aagh — times have changed, faces have changed, but I still feel privileged to be part of a community that is mine — some are clients, a lot are potential clients. We all have one basic thing in common — a desperate need to change the world we live in.

Until the insanity of today's mass arrests, there were very few political people I did not know, or at least, did not know each other. Some call it an incestuous world — at times it really seems so.

But not all my clients are political — not all of them are friends — come to think of it, she is neither. (*She points to* NICKY)

NICKY: (*raises right hand as if giving evidence in court*) I'm Nicky Donahue — Born in the R S A.

I'm 5'10", I've been 5'10" since I was fifteen. One year I was the tallest in my class, boy or girl. My boyfriend was three inches shorter than me. It was so humiliating, my poor mother. So when Glen came along — looking like he looks, and five inches taller than me, I thought he was from heaven. I don't know how old he was then — about eighteen or nineteen, but even then there was something about him. I don't know — it was the way he listened. He never spoke unless he had something to say, it wasn't that he was shy — more like a strange kind of privacy. Ja—he was the first guy I slept with. God those were fantastic days. Clifton, Cape Point, discos, his dad's car. I could have eaten him alive.

SUSAN: (*raises right hand*) I'm Susan Lang—Art teacher. Born in the R S A.

I'm 5 feet tall and I've got a fetish for boys over 6 foot one. The first time I saw Glen, and his 6'3", I was with Mia and he was walking towards us and I thought "My God he's going to talk to me—I'm going to die" —turned out it was Mia he was heading for.

MIA: It's peculiar how each case I deal with informs another. It's an endless spiral of connections. Like Glen —the first time I met him—was pretty ordinary, really. He came to see me about an insurance claim—I was the legal advisor for NUSAS at the time. Suzie was with me in the office—she was sitting on the desk just chatting away—you know Suzie, God can she talk! Glen walked in—tall, blondish. Nice enough. And suddenly Suzie just went tjoep-stil. . . . A few weeks later they were lovers!

GLEN: (*raises right hand as he moves off his platform, forward*) My name is Glen Donahue. I'm a graduate student. Born in the R S A.

When I was little I used to go into these long dwaals— Not out of boredom, just out of simple fascination with how a cloud was shaping itself or how an insect was moving. People always said to me "What are you thinking about?" I would just say "nothing" or I would just smile. Privacy intrigues people so on the whole people find me intriguing, especially women. They all have so many questions and I just smile or shrug and it drives them crazy. The reasons why I do things are usually very simple but nobody believes me. For instance I did my national service in the Police because I could stay at home, in Cape Town. Simple. And I've always been able to get on with blacks because I'm simply curious about them, not because of the whole liberal guilt thing. And I never used to join in with all the raps about sex with all the other guys at the Charge office, because I had Nicky, and that used to confuse them.

And then when I finished my training, I decided I wanted to go to Wits. I thought that I was ready for Jo'burgh. Nicky's parents let her come to Wits too. I wasn't sure about that because I was half looking forward to feeling the place out on my own.

NICKY: I argued nonstop with my parents about how much better the courses at Wits were. Well I suppose I paid for my sins. You see I used to sit right at the back of the class, completely spaced out — trying so fiercely to concentrate, and before I knew what was going on the lecture would finish and I'd come out in this total daze. So I started oversleeping, missing lectures, arriving late and too embarrassed to tiptoe in. I became a feature of the canteen, sitting under the speakers, yelling over the music. I'd go window shopping in Braamfontein, melk-tart at the station, free facials at the Carlton Hotel, and would usually end up in those T-room bioscopes with schoolboys bunking school, throwing popcorn at me.

SUSAN: After the meeting we were all talking and somehow he ended up next to me, he stood so close and I felt so miniscule. I decided that our relationship would have to be conducted sitting or lying. Well we did — lie down a lot.

NICKY: So when I fell pregnant it was this fantastic excuse to get out of it all. God I must have been such a pain. Bragging about my swelling belly, giving up smoking and then bragging about that too, and then breast-feeding in public at every opportunity. I still don't know why Glen married me.

GLEN: When Nicky fell pregnant, I became so fascinated with how her body was changing that it seemed better to marry than to stop it happening.

We were very naive in those days. I had had very little to do with politics before I came to varsity. There were things that I didn't like about the government if I thought about it, but I'd seen shit happening on both sides in the police force, and I like my life and didn't want that to change. If anything, Political Science at Wits put me off even more. There was so much bullshit flying. One thing I can't handle is bullshitters who are so goddam sure of themselves. This one guy Feigle—he was my tutor for Political Science—he nearly made me change courses. I swear that that guy's tutorials on Marxism have put me off it for life. Reagan should hire him in his fight against communism. Save him billions. Just drop Feigle in Cuba, Nicaragua, Angola, get him rapping—country a month.

NICKY: You know at first Glen's friends were wonderful. Everything my mother would have wanted for me—into art, good food, music, bit of swimming—everything I wanted too—and then he got involved with this political crowd. I don't know—they just got so boring and we'd usually end up at these multiracial parties, or curry suppers with Indians and all they could do was talk politics. God I used to get bored. I mean, well I suppose I didn't have much in common with them. I couldn't pretend to relate to them, and to be honest—some of the white people just didn't seem sincere.

GLEN: One day this guy Peter Moore phoned me up, and he says that he met me in the force. I don't remember him but I say OK, I'll meet him at the Devonshire for a drink, which I do. . . . To cut a long story short, it turns out he's a lieutenant and he's handling the campus, he says that he's heard some good things about me, we have a long chat about Marxist stuff-ups and then he says that Feigle is causing lots of dangerous shit. Would I watch him—only during classes? And they're going to pay me. First I said no, then I said let me think about it. But it wouldn't be for money. I was very confused and then I find myself in a Feigle tutorial and this guy starts rapping, way off the subject, on this heavy rap about Nicaragua. Again. And I start —just out of frustration—to take notes, and suddenly I think, hey, shit, it's happening. And I look at this guy and I think no, what you're saying—that is trouble man. Then I think no wait, wait, it's in my hands, in my handwriting. There was this double feeling you know, this feeling of my own power and of Feigle as . . . as innocent. There he was, he was rapping away with that same slick certainty I knew, but he didn't know what was happening to him, I knew, because I was happening to him. It was a new feeling, it was a good feeling and then that night, I took Nicky out to dinner. It felt like the first time in months.

NICKY: Ja, we never really went out much, as a couple I mean. We began to argue a lot about Glen's political friends. We'd fight and make up, fight and then make up and then, well, I just stopped going.

GLEN: Anyway, two days later Moore phoned me up, so I played it cool, he says howzit—I say fine. He says "how's Feigle," I said—plugging away as usual, red flags flying. And he says "ja, he's going to get a lot of nice people into very bad trouble. Did you take anything down?" I say ja, I've got some stuff, but I don't know how valuable it's going to be, but he drives over, comes and picks it up. And then, a week later there was this cheque in the post. Now look, I had intended to send this thing back, but then it lay around in various pockets, and then the next month there's another one there. I mean there was a baby coming and anyway . . . that was it, I was employed.

ZACHARIA: (*raises right hand, steps forward*) My name is Zachariah Melani, affectionately known as Zach. I was born in the R S A. I play the double bass. I came up from Cape Town to do a couple of gigs and had a hell of a time finding a place to stay, until I bumped into

Themba Mafu, a trumpeter I had helped out of serious trouble some two years ago. He had a one-year contract in Lesotho and I was welcome to use his place. That was the garage behind his cousin's place. His cousin was Thenjiwe Bona, an amazing woman. I'd followed her story for years. She and her husband were active in trade union and other things. He's been in Pollsmoor now for two years. Then she became a prime target for the special branch. She is famous for her courage. She'd been in and out of detention. In and out of house arrests. At present she was confined to the magisterial district of Johannesburg.

MIA: The first time I saw Thenjiwe, it was love at first sight. She was speaking at an inter-racial meeting for women's rights—about'72 I think. I went along with Mike, my husband. I remember just sitting at the front of the hall listening to her—you know I just couldn't believe my ears. I turned to Mike and said—"Hey, you want to take a bet?" He says "What?" I said "This . . . will be the first woman president of South Africa!!!"

ZACHARIA: Thenjiwe Bona was pretty—much prettier than her pictures. She showed me the room. It was perfect, fully furnished. All I had to bring was my clothes. She told me Themba had been saying a lot of nice things about me and if I wasn't scared of being associated with her, I could have the place. There were two girls, one was in boarding school, and a ten-year-old boy, Dumisani, who was crazy about music. She moved the bed away from the wall, it had a false bottom and hidden drawer. She opened it and says "I'm sorry but this comes with the room. It's the only safe place." The drawer was full of pamphlets, I pick one up, ANC. She looks at me and says "How do you feel now?" I said, "Shit, OK, I'll help you fold them".

GLEN: I started going to places I'd never been to before. When Nicky became a bit too much of a drag, I sort of just discouraged her from coming. I think she was quite relieved.

ZACHARIA: Nomhle, the little girl, did not take much notice

of me but Dumisani did. He was at my door with a
recorder so I taught him to play that Mackay Davashe
number, "LaKushon'i Langa." (*THENJIWE starts to sing
under ZACHARIA's voice*) It's a song I really love. It
turned out to be Thenjiwe's favourite too. So we
worked hard on that one. We had lots of fun. We
listened to tapes together. I took him to gigs with me,
he had a real feel for jazz. He became a mascot, a
buddy.

*Stage transforms to party scene, GLEN talking to SUSAN
in background, others standing in a group.*

NICKY: The last party I went to, Glen was standing
chatting to this girl, and I was just standing around,
and this black guy comes up to me, and he starts
chatting, and he takes out a joint, sucks it smooth,
lights it up, takes a couple of drags and hands it to me.
Well, I'd never smoked a joint with a black man before
but I turn around and I see Glen is watching us, so I
think—no fine—so I take the joint, and I take this
really long drag. I turn around to see if Glen's seen, but
he's got his back turned to us, he didn't see a damn
thing, no one saw. If they did, no one cared.

GLEN: I started to get a smell for the whole thing—and I
discovered how easy it is to manipulate people—to get
to know what you want to know, there's no two ways
about it. I started to enjoy it. There was this one guy,
Semple, now he was a buddy of Feigles' and he'd
started a whole series of alternative studies groups all
over the country, so they banned him and restrained
him to the magisterial district of Johannesburg. He
didn't cope with this—he decided he wanted to get
out. I organised his route and a couple of contacts in
Botswana. I said to him, "Graham, you musn't talk
about this to anyone, I'm not sure about a lot of these
guys." He said, "Well, I've only told Steve, and I'm
leaving tonight." I said "Steve?, ah no Christ man, not
Steve. Look I'll just pray I'm wrong—Good luck."
They arrested him before he got to Rustenburg, and

Steve Farmer, the rising star of NUSAS. . . . after that no one would touch him with a barge pole. Two birds, one stone. They promoted me to Warrant Officer after that. And then there was Susan. Now you see Moore had said I must get to know more about this black women worker's rights thing, they thought there was some sort of ANC link up and he'd given me a list of all the people that were involved. Now what I used to do was look at the women's names first—and Sue was the only white woman there—so I thought lekker let's go for that!

ZACHARIA: I made myself generally useful around the house —you know fixing plugs, locks and broken washing lines—that kind of thing. Dumisani helped me. I've got two kids of my own. I've never lived with either of them so I began to understand what I was missing. He was just wonderful. Thenjiwe was something else. I've never seen anybody as busy as her. (SINDISWA *moves across stage toward* SUSAN, *looking irritated*) Take it easy Sindiswa! When I woke up mornings she was usually gone. But she'd already cleaned the house and cooked for the day. When she came from the office she was busy again. You know—like young people moving, in and out, asking for help and advice. She never did less than two things at a time. If she was watching the news on TV, she was also cutting the meat for the stew or mending or ironing, or checking homework or answering the phone. And when you discuss the news afterwards she remembers more than you do.

SINDISWA: I'm Sindiswa, Thenjiwe's sister. My sister's famous because she is brave, clever and she's beautiful. I'm a school teacher in Alexandra township, I stay in the women's hostel there. I'm not famous, I'm not too clever and I'm not so beautiful either. I hear what people say about Thenjiwe but they don't have her for a sister. I go to her place in Dube some weekends and on school holidays. I love the kids . . . I love her too, she's a good sister to me, she looks after my son Dumisani but she doesn't know the meaning of the word relax, not only for herself but for everybody about her. Ag, sure, sure, I understand about using your time well and being responsible, but you must also know how to waste it . . . otherwise what kind of person are you?

MIA: The last time I saw Thenjiwe was at my birthday party. What a night! Usually I hate surprises, especially on birthdays, but . . . well that night was special. Everyone was there, Suzie—with Glen, Sindiswa, Zach. They did this whole number for me . . . they called themselves the Andrews Sisters.

SONG—THENJIWE / SUSAN / SINDISWA

They dance and sing, imitating the Andrews Sisters.
GLEN and ZACHARIA play mock drums and bass.

I never loved a man—the way that—I loved you,
I never loved a man—the way that—I loved you.
Promise me you'll never leave,
Promise me you'll never leave.
I never loved a man . . .

(*they break up, laughing*)

NICKY: It kills me, but I'm still really into his body, I mean Glen, in bed he is hot, hey. Well you lie there and you think no there's nothing—he doesn't want anything from me—and then he would start to move—really slowly, and touch me like nobody had—has! When I think about him now, I know I'm not free of him yet, it makes me so angry that . . .

GLEN: I started going to functions where I knew Sue would be. Pretty soon things were cooking. One night after supper in her flat she just wouldn't let me out of the door.

SUSAN: You know what I was just wondering—who would have to move what for us to kiss?

GLEN: Actually she's amazing, she never once said what are

you thinking about in all that time I knew her. It became a very complicated situation. One day she confronted me and I thought "Oh fuck, this is it." But it turned out to be about Nicky.

SUSAN: *(from behind, leaning over face to face)* Why didn't you tell me you were married?

GLEN: Because I'm not.

SUSAN: You are.

GLEN: Not in any way that matters. *(kisses her lightly)*

SUSAN: I didn't know how to take that, but I didn't want to let him go — not yet. I didn't know why — but not yet.

NICKY: Sometimes Glen didn't come home until five or six in the morning — I've got this job in a framing shop, so by the time I got up for work he was either sleeping or had gone out again, how's that for a marriage.

GLEN: One morning — Sue was making breakfast and I was getting dressed. I picked up this *Mad* magazine and this pamphlet fell out. I picked it up "UMKHONTO WE SIZWE." The real thing.

SUSAN: *(back turned to him)* Hey, what you doing?

GLEN: Nothing — just thinking about you.

SUSAN: Liar!

GLEN: It was a good breakfast — bacon, eggs, fresh orange juice. Gunning for Feigle had been easy — but this — this was the ultimate test — I really cared for Susan, but I felt this crazy kind of high, it was like standing on the edge of the top board waiting to jump, I decided to hand it in.

NICKY: Do you know when I knew I had lost Glen? I was driving to Braamfontein and I see Glen is standing at the traffic lights, he was waiting for them to change and there was this small girl, no — woman, and he raised his hand like this and rested it on the back of her neck, I know it doesn't sound like much, but to me his hand was so tender, so caring, I'd forgotten it was possible from him, I nearly died from it.

GLEN: They were pleased but they said that I should hang in there for a while, because they were really after this Thenjiwe Bona woman, a buddy of Suzie's, and a couple of other people that were still in hiding. Now I had met this lady at a couple of parties. She had real class. So the next time I was at Sue's place I just mentioned her name along with a couple of others.

SUSAN: Ja, I saw her the other day — she's OK.

GLEN: Well I'd quite like to see her again.

SUSAN: Well, I'm seeing her this weekend, she might be coming to the flat. Why don't you pop in — Sunday — nineish.

GLEN: Which meant that the meeting was about sixish, sevenish. I left the rest up to them. They decided to raid the meeting itself and that meant Susan too. In the end she actually asked me for a lift to the place. It was very confused — the heavies and the highs.

NICKY: When Glen moved out, everyone was very nice to me. I tried all the things other people were going for. One guy took me to his reborn church, but the noise — it really freaked me out. And then another guy took me to a Hare Krishna session. Can you see me dancing around in the streets like that? I even tried for a better job. There was a nice one going at Woolworths, but the manager was black so I didn't even stay for the interview.

SUSAN: Everyone at the meeting was quiet, tense. Thenjiwe hadn't arrived and we were scared because the last contact we'd had, she said she thought she was being followed. When we stopped for supper break, Rashid and I drove to Hillbrow for Fontana take aways. There was quite a mob. It took ages. When we came back the watchman was standing in the middle of the pavement.

ZACHARIA (WATCHMAN): (*moving forward, indicating handcuffed wrists*) Hai, Missus.

Batha thiwe ngamaphoyisa missus. [They were taken by the police.]

SUSAN: Where? Where?

ZACHARIA: Here missus. All of them.

SUSAN: We sat in the car not knowing what to do. Rashid was going on about what we should do, where we should go. I said—I don't want to go anywhere. Just take me home. He dropped me at the cafe on the corner—My phone's tapped—I left a message for Zach, I left a message for Sindiswa—Thenjiwe's sister. I knew Mia was in the Eastern Cape, so I left a message on her machine—and then I went home to sleep.

MIA: That night, I had just got back from the Eastern Cape. There had been a lot of trouble in a whole string of townships and they'd arrested hundreds of people. Now it's Klerksdorp, Krugersdorp, Kagiso, Delmas, Witbank, the Free State, tomorrow, who knows? I went down as part of a legal team—most of the detainees had no access to lawyers. It had been a terrible five days. A lot of people had been killed, wounded, and needed not only legal advice, but urgent medical attention. They wouldn't go to the hospitals— they knew the police would be waiting for them there. I was running around with bandages, washing, dressing, driving people to doctors, carrying people.

I came home feeling . . . just . . . sick to the stomach—I mean obviously about what was happening—but about myself as well—I mean I was so relieved to get away from it all—and it was so easy to do.

Ja—that's the worst part of my job—feeling guilty about having feelings, because those begin to impede your efficiency. I'm famous for my feelings impeding my efficiency.

Anyway I was home—I sat down with my files and turned the answering machine on.

(*SUSAN's voice*) "MIA, THE BWWR MEETING WAS RAIDED. THEY TOOK EVERYONE, I THINK. THEY'VE DEFINITELY GOT THENJIWE. PLEASE SEE WHAT YOU CAN DO."

then three along:

(*NICKY's voice*) "MRS STEINMAN, I'M A FRIEND OF SUZIES. SHE'S BEEN ARRESTED UNDER SECTION 29. SHE ASKED ME TO PHONE YOU. SHE SAID YOU'D KNOW WHAT TO DO".

THENJIWE: One minute I was dreaming of a fat Fontana Russian sausage and chips, and the next I was on my way to Jon Voster Square with a Boer on either side, well that's life in the R S A. They took us in three cars. That little cop, Klaasen, came to identify us. He looked me over and said "Ja, dis die kaffermaid op wie ons wag" [It is the kaffir maid that we have been waiting for] and you know I was wearing my nice clothes and they said "Ja, where did you steal those clothes from?"

ZACHARIA: One Sunday night a message came through that Thenjiwe was arrested. Now she said — if they come — say you know nothing. If they find the pamphlets, just say you know nothing. But shit I didn't feel safe — if she was arrested then they would definitely come and search and I didn't want to say nothing about anything to them. I pulled the box out — OK to the coal bin — no good — ah — toilet — on top of the toilet — ag stupid man — which neighbour could I leave them with? No that would be unfair. So I found myself running with the box through yards over fences past barking dogs to the football field. I dropped the box behind the goal posts and ran back home. I looked back once and saw Thenjiwe's pamphlets moving like ghosts across the field. In 30 seconds flat I was back in bed with the door locked behind me.

SUSAN: They came about 4:30 in the morning. I was sleeping so heavily I didn't hear the knocking on the door. My friend comes running in.

NICKY: (*SUZIES' FRIEND*) Suzie, the police are here!

SUSAN: Look don't panic and don't cry, or you'll get me started. They're here for me.

There was this blonde lieutenant woman. She kept touching all my clothes.

MIA: (*COP*) Ag, shame you're going to miss yoga tonight.

SUSAN: You seem to know a lot about me.

MIA: (*COP*) Oh, we know everything about you, girlie.

SUSAN: They searched my flat for about three hours. Then they searched my car, then my studio. Then they took me to an office at John Vorster Square.

THENJIWE: They led me through a lot of banging and clanging gates to my cell. There were two young girls spreading mats there, hey for a moment I was pleased, perhaps there was going to be company but the girls moved out as I moved in and the door was locked. I thought about Susan. Did they wait for her? Did she manage to get away? I knew the kids would be alright. I was worried about the pamphlets but my only hope was that Suzie or Rashid would warn Zach before the cops got there.

SINDISWA: Anyway, I teach at a Secondary School in Alexandra. Because of all this unrest there are no serious classes really. Some days a few students turn up and then we carry on with classes. Usually there are too few of them for us to teach. But the regulation is that we must be on the school premises at all times. So mostly we just sit around gossiping or reading magazines, and now with the way things are so many kids are in and out of jail.

ZACHARIA: About an hour later a van arrived. I heard voices about in the yard. They knocked at my door, I took my time answering. There were three whites and two blacks, they were all speaking Afrikaans. Anyway I went across to the house. The kids were sitting in the bedroom handling everything a lot better than me. I sat with them. They took me back to my room to search. I was doing a lot of praying but they never found the hidden drawer.

MIA: You get a message Thenjiwe's been taken!
You get a message Suzie's been taken!
You're hearing about friends!
You know what taken means.
You know who does the taking,
You know what could be happening to them because of who they are and what they believe in.
So what do you do?
You apply here, you apply there, you apply here, you apply there, you apply, you apply, you apply — and then — YOU JUST WAIT!!

SINDISWA: One Sunday evening I received a message from Susan. It said that Thenjiwe was arrested. Now it's not the first time I'd received a message like that — it's become part of our lives now, so I packed my bag and got a taxi across to Soweto. When I got to the house Zach opened the door for me. He was sleeping with the kids in Thenjiwe's bed. I sent him back to his room and I climbed in between Dumisani and Nomhle. After that cold taxi, they were just lovely and warm.

SUSAN: At John Vorster you just wait. I was trying not to feel anything. I was smoking a hell of a lot and then they offered me tea.

MIA: (COP) You see, we're very nice here. All the things you've heard is just people's fantasies. Just big lies, we are nice, very nice.

SUSAN: Very nice.
I wondered what was happening to Thenjiwe.

THENJIWE: There was a tap on my left-hand wall.

SINDISWA: (CELL PERSON) (whispers) Sisi. Sisi.

THENJIWE: Hallo

SINDISWA: (CELL PERSON) You're so quiet.

THENJIWE: I'm eating.

SINDISWA: (*CELL PERSON*) Have you just been brought in?

THENJIWE: Ja.

SINDISWA: (*CELL PERSON*) And you're eating.

THENJIWE: Ja.

SINDISWA: (*CELL PERSON*) Most people spend the whole week crying, not eating.

THENJIWE: Hai, Suka, I'm hungry man.

SUSAN: My cell was black cemented floors. There were three felt mats and a few blankets. There was a toilet, a cement bench, a bible, kotch green walls and that was it. No, there was a small box high in the corner — a TV camera. I moved my mats under the camera between the cement bench and the wall. I sat on the mats and I thought — OK, so this is it. Then — three policemen came running in.

GLEN: (*COP*) Move your mats! Move your mats!

SUSAN: Why?

GLEN: (*COP*) We can't see you on the TV Camera.

SUSAN: That's your problem. This is my cell — I'll sit where I like.

They adjusted the camera after that.

THENJIWE: I stayed in my cell day after day with no company, just my plates of food and the whispering from other cells. After 28 days they came for me. They led me down a flight of stairs and into an office that had been a cell. Inside there were four cops, three rooinecks and one bantu. They looked nice and fresh. They gave me a thick file with clean pages inside.

GLEN: (*COP*) Now girlie, you know what you're going to do? You are going to write about yourself — everything. From the day you were born until now. Don't leave anything out. Your involvement with the ANC, your guerilla training, this BWWR business, trade

unions — this boycott you were planning — everything,
no games hey — not like Biko or Timol or Aggett hey.

THENJIWE: I took the pen and started writing. How I found
my opening lines, Jesus only knows — but I kept on
writing. Where I was born, where I schooled, my
family and my work. I didn't care about sense, I just
kept writing. My pen stopped about the 11th page.

GLEN: (*COP*) OK, now let's see, 11 pages? No, no my girlie
— you've got another 89 pages to go!!

SUSAN: During my first supper I thought to myself, OK, so
this is it — so what have we got. There's definitely a
shower so I'll be clean. I've got food to eat — a lot of
people starve, I've got a roof over my head — a lot of
people don't. I've got blankets, so I'll be nice and
warm. I've never read the Bible. I hear it's great
reading, and if they make me wait, if they leave me
alone, I'll carry on with my work. I'll give the kids at
the centre projects to do everyday. Then I'll imagine
what they drew and I'll give them marks. I'll perfect
my yoga. I'll be very busy. I organized myself a
schedule for the next day in case they didn't call me for
questioning. And then I lay down. I closed my eyes and
I tried, I tried, I tried to picture Glen — I could see his
shirt, and his hands but not his face. Eventually I tried
to sleep. The light was on.

THENJIWE: After my fifth attempt: —

GLEN: (*COP*) You are being very stubborn. So now you are
just going to stand until you tell the truth. The only
time you will sit is when you go to the toilet, and that
will be for one minute — that's all.

THENJIWE: I thought to myself — OK, I will stand until I
die. (*She remains standing in this position during much
of the rest of the play.*)

ZACHARIA: That was a strange day, winter and rain.
By six o'clock Dumisani hadn't come back from
school, so I went out into the streets to look for him

and then from house to house. None of the neighbours had seen him. Some of them were also waiting for their kids. And outside in the main road, there was a bus burning.

THENJIWE: I stood 18 hours a day for the first 5 days. They came in 6-hour shifts.

When I went back to my cell I couldn't sit or bend. It took me ages, first to sit, then to lie down, but by the time sleep came, it was time to stand again.

My body began to swell. They swore at me. They threw leftover food and their cigarette stompies at me. They began to hit me. On the 7th day my shift was changed to 24 hours.

SINDISWA: One day we had a good attendance at the school. It was quite hot for winter, but now it looked like rain and then, suddenly, toward the end of the day — as if on signal, these children, uyazi ndisenombono wabo [I can remember vividly], they poured out of their classes into the streets, where the police were. They were shouting "Siyayinyova! We will destroy." They picked up rocks and bricks and started attacking buses and cars. Dodging the police. I ran back to the hostel and watched from a window high up. There was running everywhere, just school uniforms all over the township and shouting and chanting and screaming and burning of houses and cars. Soon the streets were lost in dust and smoke. Clouds from earth began to meet the clouds from the sky.

Then the soldiers were moved in — but they were late. We suddenly heard Qhwara! Qwhara! Qhwara! Lightning and thunder, louder than any bomb or gun. Poor soldiers, their guns came down as the rain began to fall, whhhaaaaaaaaaaa, there was no other sound. Everything went very very quiet. Just the sound of the rain. Whaaa. People started to come back from work, they walked in the rain, talking as if everything was as they had left it. There were smells of cooking in the hostel. I decided to go back to Soweto then.

SUSAN: I was interrogated every day from early in the morning until 6 o'clock at night. Their first question told me how they saw white left woman.

GLEN: (*COP*) Do you shave your legs?

SUSAN: No I was born this way.

GLEN: (*COP*) Do you like Soya Mince and lentils?

SUSAN: I prefer lamb chops.

The questions that followed weren't so easy. They kept me busy, but I watched them like a hawk. It went on for a week.

GLEN: (*COP*) We've got plenty of time, you're being very uncooperative and you're a liar, so now we're just going to leave you.

SUSAN: You know what? I've got a helluva lot of time as well. I've got no appointments. I've got absolutely nothing to do. I think the best thing for you to do is to send me back to my cell.

GLEN: (*COP*) But first a little question about Thenjiwe Bona.

ZACHARIA: When I got back home—Sindiswa had arrived—but there was no sign of Dumisani. There was a knock at the door. It was Mr Sithole, he had heard that some kids had been caught after the burning of the bus and he thought that Dumisani and his son were among them. We went with him to Protea Police Station.

SUSAN: They take lots of things away—like your shoelaces, your earrings, your comb, your mirror, even your tampax. So you start to think of ways of getting back at them. For instance, during interrogation I started my pin collection. I wasn't even sure what I'd use them for. The captain had pins on his desk on a magnet, so I stole pins. I'd pick a pin up and I'd play with it, put it down, I'd light a cigarette, pick it up, until they weren't really aware of what was happening, and then I'd slip it in my pocket. I had pins hidden all over my cell. I'd have a pin like in between the felt mats or in the folding of my glasses case or in the sole of my shoe. If they found one, it wouldn't have mattered because I had a whole selection.

GLEN: I'd been thinking a lot about Susan. I said to Moore that this whole thing was getting very difficult, but he said to me—listen come on man—you know, it's like gardening. You pull out the weeds so that the real plants can grow. He says to me I'm a landscape artist.

THENJIWE: By now my body was so accustomed to standing that I began to dread the time when they would lead me back to my cell and I would have to struggle to lie down again. Ja, I learned to sleep with my eyes open. I looked up at the ceiling and I slept and dreamt. I slept and dreamt.

SUSAN: They got heavier and heavier. They knew everything. Not only about the boycott we were organizing, but about my sex life, my contacts, my mother's bowling club. And then—they came to the point. They asked me what I'd done in Botswana.

GLEN: (COP) Do you like riding around in the backs of bakkies.

SUSAN: Depends on the company.

GLEN: (COP) Oh you mean like black men?

SUSAN: Perhaps, Depends what black man.

GLEN: (COP) And on what he's wearing?

SUSAN: That's a point.

GLEN: (COP) Like an ANC T-shirt

SUSAN: This is boring.

GLEN: (COP) Is food boring?

SUSAN: Sometimes.

GLEN: (COP) Grilled chicken?

SUSAN: No, I like grilled chicken.

GLEN: (*COP*) Do you like Molefe's grilled chicken?

SUSAN: Bit too salty. I had had grilled chicken at Molefe's the night I left Gaberone.

Then they asked about the ANC pamphlets that I had collected from Molefe and the people I had delivered them to in Johannesburg.

SINDISWA: At Protea Police Station, the black policeman at the desk was reading a photo comic. He didn't look up at us and I started crying.

ZACHARIA: (*COP*) Ja?

SINDISWA: Ntate, we are looking for our children.

ZACHARIA: (*COP*) Hai man, Hai man now why must you ask me? You must send in a written application to the Police Public Relations in Pretoria.

SINDISWA: Ntate, just look at how unhappy we all are, our children are ten years old.

ZACHARIA: (*COP*) Where were they?

SINDISWA: Dube — they didn't come back from school today.

ZACHARIA: (*COP*) Today? Nobody was brought here today. Moroka maybe — not here.

SINDISWA: He picked up his photo comic again and began to read.

MIA: I came back from court one day — company liquidations — they're getting more frequent now — when I get this call from Sindiswa.

SINDISWA: Hallo Mia, I don't know what to do, my boy Dumisane is missing!

MIA: What? Since when?

SINDISWA: Last night. I went to Protea but . . .

MIA: Ja well that's pointless. Look Sindiswa leave it to me. I'll try and find out all that's possible.

SINDISWA: All I know is a bus was stoned and burnt.

MIA: Do you think he could have been part of it?

SINDISWA: Never!

MIA: Are you sure?

SINDISWA: Oh God! I don't think so—I don't know.

MIA: Was he taken with other kids?

SINDISWA: What do you mean?

MIA: From which area? Dube?

SINDISWA: Yes!

MIA: Well then it's possible he was taken with other kids.

SINDISWA: They say I would waste my time at Baragwanath.

MIA: You would—if you know someone who works there —ask them to snoop around. Don't join those long queues yourself.

SINDISWA: And Moroka . . . maybe . . .

MIA: Listen Sindi just leave it to me—what's his name again? Dumisane Ngube. Right! I'll send a telex now. If you can, sit still. If you can't, then don't. I know how you feel. I'll be in touch.

I didn't have a telex machine in my office, so I ran upstairs to a colleague in the building—he had been a friend of Mike's—Englishman—had a lot of big commercial firms as clients. I explained the situation to him—told him a ten-year-old boy had been arrested— asked if I could use his machine, but he just shook his head.

GLEN: (*as laywer*) "Mia I'm sorry . . . but um . . . my partners feel . . . um that in these times we really shouldn't deal with MESSAGES OF THAT NATURE!"

MIA: "I only hope that one day either your children or your partners' children have conscience enough to find themselves in the same situation and that you, my learned friends, have no fucking telex machine at hand."

I sent a cable by phone.

SUSAN: When I realised how much they knew, I panicked. I dreamt pamphlets, pamphlets, pamphlets, pamphlets, in Thenjiwe's back room, in Rashid's father's storeroom. I agonized over a piece of folded paper in the boot of my car. And then I thought—no they know about the pamphlets, forget about the pamphlets, and I began to function again. I listened and I waited. I listened and I waited. I said nothing. After a whole day of silence, they told me they would send me to my cell for a month, to stew.

THENJIWE: One dream came from the sound of their boots pacing up and down around me. (*They all gather around her, back-lit, their faces dark, miming soldiers with guns.*) I dreamt that my friends, my lawyer, my sister, Zach, Suzie, Glen had gathered around me. "Hey! What are you doing here, are you crazy, there are Boers all over this place, they'll kill you." Sindiswa, ubasaphi ababantu—kanene nawe uphambene ufana nabo [Sindiswa, why are you bringing these people here? By the way, you are also as crazy as they are], but they just smiled at me, they all had guns. They gave me one too. We started to sing and dance down the stairs.

SONG—*All except* NICKY.

They all sing and dance together, miming guns. Before the song ends they dance back to their places. THENJIWE *sings the last line alone.*

"*Qiniselani, nai, maqhawe, sekuseduze lapho siyakhona, Ayanqikaza ayesab'amagwala, athi kungcono sibuyel'emuva. Tyhini Thixo! Bemkile.*" [Hold tight you *brave ones, we are almost there. The cowards are scared and confused and are contemplating retreat.]* I woke before we reached the gate.

SUSAN: The next morning I was reading my Bible and four of them came into my cell. "What is this? What do you want? Fuck off out of my cell. This is my cell. You've told me this is my space. You told me you're leaving me alone. Now just fuck off and leave me alone."

GLEN: (*COP*) You better read your Bible.

SUSAN: I have, I have, I have studied the Bible and there is no sin in opposing a state that disobeys the word of God. You know what? One day we'll both account to him to see where justice lies. Because I don't have to account to you.

Anyway they left me alone. They left me alone for 10 days and then they came at me again — harder than ever.

MIA: The other day I had this conversation, no, no — argument — with this prosecutor . . . umm ah . . . agh forget his name. We were talking about black kids — the exploitation of the children by the ANC — the brutality of the children. And I said to him "Louis," agh OK his name was Louis, I said "Have you got eyes, your bloody government has been waging war against CHILDREN since '76. You know how I see them? As our liberators — yours — mine — their parents. They are fighting for the freedom of us all!"

"Freedom?" he said, "from what?"

"From all the lies that have been . . . strangling us since . . . agh I don't know when!!"

I said "Louis, you know why we're pissing in our pants? Their blood is a mirror in which we see ourselves. You think we're scared of them — we're terrified of us. I know them man — I speak to them — they speak to me — it's you I run away screaming from, and what you are forcing them to become! Listen, and, if you're counting barbarians — we're the first in line."

ZACHARIA: *(moving to front of stage with* SINDISWA*)* The next morning we went to Moroka Police Station. It's a bus centre, a very hot spot—always buzzing with people moving to places, from places, out of places, into places—workers, musicians, fruit sellers, newspaper sellers, students, old-age pensioners, pickpockets, and of course—the police! Two of them were at the gates, with hefty R1 rifles.

SINDISWA: Suddenly there was a kwela-kwela approaching. All you could see were shadows inside, and fingers reaching through the wire mesh windows. But no—it was older men—pass offenders. And another van was coming behind it—full of students singing.

SINDISWA, ZACH, AND THENJIWE SING: Khwela phezu kwendlu ubatshele; umama uyajabula umangishaya ibhunu. Umam'uyajabula, umam'uyajabula umam' uyajabula. [Go to the top of the mountain and tell them that my mother likes it when I hit the white man.]

SINDISWA: The van stopped at the gate.

Hey mfana wami, awungisize ungibhekele umfan'omncane. UDumisani Ngubo. Una 10 years, ufunda e Dube Lower Primary. [Hey young man, please help me find my young boy. His name is Dumisani Ngubo, he is 10 years old and is a student at Dube Lower Primary School.]

and at the same time:—

ZACHARIA: Hey, my lytie, awuyazi lentwana encane U Dumisane? Ile edlala i flute. Suka efasteleni my lytie. Suka, ngifuna ukubona lentwana esemva kwakho. [Hey young man, don't you know Dumisane. He is the one who plays a flute. Move from the window young man, I want to see the other young man behind you.]

SINDISWA: The van went through the gates, the children filed out of the van. There were bigger ones and little ones. Others were crying, others were still singing. Then the policemen hit out. One of the big girls called out to us—Baba, Mama tell them to let the little ones go! But no, no one knew Dumisani. We spent the whole day at the place. Van after van passed us, but we didn't find him. (*She wanders back to her seat.*)

ZACHARIA: I just couldn't take it any longer—I sent Sindiswa home in a taxi and I wandered around Soweto like a mad man, I asked every friend of his I could find. I asked every friend's mother, father, sister, brother, but nobody knew anything about Dumisani.

MIA: Kids! You know, the other day this kid was brought into my office. Kids. Black boy—about 14 . . . 15. He sat across my desk. His mother sat next to him. He wouldn't talk to me because I was white!

He was up on a charge of public violence and had been subpoenaed to appear as a state witness in five other trials. They wanted him to give evidence against his friends!

What alternatives did he have—to give evidence and possibly be burnt alive as an informer or to go to jail for a total of 20 years.

I just looked at him—he has no doubt. He's so powerful he STINKS OF VICTORY. Aagh it's finished man—Let them take him—let them lock him up. He's got ten little brothers to take his place.

GLEN: Listen, no one in the world has any right to judge anyone else. I mean—they want to talk to us about shooting children, talk to the Americans about burning them man, Nagasaki, hey Napalm, and Philadelphia, did you hear about that bomb they dropped on those blacks in Philadelphia? Racism is a problem every-where, it's primal man. And that goes for the Feigles too. They need us to be like this, it's the new porno-graphy, we're the stars of the world. They watch us like voyeurs in some sleazy leather bar. (*kicks rostrum*)

THENJIWE: Early one morning, there was a loud bang.

GLEN: (*COP*) It's not fair, the captain is at home sleeping with his wife and I have to sit here staring at this fucken kaffermeid.

THENJIWE: It was a very young white cop. He was hitting the wall. His was a face I had seen before. I had dreamt about it, agh, shame, for a moment I pitied him. At least I was doing something I believe in. But what was his life locked up in a cell with a swaying, swelling kaffermeid with rolling eyes. He took money out of his pocket and sent the black cop out to buy him a cool drink, he watched me.

GLEN: (*COP*) How many boyfriends have you got?

THENJIWE: I didn't answer.

GLEN: (*COP*) Don't you miss them?

THENJIWE: He moved towards me. I closed my eyes and when I opened them I don't know how much later, he was still watching. I thought no, I can't believe it. "Listen man, it's no use. It'll take you an hour to get me to lie down and I'm no good at doing it standing." He just watched me. His gun was on the table. If I could just fall that way, I would land on it. The thought of using a gun for the first time got me very excited. I saw it happen, (*she mimes shooting poses*) kazoom, kazoom, again and again, kazoom, kazoom, from different angles, kazoom, kazoom, kazoom, like a crazy cowboy movie, kazoom, kazoom. Thixo, the black cop, arrived with the cool drink. Wayimosha! [He spoiled it.] I think we were equally disappointed.

NICKY: You know I could have been in Amanzimtoti when that bomb went off. This hairdresser friend of mine— well he and his boyfriend asked us to go down there for Christmas. Thank God we didn't go. And the other night, we definitely heard a bang go off somewhere in Hillbrow. It's at times like this, I really hate Glen for leaving us. Well just say I was there in Amanzimtoti with Dominic, buying an ice cream or reaching for a can of tomato soup and BOOM!

No way—now I do my shopping at the local cafe—it costs twice as much—but what's money anyway.

THENJIWE: One day my toilet escourt came for me.

NICKY mimes woman cop.

GLEN: (*COP*) Come in—she doesn't want to go to the toilet—she wants to play a little game.

THENJIWE: They were talking about me as if I wasn't there. The wardress has a little smile on her face. She stood and watched me.

GLEN: (*COP*) Klap haar. [Slap her.]

THENJIWE: I stared straight into her eyes, she didn't move.

GLEN: (*COP*) Kom nou, klap haar. [Come now, slap her.]

THENJIWE: She moved towards me, I stayed staring. Her steps got smaller and smaller, finally she stopped. I was sweating. I could imagine my fingers around her neck. Suddenly she turned and went straight out of the door. After an hour or so, she came back to take me to the toilet, this time they let me go. On the way she asked me.

NICKY: (*ESCORT*) Listen, what would you have done if I had klapped you?

THENJIWE: I would have killed you, I swear to God, I would have.

NICKY: (*ESCORT*) You know, I could see it in your eyes. Is it true you did guerilla training?

THENJIWE: Yes, I lied, I just have to touch you with the tips of my fingers like this (*she makes small, tight gesture and rasping sound*)—She never came for me again.

ZACHARIA: I went to Diepkloof to find a nursing sister that hid wounded children from the police.
I counted three casspirs along the way. Suddenly a group of boys and girls came running around the corner. Then there was chaos, gunshots, tear gas,

women screaming children's names, police jumping out from everywhere. A boy fell—bleeding from the stomach and they dragged him down a side street. An old woman stood in the door screaming "NOMAZA, NOMAZA, NOMAZA!" I saw this little girl standing at the gate crying. I picked her up and ran inside. The old woman locked the door behind us. I sat in this dark room away from the windows, hardly breathing. The old woman had wet herself. She saw that I had noticed. She held the child close to her. Look at me my son, look at what they are doing to us. It was two hours before I could leave. When I got back home—a hippo, ja, a hippo was parked at the gate!

THENJIWE: They were angry with me because they still had no statement to present to their senior. One of them held my hand, forced a pen between my fingers and tried to make me write.

GLEN: (*COP*) Ja, you and your fucken ANC. Did you hear about Mamelodi? They incite the children, but this time they learned their lesson, because not only did your children get shot, but your grandmothers too.

THENJIWE: What do you want me to do? Do you want me to cry? I won't cry for those grandmothers. I know them and they are proud because every grandmother that gets shot gives birth to a thousand freedom fighters. I threw the pen at them. One of them hit me. They dragged me back to my cell. (*She lies down.*) The last thing I heard was:

GLEN: (*COP*) (*to ZACHARIA, as fellow COP*) She's definitely Chinese-trained—if she was Russian-trained, she would have given up long ago.

ZACHARIA nods.

SUSAN: One day they threw a canvas bag into my lap. I said—Thanks.

GLEN: (*COP*) Do you know what it's for?

SUSAN: To keep things in. Now you must give me lipstick and a pencil and a notebook.

GLEN: (*COP*) Very funny.

SUSAN: What's it for then?

GLEN: (*COP*) You tell me.

SUE: Money. But I don't need any.

GLEN: (*COP*) Stop playing games.

SUSAN: OK it's the latest fashion. It's a hood. You wet it and you put it over my head and you ask me things.

GLEN: (*COP*) Nearly right.

SUSAN: Why?

GLEN: (*COP*) It's not for you.

Light flashes on THENJIWE, *hood on her head, jerking with electric shocks. Light flashes off.* SUSAN *screams.*

SINDISWA: I was sleeping with Nomhle in my arms when there was a heavy knocking on the front door. Only one kind of fist makes that kind of sound.

ZACHARIA: (*COP*) Polisie!

SINDISWA: I left Nomhle sleeping and I went to open the front door, there were two black policemen and beyond them two very young white policemen. I looked down—one of the blacks had Dumisani by the hand, I bent down and caught hold of him. But they pushed me away.

GLEN: (*COP*) You can't do that, this boy is under arrest—go inside.

SINDISWA: What has he done?

GLEN: (*COP*) Who are you?

SINDISWA: I am his mother.

GLEN: (*COP*) You are not Thenjiwe Bona.

SINDISWA: I'm her sister, this is my son — what has he done?

GLEN: (*COP*) He was found yesterday, stoning buses and cars.

SINDISWA: I don't believe it, can I ask him?

Dumisani was dirty and cold, his lip was swollen.

'Mama, angenzanga Lutha mina, I was hiding in the shelter from the rain. They were chasing other boys and they took me.

GLEN: (*COP*) Ja, that's what they all say. You can't talk to him now. You must come with us to the station.

SINDISWA: Then Zach appeared at the front door.

ZACHARIA: What's the matter?

SINDISWA: Dumisani wouldn't look at him.

ZACHARIA: Is he alright?

SINDISWA: I don't know Zach — I've got to go with them to the police station.

ZACHARIA: I'm coming with you.

GLEN: (*COP*) Wie's hy? Is hy die pa? [Are you the father?]

ZACHARIA: No, I'm a friend.

GLEN: (*COP*) Dan bly jy hier! [Then you stay here.]

SINDISWA: I put on my coat. I followed them out.
They led us to a hippo. They let Dumisani in first and then I followed.

SUSAN: Ja, they got to me. I began to do a lot of screaming. I'm not sure if it was while I was sleeping or awake. All I know is that one day they showed me a statement I had signed and that I had a new wardress. She was very young 19, 20, years old. She was very kind to me. One night she made a pack of cards out of a school exercise book. She only knew snap, I tried to teach her rummy.

SUSAN: So where do you come from?

NICKY: (*WARDRESS*) Me? Bothaville.

SUSAN: Never heard of it. Where is that?

NICKY: (*WARDRESS*) It's a small place in the Free State. My parents have a farm just outside there.

SUSAN: What do they farm?

NICKY: (*WARDRESS*) Ag, mielies mostly.

SUSAN: So, you grew up on a farm?

NICKY: (*WARDRESS*) Yes.

SUSAN: How come you work for the police?

NICKY: (*WARDRESS*) Well during Matric I didn't know what to do, and then the police sent a woman to our school and what she said sounded nice. She said it's a job where you can serve the community, really help people.

SUSAN: How come you ended in Joburg?

NICKY: (*WARDRESS*) No, they transferred me here. I don't mind because Ampie's stationed in Pretoria. So on my weekend off I can see him.

SUSAN: So who's Ampie?

NICKY: (*WARDRESS*) He's my fiancé.

SUSAN: Oh yes—you've got a lovely ring.

NICKY: (*WARDRESS*) Yes, it's a Caress. [popular inexpensive ring]

SINDISWA: The hippo didn't feel like a hippopotamus, it felt more like being swallowed by a crocodile—cold and dark. There were more white policemen inside. I couldn't see . . . I couldn't tell how many. I sat opposite my child—I just couldn't believe he was guilty. And if he was—why this mad machine? Why all these mad men, just for one child? The hippo was moving very slowly. I couldn't see out. The white policemen were very young.

I remembered stories I'd heard about women arrested and then raped. I sat back so they couldn't see my face. I just wished they'd hurry . . . for the first time in my life I was happy to reach a police station.

THENJIWE: (*sitting up slowly*) I don't know how long I slept, but when I woke up there were six plates of food untouched. I tried to work it out. How long had I slept, where was I?

SINDISWA: When we got inside, they showed me a statement they said Dumisani had written. My God, it was all there—how he had stoned buses and a Mercedes Benz and then hidden in the shelter . . . it was all there, in his scribbly little child's handwriting. I prayed—I said, please God, let them warn him and send him home with me. But he wasn't listening. They led Dumisani away and told me to go home. He was crying and calling my name. I just stood at the desk.

ZACHARIA: (*COP*) Now, what's the matter?

SINDISWA: I don't understand what you are saying to me. Let me pay bail then . . .

ZACHARIA: (*COP*) Ja, and let him skip to Botswana.

SINDISWA: Botswana? This child can't even go to Alexandra on his own!

ZACHARIA: (*COP*) What about those COSAS people? They call him a sell-out and set fire on you all.

SINDISWA: Please, let him go! He's a good child, I swear . . .

ZACHARIA: (*COP*) Is that so? We spoke to his headmaster, and he said that Dumisani never listens and always makes trouble at school.

SINDISWA: I became very confused and didn't argue anymore. They told me to come back the next morning and they sent me home.

NICKY: You know, people start to tell me things about what's happening here, and I say no man—how do

you know it's true, what proof have you got? You
know, I just want them to leave me out of it. Look—
I'm a single parent. I'm trying to bring up a child—a
boy—without a father. I just can't afford to get
depressed.

SINDISWA: The headmaster and his wife came to ask about
Dumisani. We sat down and had tea and talked about
the problems in the township. Then the headmaster's
wife said—He ntombi, do you know what happens to
little boys inside? The bigger ones use them as women!
The headmaster said—no—she must keep quiet, that
we must think of Dumisani. And then I asked him. I
said—Baba, I've been at the Police Station. They told
me you said Dumisani's a bad boy, and he always
makes trouble at school. The headmaster just shook his
head. "They are devils my child—when I said how
good Dumisani was—they said to me, but how come
his mother says otherwise?"

*ZACHARIA starts whistling "LaKushon'i Langa" as he
wanders across the stage, looking up as though at windows.*

SUSAN: One night I heard someone whistling "Lovely Lies,"
Thenjiwe's favourite song, and I thought, where in this
hellhole is she, and what's happening to her?

THENJIWE: Half-asleep half-awake, I heard this whistle. I
thought this was a wonderful dream and I tried to fall
asleep again.

ZACHARIA: (*whispering*) Thenji, Thenjiwe!

THENJIWE: There was a voice—it was from down below.

ZACHARIA: Thenji, Ma, Ma!

THENJIWE: Someone was calling, I tried to make out that
voice. It wasn't very clear. Yes, I could make out just
the shape of a man down below. His face moved into
some light. Zach! Zach!

ZACHARIA: (*covers his face, overcome*) Ma, Ma is that you?

THENJIWE: Ja though you wouldn't know me, if you saw me now. Zach! Zach!

ZACHARIA: We thought you were dead, we heard you've been missing for days.

THENJIWE: Don't worry I'm OK now. How's everyone? How are the kids?

ZACHARIA: Ma the kids are fine. (*he looks around*) I must go. Someone's coming.

THENJIWE: No, wait! What day is it?

ZACHARIA: Sunday.

THENJIWE: Where are you standing?

ZACHARIA: What?

THENJIWE: What place is this?

ZACHARIA: John Vorster Square.

ZACHARIA *backs away, giving thumbs-up sign.* THENJIWE *lowers herself to the floor again.*

THENJIWE: Aaah!

SUSAN: They told me that they were going to charge me. That meant a lot of things. That I would be sent to Diepkloof to await trial. That I would be out of solitary and with other people. That maybe Glen would come and see me—and Mia. This pleased me but otherwise I couldn't feel. I tried doing a bit of yoga, but that didn't work. I ended up pacing up and down my cell. There were lots of children in the prison. I could hear them crying and calling to each other. And then one of them began to sing. . . and the others joined in . . .

SINDISWA, THENJIWE, ZACHARIA:

ALALA ENGALELE AMABHUNU EKHAYA	The Boer don't sleep
ALALA NEZIBHAMU AMABHUNU EKAYA	They lie with guns
ADUBULA ABANTWANA	When they wake up they shoot children
ABANTWANA ESOWETOO	Children in Soweto
ADUBULA ABANTWANA	They shoot children
ABANTWANA KWALANGA	Children in Langa
AYABESABA ABANTWANA	They are scared of the children
ABANTWANA ETINARA	Children in Uitenhage
ALALA ENGALELE AMABHUNU EKHAYA	The Boer don't sleep
ALALA NEZIBHAMU AMABHUNU EKHAYA	They lie with guns
ISIBHAMU EMNYAMGO	A gun by the door
ISIBHAMU PHANTSI KOMQAMELO	A gun under the pillow.

SUSAN: (*closes her eyes, concentrating*) It was a song that Thenjiwe had taught me.

"The Boers can't sleep because they are afraid of the children. They lie with guns because they are afraid of the children. There's a gun under the cushion and a gun beside the bed. The Boers lie with their guns because they're afraid of the children. In the morning they stand up and they go to shoot the children. The Boers will never sleep because they're afraid of the children."

MIA: They say we haven't even begun to feel the force of the government. That there are mountains full of arms and mine shafts full of fuel. And I think of the men who collected it all and nothing terrifies me more. The other day I was walking in town reading all these headlines about reform. And I walked past the drillhall. The pavement was full of army recruits. Young white boys in slipslops and shorts, with strong brown legs and bitten fingernails—saying goodby to their mothers and sisters and sweethearts and I thought Christ! Where are you going to? Why are you letting them go? They tell you apartheid is dead and they send you to fight people who knew it long ago. They talk about releasing Mandela and yet arrest people like Suzie and Thenjiwe!

Don't you see what liars they are? How insane they are? Don't you see who your enemy is. Run away from them! Hide from them! Don't let them touch you! Don't let them near you!

I swear I wanted to pray—I wish I believed in God.

SINDISWA: The next day I thought we were going to court, but instead, they took Dumisani and me to a Commissioner of Oaths. I had brought him a warm tracksuit. But no, they wouldn't let me give it to him. They wanted Dumisani to repeat and sign everything he'd written in his statement. They made him stand in front of this big Afrikaans man who was the Commissioner of Oaths. They brought in another big man, a black man to translate because the commissioner spoke only Afrikaans. My child was dirty and cold.

He was shivering and he said to them: "If I tell you the honest truth, will you let me go home with my mother today? I am very cold." And they said, "Ja, tell us the truth." And so he told them the truth about how he did hide in the shelter from the rain and that is all. The other statement about stoning buses and a Mercedes Benz happened because the police were hitting him, they were threatening him and he was afraid . . .

I knew they would never let him go. They made him sign. . . . They put a pen in his hand and he signed— slowly and carefully. These huge men took the pen from him and told him to raise his hand up like this, and make an oath. I watched him and I thought:

These people have made my child swear twice. They have made him lie under oath at least once. They have stood before a child and done this to a child.

If he is innocent, or guilty, there is a place in hell for men like this. There is an even deeper hell for the men who pay men like this — they will go there . . . and they will burn together!

MIA: Susan was finally charged and I started preparing for her trial. I saw her as often as possible. She looked so skinny. (*they hug.*)

NICKY: You know something — everyone is leaving, all my friends. Look, I didn't ask for all this trouble. I didn't vote this government into power. I've never voted in my life, what's the point? I don't go out anymore. Agh, one or two people come around. They bring videos and smoke grass, but you know something, when I'm all by myself — I just can't believe that anything is real anymore. There's Dominic, yes but sometimes I can't believe there's a place like Cape Town or the Magaliesburg. You see all these places on TV — San Francisco, Hawaii, Rome, but I can't see myself going there. I don't want to walk on those streets, or talk to those people. I don't want to do that here either. I suppose I'm just one of those people who are scared of everything. I don't know.

MIA: After two and a half months they had still refused to release Dumisani into Sindiswa's custody. But I continued to appeal. I phoned every day.

Then one day, for one of their very strange reasons they phoned me:

NICKY (POLICE WOMAN): "MRS STEINMAN. LISTEN HERE. IT'S OKAY. YOU CAN COME AND FETCH THE LITTLE BLACK BOY. BUT YOU MUST COME YOURSELF. HE'S IN YOUR CUSTODY HEY. NOT HIS MOTHER'S

MIA: Well what do you know — two steps forward one step back. I drove to that magistrates court as fast as I could.

GLEN: They subpoenaed me for Susan's trial. When I walked into the dock she smiled at me and blew a kiss

—shit, that killed me. I thought she knew. Mia was there of course and a whole lot of other people that were my friends. I just watched the judge the whole time which is what they advised me to do.

MIA: That day in court when Glen was called to the witness box and announced himself as:

GLEN: Warrant Officer Glen Donahue!

MIA: Her face—her face will be imprinted here, like a third eye for the rest of my life. Afterwards he tried to talk to me. "Just stay away from me. All I can see is a nice Kentucky Necklace, a huge burning tire around your neck!"

NICKY: Susan Lang trial sensation. Lover Donahue. Police spy. And there's this picture of Glen in his corduroy jacket. I tried reading the article but I couldn't concentrate. Lover Donahue. I went into the kitchen and opened the fridge. There was a packet of Smarties I'd got for Dominic. I leaned against the kitchen stove and ate them, one by one, and watched the kitchen clock. I had to fetch Dominic from nursery school. I went to the bedroom and laid down. Lover Donahue. Police spy. I got the car keys. I reached the nursery school. I don't remember seeing a single traffic light.

GLEN: So now they've offered me a full-time job in the police—a commission. I've taken it for the moment— but I'm still not sure what I want to do. I've often thought about becoming a game ranger or a forester or something. No, I'm being serious. You must go to Soweto, you must look at these kids, look into their eyes. It looks like we are all going to have our houses burned down pretty soon so I think the best place to be is in a place with no houses, you know—like a forest.

Well, come to think of it—things are pretty quiet around here—people avoid me in the streets—they don't wave back—oh ja—Mia did—but it wasn't really a wave—only cops love me now.

MIA gives him an "up yours" sign.

ZACHARIA: I went to see Dumisani at Mia's house in Saxonwold. I took his baseball bat and his recorder. I hadn't been out of Soweto for weeks. I heard that guy . . . talking about landing on the moon. That's what Saxonwold felt like. Those houses, those gardens, that cool sprinkling water. It was insanity. I sat in a bus full of domestic servants and gardeners and listened to their chatter. This was what they saw and did and said every day. My head was buzzing. Anyway I got off at the right stop in Oxford Road. It was near the convent school. Her house wasn't as big as the others but the garden was beautiful.

MIA: My brother-in-law, Morris Steinman, is here from Australia. He was staying with me. Nothing he heard or saw moved him as much as seeing little Dumisani lying there in my spare room.

He said "Come to Sydney man Mia. How can you handle it here?"

And I said "What the hell are you talking about? I don't want to go! What do you want me to do? Leave because of the fuck-up these pricks have made!" Ja, we both burst out laughing—but as Mike used to say— "It was a very black sound, a Bittere gelechte." [bitter laughter]

ZACHARIA: Mia answered the door herself.

MIA: Zach, I'm sorry—I tried to phone you. He's under heavy sedation. I don't know when he'll wake up.

ZACHARIA: Can I see him?. We tiptoed down the passage and stopped at a door. She opened it. Dumisani was lying on his back in a big double bed. His face was swollen, his eyes closed. Everything around him was little blue flowers. The curtains. The wallpaper. The cushion under his head. He started moaning and Mia quickly closed the door.

MIA: I'm sorry Zach. Do you want some tea?

ZACHARIA: No. I must go. I just wanted to pick him up and carry him home. I walked back towards the bus

stop. I realized that I was still carrying his baseball bat
and recorder. As I passed the convent school I was still
thinking of Dumisani. The playground was full of little
white girls in their neat uniforms having their morning
break. I watched them running, laughing, and playing
and I thought, Ja, do you know who's watching you?
Your mummy told you to be afraid of me. I thought,
ja, everyone of you has a nanny. She feeds you, she
comforts you, she washes that uniform, she polishes
those shoes, and every time she leaves Soweto or
Alexandra and says goodby to her own children, she
doesn't know whether she'll see them again, alive or
dead. Ja, your nanny knows where your kitchen knives
are, she even knows where your daddy hides the
revolver. Your mommy's nanny knew too. But how
many of you do they kill? Ask her about our children,
and the soldiers who shoot them dead. Ask her what
she's waiting for? For us to prove that we can kill
children as well as they can?

Suddenly I moved through the gates to the middle of
the playground.I started to swing the baseball bat—
skulls cracked—brains and baby teeth flew—I
splintered arms and legs and spines. There was blood
everywhere. I went on swinging left and right. I was a
panther, I was a tiger, I was everything they wanted me
to be. I was their black King Kong. A bell started to
ring. I found myself on the pavement. The bell was
calling to children to go inside. I continued to watch
them play. I couldn't breathe. I turned and started to
walk up Oxford Road. I heard myself yelling Fuck you!
Fuck you! Fuck you for what you have done to
Dumisani and fuck you fuck you fuck you for what
you are doing to me.

GLEN: Thenjiwe still wouldn't make a statement. So they
wanted me to go in and talk to her. I knew that it
would be useless, but they insisted. I had this whole
line worked out before I went to see her in her cell. She
let me get quite close and then she spat in my face. Ja,
I said you and Mia, come the revolution you want to
burn a nice big truck tire around my neck. "Don't
worry," she said, "You're not worth the match."

THENJIWE: One morning I was told to pack up my things because I was going on a little trip. I discovered at the desk that I was being transferred to Diepkloof Prison. I was going to be charged. I didn't know what for. There was one other lady and about ten men. We were stuffed into the back of a van.

As we drove off I began to cry for the first time. I didn't know what Diepkloof Prison would bring. John Vorster Square I knew very well. For this swollen lady it was like leaving home.

When we reached Diepkloof they hustled us out of the van. There were more people in the lobby — people detained under Section 10. Hey I was so excited — so many of them were my friends. Ndondi, Thembi, Topsie — I forgot my guard and ran to them. For a moment they didn't recognize me — just for a moment. But then we were hugging and kissing each other and laughing and crying.

We all started to SING:

THINA SIZWE ESIMNYAMA SIZOFELA IZWE
LETH ELATHATHWA NGAMABHUMU
[We the Black nation will die for our land taken from us by the Boers.]

The guards moved in on us. We didn't care.

In the spotlight the song builds and builds. THENJIWE *dances wildly, passionately, ululating, whistling, calling out the actors, singing and clapping in the darkness along with her. Behind her, movie images of defiant placards and police armored cars. Fade into Blackout. The music on tape continues and movie continues as audience leaves.*

SONQOBA SIMUNYE

ASINAMALI!

Mbongeni Ngema

Out of the anger and passion of the residents of the Lamont-ville township came the leader Msizi Dube. Passionately demonstrating against proposed rent increases, he led the masses with the cry *"Asinamali!"*—"We have no money!" this rallying phrase provided a focus for the disenfranchised as well as a poignant description of the condition of Blacks throughout South Africa.

Dube was later gunned down by government forces, a martyr to his cause; but from his leadership emerged a group of "committed artists" whose primary goal was the revelation and ultimate eradication of racial and social inequality in South Africa. Out of this concern Mbongeni Ngema's *ASINAMALI!* was born. It is not just a play, but a venture into the reality of apartheid.

The play is set in a South African jail. The five male protagonists recount, through word, song and dance, the events that have brought them there: Bheki Mqadi, the unfairly condemned man, is victim of his own skin color; Thami Cele is guilty of violating the Immorality Act as the result of a momentary indiscretion; Bongani Hlophe is a migrant laborer whose struggle to find a job propels him to commit murder; Solomzi Bisholo is a con man and pickpocket who practices his trade on the unsuspecting at mass funerals and demonstrations; and Bhoyi Ngema plays a young activist who worked with the martyred leader Dube. These five bring to the stage a combination of drama, satire, humor, music, and spirited passion in portraying the evils of apartheid in the forms of poverty, unemployment, influx control, insurrection and arson.

ASINAMALI !
Mbongeni Ngema

CHARACTERS

SOLOMZI BHISHOLO
THAMI CELE
BONGANI HLOPHE
BHEKI MQADI
BHOYI NGEMA

The play is set in a prison cell at Leeuwkop Prison, outside Johannesburg. The five prisoners, wearing short khaki prison clothes, relate their stories to each other using mime and strong music to drive their points home.

SCENE ONE

The stage is bare, save for five prison chairs at the center and to the lefthand corner a coat rack that is suspended from the roof. It serves two purposes, as a coatrack, then a window. There are two coats and a hard hat.

Five actors walk to the stage in semi-darkness. Four of them are in khaki prison attire and one is in his regular clothes (BHEKI). They sit on the chairs.

SONG: "Fanakalo"

BHEKI: (*Jumps up mid-song and moves downstage, on top of the music*) I come from Zululand. I got a place to stay in Lamontville township, near the white city of Durban. During that time this man (*he points to his T-shirt which has the picture of a man*) Msizi Dube, a very strong leader and a powerful voice for our people, was killed. They killed him. The government spies killed him. The reason for his death was that he maintained that we have no money. A-SI-NA-MA-LI! So we cannot afford to pay the government's high rent increase. People took up this call: "AAASSSIIINNNAAA MMMAAALLLIII!" and the police went to work. Many of us died and many of us went to jail, and it is still happening outside.

SONG: "Heshe Nsizwa"

Heshe Nsizwa
Namhla Ngelamanqamu
Uyoshika-Shika
Uyohlinz'Azadel'Udokotela

Kwa Ginqik'Indodo
Kwa Shisw'Imizi
Kwa Qhum'Inganano
Awu! Baphel'Abantu Elamonti

> [Today is the day
> We will face each other as men
> The doctor will operate till the end of the day
>
> Men are falling
> Homes are on fire
> All we hear these days
> Is the sound of machine guns
> Awu! People are dying in Lamontville]

BONGANI: (*moves downstage, stuttering*) I come from Zululand too. I left my four wives and twelve children back in Zululand. My cousins got me work in . . . in . . . in . . .

ALL: (*in rhythm with the song*) Johannesburg.

BONGANI: Yeah! At a road construction. After many people had been fired for asking for more money. My white boss thought I was no good. A trouble maker. A follower of Msizi Dube. I lost my job, but I remained in . . . in . . . in . . .

ALL: Johannesburg.

BONGANI: Yeah! I got a girlfriend, a bitch. She fell pregnant. But there was no money to support the child. So she strangled the child in the toilet. I killed her too. And that's why I . . . I . . . I . . . (*motions with his hand to indicate that he wants to say I am here in prison*)

SOLOMZI: (*moves downstage, still on top of same song*) I also knew about this man, Msizi Dube. But was not impressed. I come from Soweto. I never really got involved with politics, I got involved with Brother Anthony (*says it with admiration*), we called him "Bra Tony." Heh, heh, heh (*laughs*). Bra Tony, he was a good man. Brilliant pickpocketer. Very intelligent. He knew exactly where the money was in a man's body. He understood a man's body very well. Haaa Bra Tony, he was like Dr. Chris Barnard.

THAMI: (*moves downstage*) I come from the Afrikaaner farm in Bloemfontein, Orange Free State. Me and my white boss' wife, Mrs Van Niekerk . . . heh, heh (*indicates that they were making love*). Ya, and she liked it.

BHOYI: (*moves downstage*) I come from Lamontville Township, Durban. The follower of Msizi Dube. I was one of the people who were cleaning the streets of the township. The streets of the township were dirty, full of informers. Government spies. But we did it man. We cleaned them up (*indicates by running his hand across his throat to show a cut-throat motion*).

SONG: "Heshe Nsizwa"

They do a Zulu dance and then rearrange the five chairs to prepare for the court scene. Fade.

SCENE TWO

BONGANI — court orderly
BHOYI — interpreter
THAMI — judge
SOLOMZI — court clerk
BHEKI — accused

BONGANI: Rise in court! Sukumani. Silence. The court is now in session.

SOLOMZI: Does the accused speak Afrikaans?

BHEKI: No Baba.

SOLOMZI: OK. Mr. Ngema will translate into English.

THAMI: (*speaking in Afrikaans*) Is jy Bheki Makhadi?

BHOYI: Are you Bheki Mqadi?

BHEKI: Baba

BONGANI: Khuluma kakhulu kuzwakale mbombo kanyoko. [Speak louder so you can be heard.]

THAMI: Waat was daai? [What was that?]

BHOYI: It's his name, your worship.

THAMI: Op die vyf en twintigste Mei was u in onweaste vergadering in St. Simons Kerk, Lammontville gevind.

BHOYI: On the twenty-fifth of May, you were in an unlawful and undesirable gathering in St. Simon's church, Lamontville township.

BHEKI: (*shaking*) Cha!

BONGANI: Thula! [Shut up!]

THAMI: Jy moet verstaan dat toe die polisie na die huis van god ingekom skuldig gewete het party van julle uit die kerk uitgejaag ma die straate van Lamontville.

BHOYI: It is clearly understood that when the police came into the house of God the guilty conscious pushed you and your friends out of the church of God into the streets of Lamontville.

THAMI: 'n paar oomblik later, was jy slapend gevind op'n vrou wie jy se is jou vrou. Waar of nie waar nie?

BHOYI: A few moments later you were found sleeping on top of a woman who you claim is your wife. True or not true?

BHEKI: Okunye yiqiniso Okunye akulonq. Iqiniso . . . [Some of it is true and some is not . . .]

BONGANI: Ungaqhaqhazeli [Do not tremble]

BHOYI: It's true your worship.

THAMI: Is julle twee getroud.

BHOYI: Are you two married?

BHEKI: Yes Baas.

THAMI: Waar's jou huwelike sertifikaat?

BHOYI: Where is your marriage certificate?

BONGANI: Isitifiketi somshado! [Marriage certificate]

BHEKI: Asisayinanga enkantolo nkosiyamakhosi. [We did not sign in the court of law.]

BONGANI: Ha! nanikipitile! [Ha, you were shacking up illegally!]

BHOYI: We did not sign in the court of law, your worship.

THAMI: Wie is Johannes Zulu?

BHOYI: Who is Johannes Zulu?

BHEKI: Angimazi!

BHOYI: I don't know him

THAMI: Is hy nie jou seun nie?

BHOYI: Is he not your son?

BHEKI: Cha!

BHOYI: No, your worship.

THAMI: Is dit nie waar nie dat jy verlede week vir die hof gesê het dat jy vir Johannes Zulu 20 litres petrol gegee het om Meneer Gasa se huis af te brand?

BHOYI: Is it not true that you told the court last week that you gave Johannes Zulu 20 litres of petrol to go and burn Mr Gasa's house?

THAMI: Is dit nie omdat Mnr. Gasa een van die mense is wat vermoed is omtrent die dood van Msizi Dube?

BHOYI: Was it not because Mr Gasa has been suspected as one of the people who killed Msizi Dube?

BHEKI: Yes!

THAMI: Is dit nie omdat Mnr Gasa vir Johannes Zulu hegtenis geneem het . . . nie?

BHOYI: Was it not because Mr Gasa arrested Johannes Zulu . . . ?

BHEKI: Yes!

THAMI: Wat jou seun is?

BHOYI: Who is your son?

BONGANI: (*to the accused*) Lalela inkantolo. [Listen to the court.]

THAMI: Se hy nie papa na jou nie?

BHOYI: Does he not say "papa" to you?

BHEKI: He is my son, yes, kodwa akuyena owesende. [But he is not my blood son.]

BONGANI: Aha!

BHOYI: He does, your worship.

THAMI: Mama mia! En verder, weet jy dat hy is 'n terores?

BHOYI: Do you know that Johannes is a terrorist?

THAMI: Weet jy ook dat hy een van die mense wie Konstabel Gasa se huis af gebrand klippe ingegooi?

BHOYI: Do you know that he is one of the people who stoned, burnt, Konstable Gasa's house, calling him an informer?

THAMI: En verder, weet jy dat hulle besig is om deur die strate te beweeg en onskuldige vroue te verkrag?

BHOYI: And further, do you know that they are busy moving up and down the streets, terrorizing, robbing and raping innocent women?

THAMI: WAT weet jy omtrent van die wagwoord ASINAMALI?

BHOYI: WHAT do you know about the slogan; ASINAMALI! Assinamali! Asinamali?

BHEKI: Yebo, Cha . . .

BONGANI: Ngithe thula! [I said shut up!]

BHOYI: Yes and No! Your worship. (*slight pause*)

THAMI: Jy dink ons het tyd om te speel?

BHOYI: You think we have time to play?

THAMI: Of verwag jy ons moet saam met julle sit en glimlag terwyl julle kinders besig is om huise in Lamontville af te brand.

BHOYI: Do you expect us to be friendly and smiling with you while your children are burning houses in Lamontville township?

THAMI: Of is julle onder die indruk dat die'n sheeben laangsaan is, waar dans en tekere gaan terwyl anders sterf?

BHOYI: Or do you think this is a shebeen, next door, where people are laughing and dancing while others are dying?

THAMI: Wat het jy gesê verlede week in die hof?

BHOYI: What did you say last week in court?

THAMI: Wat het jy gesê van operasie Instroming Behee in Durban?

BHOYI: What did you say about the rent strike in Durban?

THAMI: Wat van Johannes Zulu se naamlose reis na Lusaka.

BHOYI: What did you say about Johannes Zulu's secret trip to Lusaka?

THAMI: Wat van terroris se vergarderings in jou huis?

BHOYI: What about terrorist gatherings in your house?

THAMI: Wat het jy gesê in die sel? Vandag Ja! More, Nee!

BHOYI: What did you say in the cell under interrogation? Today Yes! Tomorrow, No!

BHEKI: They were kicking me, they were beating me.

BONGANI: Kade ushaywa wubani? [Who was beating you?]

THAMI: Wat was daai? [What was that?]

BHOYI: Bullshit. Hawu! (*covers his mouth in embarrassment, laughs sheepishly*) They were beating me. It's nonsense, your worship.

THAMI: Skuldig

BHOYI: Guilty!

THAMI: Verwarring van die hof.

BHOYI: Confusing the court

THAMI: Herbeging van terroriste!

BHOYI: Harbouring terrorists!

THAMI: Verkeerd infomasie!

BHOYI: Wrong information!

THAMI: Geen huis permit!

BHOYI: No house permit!

THAMI: Geen troue sertifikaart!

BHOYI: No marriage certificate!

THAMI: Ongewenste verrgadering!

BHOYI: Undesirable gathering!

THAMI: Op stooking van die mense!

BHOYI: Instigating the people!

THAMI: Klippe gooiery!

BHOYI: Stone throwing!

THAMI: Afbrandig van lokasie!

BHOYI: Burning the township!

THAMI: Sewe jaar!

BHOYI: Seven years!

THAMI: Durban Sentraal tronk-Hof verdaag.

BHOYI: Durban Central Prison-Court adjourned.

> *Lights fade. They rearrange the chairs,* BONGANI
> assumes policeman's role.

SCENE THREE

> *On stage are* BONGANI, *taking prisoner's fingerprints,
> and* BHEKI, *who is still in his street clothes.*

BONGANI: Right! You've got to give me your name, your
address, your identity number, loud and clear. What's
your name prisoner?

BHEKI: Bheki "Slow Motion" Mqadi.

BONGANI: WHAT?

BHEKI: Bheki "Slow Motion" Mqadi.

BONGANI: (*kicks him*) I said what's your name?

BHEKI: Bheki "Slow Motion" Mqadi

BONGANI: Don't you have a voice?

BHEKI: Bheki "Sloooowww Motion" Mqadi

BONGANI: That's better.

BHEKI: Thank you!

BONGANI: Age?

BHEKI: 36 years.

BONGANI: Address?

BHEKI: Lamontville Township

BONGANI: I said address, you bastard!

BHEKI: Oh! 779 North Road, Lamontville Township. Durban. South Africa.

BONGANI: Comedian, eh? Nidla nabafazi babantu ninjalonje! [You even sleep with other people's wives!] Woza la. [Come here.] Relax your hand.

BHEKI: I'm sorry.

BONGANI: I said relax your hand you bastard.

BHEKI: I'm very sorry, baba. My fingers are short.

BONGANI: Hey, what is written over there? (*points to the wall*)

BHEKI: Flexible fingers, easy experience.

BONGANI: Easy experience, OK?

BHEKI: Yeho Baba.

> BONGANI *tries once more to fingerprint* BHEKI *but his hand is stiff.*

BONGANI: Easy . . .

BHEKI: Very easy . . .

BONGANI: Easy!

BHEKI: Very easy!

BONGANI: Easy come, easy go.

BHEKI: Thank you very much baba.

BONGANI: Easy.

BHEKI: Flexible fingers.

BONGANI: Mana lapha s'boshwa. [Stand over there, prisoner.] Top off. (BHEKI *takes off his T-shirt.*) Open your arms. (*He obliges.*) About turn. (*He obliges and forgets to keep his arms open.*) Ngithe vul' amakhawapha! [I said open your arms!] Pants off!

BHEKI: All off? (*surprised*)

BONGANI: Khumula! [Take it off!]

BHEKI: I'm so sorry, nkosi yanakhosi [king of kings]. (*He takes off his pants.*)

BONGANI: Open your legs. About turn. I said open your legs you bloody shit. About turn. Size.

BHEKI: 32

BONGANI: (*going over to pick up prison clothes for* BHEKI, *cannot find the right size*) Hey, 46. (*throws the clothes to* BHEKI, *who grabs them and begins to put them on while dancing around*)

BONGANI: Shesha! [Make it snappy!]

BHEKI: I'm very fast, I'm sorry, I'm sorry.

OTHER PRISONERS: Fast, you bloody fool.

BHEKI: I'm sorry. (*quickly dresses*) I'm finished.

BONGANI: Fuck-off! They are sending you to Leuwkop Prison in Johannesburg. Prisoner number 1-2-3 stroke 7, that's your name, prisoner.

BHEKI: Dankie Makhosi. [Thank you lord.]

SCENE FOUR

*In the prison yard, the prisoners identify themselves by
prison number before an invisible prison warder by
jumping simultaneously to down center stage and each
thrusts his right hand forward and calls his number.*

BHEKI MQADI—Prisoner number 123-7 Dankie Makhosi
SOLOMZI BHISHOLO—Prisoner number 123-6 Dankie
baba
BHOYI NGEMA—Prisoner number 123-5 Dankie Pitoli
BONGANI HLOPHE—Prisoner number 123-4 Dankie
Makhosi
THAMI CELE—Prisoner number 123-3 Dankie babaton

*As they finish, they form a straight line like men
working on the roads. They start pulling an invisible
cable as they chant the popular song: "Abelungu Wo–
Dam."*

SONG:
Abelungu wodam
Abelungu wodam
Ngifice abafana bethunda nam ngathunda.
Ngabhajwa ngqi.
[Damn the Boers. Damn the Boers.
I found the boys ejaculating.
I ejaculated.
I got V.D. on the spot.]

*Late in the afternoon all five prisoners work in the
quarry. They kneel still in a straight line formation and
swing their mimed hammers, and they sing their song
of frustration:*

SONG:
Welimpompo sithwele kanzima sikhala
Sikhala kuginquka Ibhunu kukhala elinye
Ibhunu, kubaleka ibhunu.
[This side of the Limpopo we are suffering.
But now the Afrikanner is crying,
The Afrikanner is dying and yet
Another is running away.]

As they work, a speck flies into BONGANI's *eye. He screams, puts a hand over his eye and runs upstage. He then puts on a warder's cap and walks back down-stage, directly in front of audience as a warder. He begins a new song over the previous song and the other four actors immediately break and run around the stage singing. They then form a line and are prisoners ready to be searched by the warder.* BONGANI, *as the warder, does a pat–down search of all of them. He examines their mouths and searches their pockets.*

SONG:
Buti omuhle sewuzawufela ejele;
Sewuzafela ejele butu omuhle
Mina nawe siboshwa sofela la.
   [A handsome guy will die in jail.
   Go on, you'll die in jail. Me and you
   prisoner, we'll die here.]

BONGANI: *(searching* BHOYI) A cigarette! Heh! A cigarette! Uphethe ugwayi, siboshwa?

He kicks BHOYI.

BHOYI: Dankie baba! Dankie baba!

BONGANI chases him while song continues.

SONG:
You can go to Central Prison
You will find Warder Sondofish
You can go to John Voster Square
You will find Makhandakhanda —
   many-headed warder.
Come here to Leeuwkop prison
You will find indod'emnyama — pitch black man.

Prisoners go into the cell. BONGANI *joins the other prisoners again.*

BONGANI: Dankie baba!

They all sit down and suddenly they hear the warder's footsteps coming their way.

BHEKI moves upstage. He stretches his arm forward and using his thumb and forefinger he creates a peep-hole. He mimes the door and starts talking to a warder, who is apparently passing by outside the cell.

BHEKI: Hey Sergeant! Sergeant! My basie! Hey Sergeant! Sergeant Nel! Sergeant Nel! My basie! Hey Sergeant: Dankie baba: Hey you know what? This place would be shit without you baba. We like you baba. We really do baba, cause you are the best white man in the whole world. You're the only one who puts salt in our porridge, ja. But Sergeant that new constable from the depot, Constable Schoeman yisifebe nja. He's a bitch. He kick me like a dog this morning. He kick Boy. He kick Thami. He kick everybody. I want to report him to you.

BHOYI: Wangishaya la ezimbanjeni. [He kicked my ribs.]

ALL *become very angry at this point and start cursing and shouting in Zulu.*

THAMI: Ja Sergeant, he kicked him very bad.

BHEKI: (*continues*) Sergeant, between you and me that man is going to cause trouble. But please don't tell him about me. Just watch. That man is going to cause trouble. Good night Sergeant.

BHEKI joins the other prisoners. They play marabaraba (game) shouting loudly. The prison warder comes to tell them that it is time to sleep and switches off the lights. Banging on the door is heard.

BHEKI: Sleeping time, siboshwa. Hayi lalatime siboshwa njalo! [Prisoners, sleeping time.]

BHOYI: (*goes to the keyhole*) Sergeant. Only one cigarette baba. One for the night. Agg asseblief my bass. [Please my boss.]

See cigarette coming through keyhole.

Jy lyk soos'n koning my basie! You look like a king!

BHEKI: Lights all the night baba. Keep the spirit moving baba.

SOLOMZI: Everything is sweet baba. Holiday Inn baba. Stay fresh and young baba.

BONGANI: (*stutters*) Good night baba. You are beautiful baba.

SCENE FIVE

All five men huddle together in some kind of abstract sculptural formation to give each other warmth.

SONG:
Wemali usegoli
Wemali yami
Ngalamba Ngayibopha
Wemali usegoli.
[My money is in Johannesburg
I starved and I decided to fast,
My money is in Johannesburg
Because that's where all the goldmines are]

BHEKI: (*breaks away from the group and stands up*) Hey, Hey, we madoda [Hey men]. This country is very funny. I tell you. Everybody is mad. Wherever you go there is a policeman waiting for you. 'Let's see your passbook. Let's see your passbook. Hey you over there, let's see your passbook.' And then they arrest you. Inside the prison there is another one, waiting for you. And even at home, your children are crying: (*imitates a child*) 'Daddy, daddy, I want money for school fees. Hay baba, even my teacher has started calling me names because, because I haven't got a uniform and I haven't paid my school fees. Hayi Baba.'

And if you are looking for work; 'where is your work seeker's permit?' and if you've got a work seeker's permit, that big white man will come; 'where is your special permit to be in the city?' You know what they looking for? I will tell you my friend. I've been through it all. Me. I'm a man from Zululand. I have no place in the city. I don't qualify to work in the city. You know what they are looking for? A stamp in my passbook so that I can go and work in the city. But it's funny you know, I will show you, right now; you wait and see. Let us go to their offices.

BONGANI has already positioned himself in a separate chair and is a clerk waiting at the pass office.

SCENE SIX

BHEKI: Molo mabhalane [Good morning Mr Clerk]

BONGANI: E! E! E! E!. Why do you people always come behind my back?

BHEKI: I'm sorry baba.

BONGANI: Right!

BHEKI: I'm looking for a special permit.

BONGANI: (*laughs*) A special permit

BHEKI: A special permit.

BONGANI: For you?

BHEKI: For me. I've been looking for work here in Durban for a long time I went to the work seeker's office. The work seeker's office sent me to the junior clerk. The junior clerk sent me to the senior clerk. The senior clerk sent me to employment office. Employment office sent me to you and . . . (*hands over his passbook to the clerk*)

BONGANI: (*looks at the passbook*) Where do you come from?

BHEKI: Zululand.

BONGANI: O.K. Listen, I can help you. You must go back, to your District Chief in Zululand. Your District Chief will give you a form.

BHEKI: (*nodding his head*) Yes baba.

BONGANI: You must fill in the form. Can you read?

BHEKI: A little bit.

BONGANI: Okay, can you write?

BHEKI: A little bit, baba.

BONGANI: Good, if you're not sure ask any school child to do it for you. Then take it back to your District Chief. Your District Chief will look at the paper and stamp the paper and he will send you to your District Bantu Affairs Commissioner, your District Bantu Affairs Commissioner will look at the paper and stamp the paper and he will send you to your District Government Doctor. Your District Government Doctor will examine you, look at the paper and stamp the paper and he will send you back to your District Bantu Affairs Commissioner. Your District Bantu Affairs Commissioner will look at the District Government Doctor's stamp and stamp the paper and he will send you back to your District Chief. Your District Chief will look at the paper again and again and stamp the paper and he will send you back . . . (*pauses*)

BHEKI: To the doctor!

BONGANI: TO ME! I will look at the paper, look at your passbook, look at your face, and . . . stamp the paper. And I will give you a big stamp in your passbook and that will be your Work Seeker's Permit.

BHEKI: Work Seeker's Permit?

BONGANI: Only when you've gotten a job, came back to me. I will give you a . . .

ALL: Special permit in your passbook!

SCENE SEVEN

Back in the jail cell, ALL are seated on the floor except BHEKI who is sitting on one of the five chairs.

BHEKI: And then I went back to Zululand.

SOLOMZI: For a special permit.

THAMI: You got a special permit?

BHEKI: Ja, no problem they gave it to me.

BHOYI: You were very lucky.

BHEKI: And then I came back to Durban.

BONGANI: Lamontville.

BHEKI: No, by then I had no place to stay.

BHOYI: Where did you stay?

BHEKI: E [at] Durban station.

ALL: Durban station.

BHEKI: Every day I pretended as if I've missed the last train, and whenever a white railway policeman came by, I would grab my suitcase, look at my watch which was not working either, shake my head and mumble some words in Zulu.

SOLOMZI: In Zulu?

BONGANI: What about your luggage?

BHEKI: Luggage? One suitcase. During the day in my hand, looking for work. At night it became my pillow! At the railway station! (*They all laugh.*) And for four months, I would go up and down looking for work. Standing in those long lines with my passbook in my hand and ten times a day I would get that same answer:

ALL: No jobs available!

BHEKI: Ha! I nearly forgot something very important.

ALL: Yes?

BHEKI: Those people I had seen the first day at the station, who looked like they had missed their train . . . when I first came to Durban Station. Most of them were like me. Their home was Durban Station! (*laughter*)

BONGANI: Ikhaya lethu [Our home].

BHEKI: Yes! We would bump into each other in front of a factory gate looking for work: CONSOLIDATED . . .

ALL: CONSOLIDATED . . .

BHEKI: FRAME!

ALL: FRAME!

BHEKI: COTTON

ALL: COTTON!

BHEKI: CORPORATION!

ALL: CORPORATION

BHEKI: LIMITED!

ALL: LIMITED!

BHEKI: And a huge sign;

ALL: No jobs available.

BHEKI: (*moves downstage*) One morning I opened my suitcase, took out my best clothes. (*starts to sing*) Sharp point shoes down below.

ALL: (*in a sing-a-long*) Ooh hooo!

BHEKI: Blue and yellow pants

ALL: Hay bo!

BHEKI: Red and khaki jacket

ALL: Oh yes.

BHEKI: White shirt

ALL: Aha

BHEKI: Black tie

ALL: Shisa!

BHEKI: (*has stopped singing*) Down Victoria Street. One of the biggest streets in Durban City. (*using chairs as if walking in street*)

ALL: Victoriiiiiaaaa Street

BHEKI: As I was walking down Victoria Street, right in front of my eyes were three gangsters who were busy running, exchanging a handbag like a basketball. A handbag which they had snatched from a woman.

BONGANI: And what did you do?

BHEKI: I grabbed it. I grabbed the handbag. And right next to me, were two Big Afrikaaner policemen. I got in between them. I looked at the policemen. I looked at the gangsters. (*pause while giving the gangsters a serious face*) And I said: Zinja [dogs] come! Don't run away. You've touched me. This is the day. How can you touch a lion? How can you touch a tiger? Here is the source of power! (*grabbing his genital area*) How can you touch me? (*he starts singing his praises in Zulu*)

All the prisoners jump up and go towards him and also sing his praises. They almost lift him up from the floor as they shout his praises.

SOLOMZI: (*when the confusion dies down*) And what did you do with the handbag?

BHEKI: The handbag? I gave it back to the woman.

SOLOMZI: And then?

BHEKI: And then we went down to the station together.

SOLOMZI: And what about the gangsters?

BHEKI: They ran away.

There suddenly is a bang on the cell door, a policeman. All prisoners dive to the floor and pretend to be asleep.

BHOYI: (*a policeman's voice*) Sleeping time prisoner! This is not a shebeen.

Different voices, in the semi-darkness, plead to BHEKI to continue with his story. He creeps up and peeps through a keyhole to see if the policeman is still around and he shouts again.

SOLOMZI: (*whispering*) Yes, the thugs, what about the thugs?

BHEKI: They ran away.

ALL: (*jumping to their feet and relieved that the cop is gone*) They ran away.

BHEKI: That woman was staying in Lamontville township, so we took a train back.

SOLOMZI: Who paid the train fare?

BHEKI: (*excitedly*) Don't worry, she paid for me.

BONGANI: Hawu, another man's wife?

BHEKI: And outside the station, we were standing until it was dark.

BONGANI: Where?

BHEKI: Under a tree.

BONGANI: What were you doing?

BHEKI: Discussing.

SOLOMZI: Discussing what?

BHEKI: What do you think.

ALL: Boy! Hayi umqadi. [Heh this guy.]

BHEKI: And ultimately she started to tell me about her family problems.

boy: Was she not married?

BHEKI: Her husband died in the mines long time ago. She had only a son, Johannes Zulu. As she continued telling me her sad stories I found myself holding her. Consoling her.

BONGANI: Consoling her wena futhi. [You, consoling her.]

BHEKI: And it all happened man! And then I went to Durban Station to say goodby to a friend because now I had a home in Lamontville and now I was a boss in a dead man's home.

BOY: So you've come a long way!

ALL: From Zululand to Durban Station. From Durban Station to Lamontville. From Lamontville to jail!

THAMI: (*stands up*) Me and my white boss' wife, Mrs Van Niekerk, had it differently. You see, I was looking after their pigs. The had about two hundred pigs in their farm. Can you believe it? I knew them all by their names. They knew me too. They knew all my sounds. I would sit in the center of the pigs and listen to their voices as they talk to each other; Hoink! hoink! hoink! Mrs Van Niekerk always called me to come help buy her groceries on Saturdays. I would sit at the back seat of the car.

BHEKI: Like a boy [servant].

THAMI: And she would be in the front seat, driving. Asking me about my past relationships. One day she started to ask me; 'how do you feel when you see a white woman?'

BONGANI: And? What did you tell her?

ALL: (*getting closer to hear the answer.*)

THAMI: I WANT THEM! (*and covers his face in mock embarrassment*)

There are varied responses from the other prisoners, some approving and the others disapproving.

THAMI: Mmmmmmm! That woman! But I was shy.

ALL: Oh, why?

THAMI: She developed a habit of touching me when she talked to me (*touches himself all over to indicate where she would touch*). And sometimes she would offer me a cigarette.

SOLOMZI: Inkunzimalanga [a great guy]

THAMI: Mr Van Niekerk went to the army at the border.

ALL: Opportunity!

THAMI: One night she called me in; 'Thami, Kom hier, come into the house.' A child asked from another room; 'mommy, who is speaking Zulu in the house?' she said; 'Ag man, it's Radio Zulu, I am trying to learn Zulu, go to sleep honey.'

They all laugh.

BHEKI: These white women are clever.

THAMI: Shit! It happened. It became a daily bread. One day when I was feeding the pigs in the pigsty, I heard footsteps. When I turned around, she was there. She held me.

SOLOMZI: In the pigsty?

THAMI: . . . and I embraced her with my dirty hands full of the pigs' food and it was the daily bread again.

The prisoners respond with exclamation and laughter.

SOLOMZI: Uyinkunzi mfana, uhlab'umlungu. [You are great, man, you screw a white woman.]

THAMI: . . . I don't know what happened. It was like a dream. But when I opened my eyes, after that daily bread (*pause*) all the pigs were out. She had forgotten to close the gate when she came in . . .

BHEKI: She was in a hurry . . .

SOLOMZI: Waxoshwa. [This man is about to be fired.]

THAMI: . . . all the cabbage in the garden had been eaten. I looked around the pigsty, even the little ones, with no names, were out and Mr Van Niekerk was running towards us in his army uniform . . . (*shadow-boxes, to indicate a scuffle between him and Mr Van Niekerk*)

SOLOMZI: (*amid the confusion*) . . . and what happened?

THAMI: Shit happened! Tha't why I'm here.

SCENE EIGHT

BONGANI: (*stands up and begins to stutter*) MY . . . my . . . my . . . kh . . . kh . . . kh . . . khh . . .

BHEKI: Cow? (*BONGANI shakes his head, no.*)

SOLOMZI: Cowboy? (*BONGANI shakes his head as he continues to stutter around the kh . . . kh . . . kh . . .*)

THAMI: Country (*no*)

SOLOMZI: Carpert? (*no*)

BHEKI: Car? (*no*)

BHOYI: Cousin (*BONGANI nods a big yes.*)

BONGANI: Kh . . . kh . . . cousin (*they all congratulate BHOYI*) took me from Zululand to Johannesburg. Not to look for a job but to . . . to . . . (*he struggles with the word work until the cast helps him . . . work*) because his boss wanted a boy.

BHEKI: (*who has left the group and gone over to the coatrack, puts on one of the coats and a hard hat to play the boss*) Nduna! [Headboy!]

BHOYI: Yes baas!

BHEKI: You see, you must go and look for a nice boy like you in Zululand.

BHOYI: Yes baas!

BHEKI: A boy who is going to stay at Soweto men's hostel like you.

BHOYI: Nkosi yamakhosi. [King of kings.]

BHEKI: A boy, who is not going to be worried about rent increase. A boy, who is not going to be worried about ASINAMALI. A boy, who is not going to be worried about Msizi Dube. A boy, who is not going to be worried about the state of emergency. A boy, who is only going to be concerned about me, his children and his work.

BHOYI: (*who has been nodding yes sheepishly all along*) I've got a cousin bass. He is very fit, like a bulldozer.

BHEKI: Great. Tomorrow, I give you the money, go fetch him. I will fire all these lazy stupid Blacks.

BONGANI: Now in Johannesburg the boss drove me to the V.D. office to get a special permit to work in Johannesburg.

SOLOMZI: And then when you got to the V.D. office did they check your man(hood)?

BONGANI: Yes, up and down!

SOLOMZI: Shit! These white boys have got us.

BHOYI: Aaah! Do they have a pipi office in Johannesburg?

BONGANI: Yeah!

BHOYI: There's a big one in Durban.

SOLOMZI: Cape Town is bigger.

THAMI: It's worse in Bloemfontein.

ALL: X-Ray! Vula! Vala Pipi office [Open and close your penis.]

The prisoners all fall on line to get their X-Rays. BHEKI, who has already assumed the doctor's role, is ready in front of an imaginary X-Ray machine.

BHEKI: Woza number one [Come number one].

THAMI: Thami Cele for X-Ray baba!

BHEKI: (*takes a passbook out of his coat pocket*) Is this your passbook?

THAMI: Yes sir!

BHEKI: Get on the machine. Head up, chest up! Don't look at me look at the X-Ray. (*imitates the sound of the cameras*) Click! Click! Gadla! Gadla! Pssst! Pssst! Next!

SOLOMZI: Solomzi Bhisholo for X-Ray.

BHEKI: (*gets another passbook from pocket*) Is this your passbook?

SOLOMZI: Yebo baba . . .

BHEKI: Get on the machine! Chest up. Head up. Don't look at me, look at the machine. (*imitates X-Ray*) Next!

BONGANI: Bongani Hlophe for X-Ray

BHEKI: Is this your passbook?

BONGANI: Ye . . . Yes . . . No. It's not my passbook. . . .

BHEKI: (*impatient*) Get on to the machine. (*same procedure*) Next!

BONGANI: Have you finished Baba?

BHEKI: Fuck you!

BONGANI: Hawu!

BHEKI: Next!

BHOYI: Bhoyi Ngema for X-Ray

BHEKI: Is this your passbook?

BHOYI: Hayi! No, mine is new, this one is old . . .

BHEKI: Get on to the machine. (*same procedure*) Next!

BONGANI: Baba, this is no my passbook this one. (*He is ignored, but* BHOYI *comes over to him. On examining their passbooks, they find out there was a switch and they happily exchange as* BHEKI *starts a song.*)

SONG:
Khanda libuhlungu wesikhandamayeza.
Khanda libuhlungu wesikhandamayeza.
S'khandamayeza wesikhandamayeza
S'khandamayeza wesikhandamayeza
Mina ngisemncane angazi lutho ngo Botha
Mina ngisemncane angazi lutho ngo Botha
S'khandamayeza wesikhandamayeza
S'khandamayeza wesikhandamayeza
    [I've got a headache, medicine man
    Medicine man oh medicine man.
    I am still young and I know nothing
      about Botha
    Help me medicine man and mix your
      herbs

I have a headache because of what
    goes on in this place,
Medicine man]

THAMI: (*who has assumed the role of an inspector at the
    V.D. office, calls on the other men, who have formed a
    line with their passbooks in hand and have to show
    him their penises as he checks for V.D.*) Kom! Come!
    Kooooooommmmmmmmm!

When it comes to BHOYI's *turn, he fails the physical
because he has* V.D. THAMI *covers his face because of
the smell as he stamps* BHOYI's *passbook.*

Reject! Reject!

BONGANI: (*as the others assume places sitting around him
    back in the cell*) Johannesburg, is not like Zululand. It's
    different, you know. No one has ever seen my man,
    except my older wife, maZulu. The other three . . . no
    way! They can't even touch it. Phela akudlalelwa la. By
    the way, this is no playground. I call one at night in
    my room and she sleeps on the floor. All of them.
    maCele, maMtshali, maDlamini, maZulu herself, the
    older one. She only comes when I need her. 'maZulu,
    honey, I love you.' She comes up, and when we finish,
    she goes back on the floor . . .

BHEKI: Respect!

BONGANI: . . . fifteen years with my four wives and my
    twelve children, no one has ever seen my man. But the
    first day I come to Johannesburg, a white boy com-
    manded me to open my fly and show him my man.
    Heh . . . Johannesburg. . . But after that I got a job my
    cousin promised me at Savage and Lovemore Road
    Construction.

ALL: Savage and Lovemore Road Construction Develop-
    ment Foundation Pty. Ltd.

They quickly form a line of construction workers as
BHOYI (*headboy/supervisor*) *starts a song and watches
them as they work.* BHOYI, BONGANI's *cousin, keeps
poking* BONGANI *indicating that he should work harder*

and a fight develops. During the fight BHEKI *leaves the line to assume the boss role.*

BHEKI, *the Boss, comes in and stumbles into workers fighting.* BHOYI *takes aim at* BONGANI *and misses and almost hits the boss.*

BHEKI: You fighting, heh. you fighting hey. (*He looks scared, keeping a safe distance from the workers.*)

BHOYI: (*pointing to* BONGANI) It's him bass. Fire him. Big Boxer.

BHEKI: You are a big boxer, you're a big boxer, Muhammad Ali. Champion, Come. Nduna, come, Muhammad Ali. Come to my office. (*He walks to the other side of window as all the workers follow and kneel a few feet away, all looking apologetic*)

I've been watching you (*to* BONGANI) for a long time. I've been listening to your politics. Nduna, my eyes have been on him since he came here. I know he has been telling the workers to go on strike. I know he has been telling the workers to ask for increase. I know he has been telling the workers to hit white people. Something passed over my head like a bullet, when I was there. Nduna!

BHOYI: Yes baas.

BHEKI: Tell him to go home.

BONGANI: Awu baas, my children will starve . . .

BHEKI: Fuck your children. Go home.

BONGANI: Forgive me baasie, please.

BHEKI: Nduna! Tell him I don't want to see his face here.

BONGANI: Please Baas last chance.

BHEKI: Nduna! Tell him no last chance.

BHOYI: Uth'umlungu ayikho nje leyonto okuthiwa yi last shansi. [The whiteman says there's no last chance.]

BONGANI: Please baas, forgive me.

BHEKI: Nduna! Tell him I'm losing my temper.

BHOYI: Uth'umlungu Ulahlekelwa yinhliziyo. Hamba ekhaya ndoda. [The whiteman says he is losing his heart, go home.]

BONGANI: Please baas!

BHEKI: Jou moer! [Your arse]

SONG: "Madala"
Wemadala bo
Wazungelez'umuzi wenyindoda
Owakho bo
Owakho wawushiya nobani.
    [Old man
    You keep circling another man's house
    Who did you leave yours with.]

BONGANI: Hey this man, my cousin, Nduna, he is a sellout. A friend of white people. MaZulu, my first wife, how am I going to support your children.
MaDlamini, my second wife, how am I going to send your children to school.
MaMtshali, my third wife, believe me, I am not going to be able to buy your children secondhand clothes anymore.
MaCele, MaCele, my fourth wife, please bear with me my wife, understand my wife that I am not going to be able to get groceries on credit from that Indian store anymore.
Wewu, waze wangilaya umzala. [Oh no, my cousin really did me in.]

SONG: "Madala"

SCENE NINE

SOLOMZI: Well me and him are totally different. He is what we call in Johannesburg abo bhari. Stupid. I want to tell you something. Robbing and stealing, beautiful job. Especially if you work with guys like, Bra Tony! Ha ha ha! (*laughs*) Bra Tony, he was a good man, a very close friend of mine. We were always together, just like twins. Hey man, that guy, he was always very neat. Ten gallon Stetson hat on top. China eyes sunglasses like those of Ray Charles or Stevie Wonder. Double-breasted Jacket. Pants? Brooks Brothers. Down below Florsheim shoes A very thin belt, he used to call it a lizard skin. Beverly Hills Shirt straight from the U.S.A! Ahahahaha! Bra Tony, he was a good man. A big name in robbery. All newspapers got his name. Johannesburg Star extra headlines: 'Bra Tony.' Cape Times, London Times. New York Times. Radio Zulu, Radio Freedom. John Voster Square police head-quarters: 'Watch out for Bra Tony.' Brixton Murder and Robbery Squad files: 'Bra Tony!' Johannesburg Stock Exchange; 'Watch out for Bra Tony!' South African Defence Force, Army and Navy: Bra Tony! Bra Tony Bra Tony! Jaaaa Bra Tony, he was a superstar. Do you rememeber that greatest train robbery in Johannesburg that hit international headlines. That was us. Do you still remember that airplane that was robbed in the Transkei airport in 1976. Operation Prime Minister Matanzima's Private Flight! That was us. 1977, Putco bus robbery, Durban, 1979 Ford Motors, Johannesburg. 1980 Coca Cola Industries, Durban, the very same year Operation Underground Backlys Bank, Krugersdorp. 1981 Zimbabwe Embassy, Operation Immigration. Where were you in 1982, Holiday Inn, Johannesburg Airport. 1983, IBM wage office, payday. 1984, Shabalala Incident, Soweto . . .

BHOYI: COME along

They all jump up and grab placards with slogans, similar to those used during political demonstrations in the townships. They join in the chant.

Winnie Mandela Hai
Is our mother Hai (*repeatedly*)
Mrs Botha fuck you
Uzal'izinja [she gives birth to dogs]
Voetsek Voetsek.
Bishop Tutu Hai
Is our hero

Bishop Tutu is our father Hai.
Kuthang'hlanye kukhon'impimpi
   [I am going crazy because there is a spy here]
Mub'umakhelwane esithi sakhelene
Abethuth'izindaba ethuthel'amabhunu
Mub'umakhelwane. . .
   [My neighbor is wicked
   Because even though we are neighbors
   He reveals secrets to the white man.
   My neighbor is a wicked person.]

ALL sit down except BHOYI *who moves forward.*

BHOYI: And all around us in the townships. There were new sounds on the people's lips. What triggered the whole Asinamali protest in Lamontville Township was the death of Msizi Dube.

SOLOMZI: An ex-Robben Island prisoner.

BHOYI: Awu i' nsizwa amakhosi [a man among men].
It was him and me next to him and my friend Bhekani next to me and the children in the streets and the people all over. In the cars, in the busses, in the trains, at work . . .

SOLOMZI: (*shouting*) We will not pay the rent increase!

ALL: AAASSSIIINNNAAAMMMAAALLLIII!

BHOYI: We don't only have no money. We refuse to get out of these tiny houses they have given to us. Niyabesaha na? [Are you afraid of them?]

ALL: Hai, Asibesabi, siyabafuna! [No we are not, we want them!]

BHOYI: Shhhh . . . and the government informers killed him. I think I see an informer in the audience.

ALL: WHERE?

They all jump and go to different places in the audience picking out people indiscriminately and warning them. After a few hot moments they all come back to the center of the stage.

BHOYI: That anger was not only the problem of Lamontville township. But it became the problem of the whole of South Africa. But now, understand. It is not only about the language Afrikaans. It is not only about rent increases. It is not only about job reservations and working conditions. It's not only about gold. It's not only about diamonds, not about sugarcane plantations in Natal nor the wineries in the Cape, it's not only about bloody fucking passbooks. Not only about the vote. What is it? hey! What is it? You. (*points to a white member of the audience*). You, stand up. Hey mthatheni Bafana! [Go for him boys!]

ALL: (*jump up and go towards the person in audience*) STAND UP!!!

BHOYI: What is it? Talk! You think I'm playing games with you. You think I'm acting. Sit down. My friend. You've got to look for it. It's deep down in your heart. Niyabesaba na?

ALL: Hayi asibeshbi siyabafuna. . . .

SOLOMZI: (*stands up as the rest of the cast retreats to sit in a semi-circle behind him*) Heeeee. . . . Bra Tony! Majita. He took me to this factory on a Friday afternoon. Payday. He knew how to deal with workers on a payday. But inside that factory, it was happening.

They all jump up and assume different positions to symbolize machines in a factory. After the song starts all of them mime different machines in unison with the song. The song is more a rhythmic chant without specific words.

SCENE TEN

BHOYI emerges from the confusion of the factory wearing a hat and dark glasses with playing cards in his hand, to play the mystic 'Bra Tony.'

SOLOMZI: Take them Bra Tony, take them.

BHOYI: Here is your winning card. Here is your gold. Here is your jackpot.

ALL: Bra Tony! Bra Tony! Bra Tony!

SOLOMZI: Take them Bra Tony, Take them. Tell me Bra Tony, if I put fifty rands, How much are you going to give me?

BHOYI: Aha . . . That is very easy. I am Bra Tony. I am the money-maker. I am multi-racial. Any one of you is free to take money from Bra Tony. Black or White. No segregation.

ALL: Bra Tony!

BHOYI: If you put fifty rands, you get hundred rands.
If you put 100 you get 200.
If you put 200 you get 400.
If you put BMW 323i you get BMW 733i.

ALL: Bra Tony.

BHEKI: I put five rands.

SOLOMZI: I put hundred.

BONGANI: Fifteen rands Bra Tony.

THAMI: I'm still deciding Bra Tony.

BHOYI: Still deciding? How much you put?

THAMI: My shoes!

BHOYI: Get lost!

THAMI: My shoes Bra Tony, ah Bra Tony, my shoes. Ten rands Bra Tony.

BHOYI: Fuck you.

THAMI: Ah. Bra Tony. Ten rands, these shoes are expensive, Bra Tony.

BHOYI: Okay five rands. Take it or leave it.

THAMI: Okay Bra Tony. But my shoes, Bra Tony.

BHOYI: It's not here, and it's not here (*showing the two*

cards in his hands and tossing them to the floor thereafter. He opens the card that was on the floor.) This is your winning card. It's not here it's not here. *(He shuffles the three cards on the floor.)* Point to the winning card.

BONGANI: *(amid the confusion rushes forward)* I know, I know. *(picks up one of the cards)* Here's the winning card.

ALL: Lose!

BONGANI: Ouch! I'm sorry, I'm sorry.

SCENE ELEVEN

SOLOMZI: Ja Bra Tony, he was a good man. A very close friend of mine. I remember this Indian woman we met at Verulem Station, a small railway station miles away from Durban City. It was a very dull day for Bra Tony and myself. We found this woman in the waiting room at about 9:30. She was waiting for a train from Durban to Zululand. Majita! [Guys!] She was very pretty. We started chatting and within a short space of time we had become friends. She started telling me that she had resigned from her job. That woman was beautiful. You know that feeling when you see a pretty woman! I tell you, that woman was divine! We started touching fingers. My God. I don't know how Bra Tony got to know that she had money. He stood up, pulled out his big knife. She was looking at me, pretty thing man, in shock. She trusted me. Bra Tony just *(slap!)* slapped her so hard that saw tears flying out. Bra Tony said; 'The money!' and she said; 'I . . . I . . . I have no money.' Bra Tony repeated that action. He hit her face again. The stomach. The back. The head, the bottom. Her skirts were flying in the air. When she turned around to look at him, Bra Tony was there. He looked at her. Directly in her eyes. 'Give me your panties.' She said; 'I . . . I . . . I'm having my period.' 'My baby, sweetheart, give it to me.' You know what she did? She pulled down her panties and Bra Tony grabbed the whole thing. A big roll of money came out man.

The other prisoners snore loudly. SOLOMZI *notices and turns around to face them.*

Nilele, minqundu yenu. Ndithetha ndodwa ngathi ndisibhanxa. [You bastards are asleep. I end up talking to myself as though I was crazy.] Ha . . . Bra Tony (*he joins them and lies down*) Bra Tony, Bra Tony (*in a voice that fades with sleep*)

As the prisoners lie a warder's knock on the door wakes them. They jump up and then squat in a line, one after the other with BHOYI *in front.*

BHOYI: Good morning, Sergeant.

ALL: (*in unison, addressing, the invisible warder*) Good morning sir, we are ready to go to the bush! Ready to chop the trees!

BHOYI starts a siren sound and ALL resume positions as though in the forest. They swing imaginary axes and chant as they work on the trees. BHEKI *motions to the others that his tree is about to fall. They all jump up stage and take positions to prepare to lift the log.* BHOYI *leads them in the chant as they lift the log.*

BHOYI: Sandla ngena–la. [Hands take your positions.]

ALL echo the chant as they move in synchronized movement downstage toward the audience. At the edge of the stage they throw the tree towards audience and sigh in relief. They all wearily walk back upstage, their bodies reflecting exhaustion. Leads to new scene.

SCENE TWELVE

BHOYI: Thousands of people gathered in an open field in Lamontville Township. My friend, Bhekani, and I were among the first people who heard Msizi Dube shout: ASINAMALI for the first time. And after that gathering, the whole township understood . . .

ALL: (*in a powerful, slow deliberate whisper*) ASINAMALI

BHOYI: We the youth went into the streets. It was finally happening, my friend Bhekani and I were in front. That guy, Bhekani, Bhekani he was a beautiful stone-thrower. He never missed an informer with a stone. One day soldiers and police came to our school. Bhekani picked up a stone and hit one soldier who was on top of a tank. That was the beginning of shit. We scattered. I threw myself under the barbed-wire fence and I saw Bhekani's feet passing over my head running down the vegetable garden, a policeman right behind him. Ay, that policeman was running like Zola Budd man.

They all laugh.

He caught Bhekani by his shirt. Bhekani came out of the shirt and this policeman had Bhekani's shirt, in his hands. His police hat was flying up, his boots were heavy and he was running. We were laughing.

They all laugh and scream.

Bhekani was laughing too. Just around the corner, I saw one policeman pick up a machine-gun. Tratatatatatatata. (*pointing it towards* SOLOMZI *who then falls in response*)

And then I saw Bhekani taking long strides, lifting up into the air, over the vegetable garden fence and then a somersault. And then he hit the ground. That man, my friend, he lay there and he was no longer the man I knew.

SCENE THIRTEEN

BONGANI starts the funeral song. They all carry SO-LOMZI like they would a coffin and finally lay him down.

SONG: "Isibham sami"
    Oyibambeni we bafana
    Yibambeni we zinsizwa

Oyibambeni we bafana
Yibambeni we zinsizwa,
Isibhamu sabafana
Sesing' khumbuza e Mozambeque.
　　　[Hold tight guys
　　　The sound of warriors' guns
　　　Reminds me of the guerilla war in
　　　Mozambique.]

BHOYI: And then we buried my friend Bhekani. Like all our heroes, we carried his coffin on our shoulders. That was a funeral of courage, hope, but during that funeral, people got very angry. People got mad. My mother just pointed out a grave of a government spy right next to my friend Bhekani's grave. People started throwing stones and dancing on top of the grave, and spitting on the grave. And then someone shouted; 'let us dig the informer out of the grave.'

SOLOMZI: Makambiwe! [Let him be dug out!]

ALL: Makambiwe!!!

BHOYI: Hey, within no time, we dug out the dead informer. We got him out of the grave and took the corpse down the street to his wife and his children.

ALL: (*they shout different things to the family in mass confusion*) Here he is, your informer, he has resurrected. Like Christ.

BHOYI: But back at the graveyard where my friend Bhekani was lying peacefully, police moved in. You know what they did? They shot women and kids inside the graveyard, and we, the men, they did not see us. We were hiding up there next to that informer's house. We just watched with nothing in our hands but stones.

SONG:
Sonke sithi ngalonyaka womanyano
Sonke sithi ngalonyaka womanyano
Sonke sithi ngalonyaka womanyano
S'khulule bawo
Ngo bhazuka ne mota ne akai
S'khulule bawo.

[In this year of unity set us free
In this year of unity set us free
In this year of unity set us free
With the help of bazookas and mortars and AK47s
Set us free.]

SOLOMZI: You know what happened in that township of
Sebokeng. For the first time there were soldiers in every
corner of the township. Heh! Those guys came with
hippos, saracens, tankers, spiders, thunder chariots, and
all those big machines! It was like in the movies! Yoo
—the whole township was full of dust, smoke, and
fire. Children, old men, old women, women with
babies on their backs—and then there was the fire—
and then there was the people. A stone in one hand, a
garbage can lid in the other. And then there was the
teargas. And then there was the policemen in camouflage uniform. And then there was the rattling sound of
the machine gun again. Windows of our homes were
shattering, pieces of glass were flying through the air
each time a white policeman turned his automatic
machine gun toward our four-roomed matchbox
houses. And then there were the screams. And then
there were the shouts. Some of us were left lying on the
ground. Ningahlehli madoda. [Don't retreat, go forth.]

ALL: Asiyeni bafowethu ningahlehli; forward comrade
niyabesabe na? [Let's go forward brothers. Don't
retreat. Are you afraid of them?]

SOLOMZI: It was the fire! The smoke, the people, the TV
crew, and those brave newsmen were taking pictures
amid confusion. It was chaos. People were running
from different angles to different directions.

SOLOMZI takes pictures.

But I ran for my life. The next morning I was on the
front page. When I turned around the street corner I
was face to face with a white policeman holding a
machine gun, just when he was about to set the
machine gun. The schoolgirl Nomthandazo, the pretty

one from the corner house, she threw a stone on his back. I heard the rattling sound of the machine again which left me paralyzed in shock. The white boy was firing up to the heavens as he was going down on his back. Yi mci, I swear he wished Pretoria taught him how to use stones. And there was the people with stones, big rocks, pipes, forks, tires, matches. We gave him gasoline to drink, and then we put on him a necklace. In less than two minutes man he was fire. I didn't wait to see the end. I ran as hard as I could. Jumping from fence to fence. Somewhere at the end of Zone 14 I heard someone screaming, shouting from the ditch, hey it was no time to help anyone. I even saw Sgonfana the lawyer leaving his wife behind.

Ngilinde baba ka-Sbongile
Woza ungilandele
Awu Honey
Honey uyongithola ekhaya.
 [Wait for me, honey.
 Honey follow me.
 You will find me at home.]

They all laugh.

THAMI: He was a coward.

SOLOMZI: This man kept on shouting, calling my name, and now it sounded like Bra Tony. I kept on running, but something kept telling me that I should go back. I found Bra Tony right inside the ditch, his whole body was covered in blood. He looked at me, I looked at him, he smiled; 'Ja, big-boy.' That's how he used to call me. And that was the last time I heard that voice. His body was among the many police victims that we buried that weekend. The very same evening soldiers and police distributed pamphlets all over the township. The pamphlets had good pictures of happy Black families. Children going to school in school uniforms, parents waving, parents reprimanding. But even then with all those good pictures distributed all over the township, people still maintained:

ALL: (*in a powerful whisper*) ASINAMALI.

> BONGANI *emerges with a prison warder's hat and starts applauding. The other prisoners quickly fall into a line. He motions to them to applaud too. They look at him perplexed, but they reluctantly join in the applause.*

BONGANI: Okay okay, okay. Today, we are celebrating Happy Birthday Leeuwkop Prison. (*applauds and motions to the prisoners to do likewise*) This means fifty years since these prison walls were erected. (*applause*) Ladies and gentlemen, we have some of the big guys, in here today from the Justice Department. From right to left starting with the top guy. The honorable, Major General Mr Jan Coetzee. (*he applauds, and everyone follows suit*) Brigadier Mr Van Der Merwe. (*applause*) Major General Mr Bezeidenhout. (*applause*) Good citizens of South Africa, how can we forget the pillar of 1976 Soweto riots. Who crushed the naughty school children with great force, Lt. Swanepoel. (*a stunned look on the prisoners' faces is replaced with grins as they start applauding when he looks at them*) Children of God, I have a reliable choir standing right in front of you. My Boys.

ALL: Baba.

BONGANI: Bafana bam, smile, So me do, (*gives them the right pitch*)

ALL: (*with frozen smiles on their faces, singing the harmony*) WHOOOOOOOOOOOOOOOOO!

> *With* BONGANI *conducting, they sing an inspired Happy Birthday song and burst into applause when they finish.*

BONGANI: Major General, Mr Jan Coetzee will be here tomorrow morning to talk to you. You must be clean, you must be neat. Well shaved, well behaved. Show him some responsibility, and most of all, respect. By the way, ladies and gentlemen, I have a bombshell for you. (*addressing the audience*) I've been asked to announce to you that their sentences will be reduced by a five year remission.

The prisoners are stunned, and break into excited shouts.

ALL: Remission? Remission? It must be some kind of prank.

BONGANI: (*still as the prison guard*) OK Boys, OK, smile! So! Me! Do! Woo! Woo! Woo! Chord!

ALL: (*singing more joyously after the announcement*) Wooooooo!

BONGANI: two, three, four!

ALL: HAPPPPPYYYYY!

BONGANI: Leeuwkop Prison!

When the song ends there is a little celebration with guys slapping each other's hands, excited at the prospect of leaving jail. BONGANI rejoins the others and is back to his role as prisoner.

SOLOMZI: Remission? I hope he's not pulling our legs.

THAMI: Back to the pigs!

BHOYI: I'm going to see my mama!

SOLOMZI: I'm going to see Bra Tony's wife.

BHEKI: Did you hear, there are no more passbooks. I don't believe it!

BONGANI: (*stuttering*) I'm going to see my four wives!

SOLOMZI: I hear that the Immorality Act is gone too.

THAMI: (*jumping up with joy*) Mrs Van Niekerk! Here I come!

ALL *the prisoners jump and embrace in excitement.*

BHOYI: Ayihlale phansi [Sit down]

They ALL join him in a chant:
Ayihlale phansi,
ibambe umthetho
    [Let's all sit down
    and hold court]

BHOYI: Madoda, we have been here for a long time. There have been bad times when we fought for a spoon of porridge and there have been good times when we talked about our loved ones and families. But for a moment, I ask, let us think of those who will not be given a chance to get out.

The other prisoners respond with confusion, some agreeing, others puzzled.

BONGANI: I know that, I know that . . .

BHOYI: Some of you will think that this is not important.

BONGANI: People like him (*pointing at* THAMI) who come here for stealing pigs. (*The others are stunned into silence, because* THAMI *is one of the most feared prisoners.*)

THAMI: (*screaming with anger and going for* BONGANI) Hhhhhhaaaaaaaiiii! Who stole pigs! Hey you. You will tell me the truth today. Who stole pigs?

He goes for BONGANI, *but* BHOYI *and* SOLOMZI *restrain him while* BHEKI *and* BONGANI *dash for cover.* BHEKI *is the most terrified.*

BHEKI: Bhoyi, Solomzi, please hold him, Hold Thami, he's very dangerous. Please tell him to sit down. Thami, we are friends, we are together. Tomorrow we are going out. You are also going out. Bongani was only joking. Thami, please sit down. Show them that you are a nice man. (THAMI *retreats and sits down.*) Thank you very much Thami. (BONGANI, *who had been standing at a distance, holding a chair as though he was ready to fight, also comes and sits down. Order is restored.*)

SOLOMZI: (*who is sitting next to* BHOYI) What he (to BHOYI) is talking about is very important. I know I'm a criminal. But I respect people like Himmmmm! (*hugs* BHOYI) Madoda, I have a long experience in prison. I've been to many prisons. I've been in with strong guys, real leaders of our people. Strong guys like him. (*hugs* BHOYI *again*)

THAMI: (*who has been sullen all the time along, jumps up*) Fuck them strong guys, man. Who! Stole! Fucking! Pigs! (*All hell breaks loose again as the guys run for cover except BHOYI.*)

BHOYI: (*irritated*) Hey you guys. Thami, Bheki. You guys hold it. Thami come here. Come here. (*pulls him closer and talks to him like a big brother*) You see, Msizi Dube spoke about those people. And always when he spoke about our leaders he spoke about waste. Wasted people. (*THAMI nods in agreement*)

THAMI: Nabo-ke abantu es'ngakhuluma ngabo. [Those are people we can talk about.]

BHOYI: Most of those people are wasted six feet underground. Others are in death cells waiting for the hangman. If they are not in the death cells they are wasted in detention. If they are not in detention they are wasted in prison.

BHEKI: Khuluma mfowethu! [Speak brother, speak!]

BHOYI: Heeeeeeeh! That man, Msizi Dube, knew he was going to die. He knew that informers were after his life. They got paid for that. They get paid for informing on us, to put us in jail for 90 days or even death sentence for our beliefs. Informers get paid for that! Where are our leaders today. Where is Griffiths Mxenge and his wife, Victoria Mxenge. U Victoria Mxenge muphi! [Where is she!]

ALL *the prisoners jump up and start shouting out names of heroes past and present:*

ALL: (*alternating*) STEVEN BIKO, NELSON MANDELA, WINNIE MANDELA, LILLIAN NGOYI, AHMED TIMOL, ROBERT SOBUKWE, ZEPH MOTHOPENG, ABRAM TIRO, HECTOR PETERSON, SCAR MPETA, PHAKADE MAGWAZA, BOBBY TSOTSOBE, GOVAN MBEKI, JOE GQABI, KHOTSO SEATHLOLO, WALTER SISULU, NEIL AGGETT, RUTH FIRST, BRAM FISCHER, NDODA XABA. SIBUSISO ZONDO

Towards the end of the list BHOYI *starts a song and they all join and do indlamu, a Zulu dance.*

SONG:
Elamanqamu namhlanje, namhlanje zinsizwa
Elamanqamu, elamanqamu namhlanje
Kwaphel'izinsizwa, kwasal'amavaka ayobaleka
Elamanqamu, elamanqamu namhlanje.
   [(Today is the D-Day, today is the day)
   Gone are the brave men,
   only the cowards remain
     and they will run
   Because today is the day
   It is the day of reckoning.]

They then come together to form a phalanx of resistance.

SONQOBA SIMUNYE

CURTAIN

BOPHA!

Percy Mtwa

Written by one of the co-creators of *Woza Albert!*, *Bopha!* examines the lives of those blacks enmeshed in the web of apartheid. Using one family, Mtwa pits father against son and brother against brother to examine the contradictions of life in South Africa. There are three principal characters: the father, a career policeman who upholds and enforces the government's rigid and abhorrent laws; his son, a radical student and leader of young students set on destroying the very ideals that his father bases his livelihood on; and an uncle, the policeman's brother who, without a proper pass, comes to the city from the homelands in search of a job. The uncle is arrested under the pass laws, but his brother promises him freedom and a new "fixed" pass if he joins the police, which he reluctantly does.

As the characters are placed in a situation of mounting unrest in the townships, they are also confronted by their own conflicting loyalties. The activist son refuses to tow his father's line and is subsequently arrested, landing in his father's jail; the father and uncle are called upon to quell the riots, but the uncle refuses to take up arms against his own. He breaks the policemen's code of conduct by arresting white people and questioning the nebulous laws. Finally the family house is set on fire by angry protesters, the policeman's wife is gunned down by policemen who are after the angry students, and the father comes to the realization that he has become an enemy of his own people.

Bopha! portrays the brutality of life in South Africa in all its nakedness; but Mtwa also succeeds in presenting a humorous look at sadness and despair. The stage craft used is similar to most of the plays coming out of the townships in present day South Africa. *Bopha!* is strong, vibrant and "just in time."

BOPHA!
Percy Mwta

CHARACTERS

NJANDINI — a Black policeman
NALEDI — the policeman's brother
ZWELAKHE — the policeman's son

There are also twelve other minor characters whose roles
are interchanged by the three actors, as they appear:

COMMISSIONER STAFANUS DE VAN GENOUBI
WHITE EMPLOYER
CONSTABLE DUPE
SERGEANT BUFFALO
POLICE RECRUITS
POLICE MAJOR
CAPTAIN VAN DONDER
MPANTSULA
DARKTAIL
STYLES
MAGOGO
PIET

BOPHA is Zulu for Arrest

*A wooden bar, three yards wide, is attached across the
wall on which the actors hang their costumes. Four mus-
taches of differing colors hang on the bar which the actors
use to portray the white officers. A pole is fixed on the
floor in the middle of the stage, about three feet from the
wall, on which hang four police caps. Three brown, for the
black cops, and one blue for the white officers. Two chairs*

are placed on either side of the pole and a small bench is placed against the wall. A blue police light on top of the pole is the preset and will always be on during the scenes that indicate a police-station (precinct).

SCENE ONE

GRADUATION CEREMONY

(Njandini comes forward.)

The actors are dressed in police cadet uniforms, sweat pants, striped vests and running shoes. As the house lights go down the three actors run onstage and take positions. Stage lights fade up as they begin their police display routines. The physical training display is followed by the police drill and all the cops have on their police caps. The routines are transformed into a dance and towards the end of the dance a black sergeant comes forward.

NJANDINI: Thank you ladies and gentlemen. This is yet another proud moment in the Republic of South Africa. The South African Police Passing Out Parade. And today I'm very proud to present to you The Commissioner of Police, Mr Stefanus De Van Genoubi!

SALUTE.

(The Commissioner comes forward—one of the actors, with the use of blond mustache, becomes the Commissioner)

COMMISSIONER: *(with pride and arrogance) Dankie! Dames en Here!* Our Policemen have carried out their duties with such high grade competition that the whole world is jealous! Ja! The whole world hates Suid Africa today because of the clever ways in which our policemen know just when and how to prevent crime and other disturbances from going too far!
    Even Great Britain is jealous, because the percentage of arrests made by our policemen is higher than the

percentage of arrests made by their highly praised Metropolitan Police of London.

The fact is that only one percent of our policemen are not fit for this cap, but that is a far better average than you would find in the Roman Catholic Church.

And I'm telling you Ladies and Gentlemen, the Suid African [sic] Police will stand no shit !!! *Agh verskoon my fok* . . . no nonsense! That is why we as Policemen will always at all times live up to our motto, "We serve and protect." *Dankie*. [Thank you]

DIE STEM VAN SUID AFRIKA

Blackout

SCENE TWO

NALEDI: (*with his police cap in hand narrating to the audience*) I was there in Hammanskraal. 360 Bantu constables in a passing out parade and I was one of them. "Bantu Constable Naledi Moloi" Yes Serge, there were lots of people, friends, families and relatives, Ministers, Generals, Lieutenants, and Bantu Constables. It was a great day for all of us. Policemen jumping with joy and throwing their caps in the air. "Hura" [Hooray] But there was one problem. We all came from the homeland. Some of us were recruited from the mines and we all knew that the only way to beat the influx control was to join the police force.

Hanhle hanhle [truthfully] I didn't want to be a policeman. I come from Qwaqwa. I came to Jo'burg because my brother Njandini was here, a whole policeman Sergeant. I wanted him to help me fix my pass, so that I can get a job, but he refused. *Kemuth amubi!* He is so madly in love with the police force that he wishes every member of the family to be like him.

SCENE THREE

The set is bare save for a few chairs. Njandini is sitting when his son, Zwelakhe, enters.

HOME 1

NJA: *(furiously)* And then? And then?

ZWEL: *(stops abruptly)* And then what Baba?

NJA: *Hey wena* [Hey you] it's 10 O'clock. Where do you come from?

ZWEL: I'm from the school meeting.

NJA: School meeting *se gat.* [Fuck the school meeting.] How many times must I tell you about these meetings *Kwedini?* [Son]

ZWEL: *Kanti* [But], what's wrong with these meetings baba?

NJA: Zwelakhe! Zwelakhe! I'm watching you my boy— You and that bloody friend of yours Pule—comrade— comrade.

ZWEL: But there's a lot wrong in our school—age limit, corporal punishment, wrong education. Right now, in 1976, they wanted us to do mathematics in Afrikaans. *Bangayenza leyonto Bangayenza?* [How can they do that?]

NJA: You can do Biology in Afrikaans—English in Afrikaans, Afrikaans in Afrikaans, Zulu in Afrikaans *Kuyafana* [It's the same] it's education—if you don't want to go to school forget it man. *Mayibuye, Mayibuye i Afrika Beyi yephi?* ["Let Africa come back"]

ZWEL: The problem is that you're a policeman wena baba! [You daddy]

NJA: *(Chases Zweli)* Uthini, what did you say my boy— sewu fuze unyoko and that bloody Uncle of yours, Naledi, and yet I'm working for you and your bloody education—Swine! You eat the police—you shit the police and you sleep the police, damn it! This is my job man—and I'm doing my job—ngithi my job my job man! *Seliya qina isende kwedini*[You're too big for your boots]—just say police—say nywe shit! Where were you when I was an idiot, a vagrant, no money, no house, no wife, no nothing, where were you man?

(Exit Zweli. To audience)
The law is the law. The police are not the law. The police are the protectors of the law and the law is made by the white man there in Pretoria—Police—Police. Comrade le e Pitoli (Pretoria) not in my house. I'm proud to be a sergeant today. A true gentleman. A man amongst men. A policeman of strength and loyalty! *Unjandini lo*—No fucking school boy is going to tell me what to do with my life in my house.

(Calls Zweli. Zweli re-enters)
Kwedini tshayisa—Attention la! *Yizwa* [listen] *la* in this house you're going to follow in my footsteps. When I say left, I want your left foot there and when I say right—*khonala futsek*! [young man, come here]

(Enter Naledi wearing a blanket around his shoulders, furious)

NAL: Abuti man! [My brother] Abuti man! Left, right, left, right, this is not a charge office.

NJA: Good evening! Culprit no. 2. Did you find the job? *Uwutholile umsebenzi?*

NAL: How? (*Takes out his passbok and throws it at his brother's feet*) Fix my pass.

NJA: (*Picks the pass up and throws it back to Naledi.*) This is not a pass office mfo! [brother]

NAL: Right! Let's go to the pass office. Sgt. Ngobese your friend is waiting for you just to come and sign that I was born right here in Jo'burgh. *Wena hahubatle.* [You keep refusing.] Aai, you beat me abuti!

NJA: *Vele* [It's true] if you can't beat them, join them.

NAL: No! *Akebatle!* [I don't want to]

NJA: Then that is very easy—very easy mfo. Pack your things and futsek [leave]. Tomorrow morning I don't want to see your face in my house. I'm trying to make you a man. *Wena uzonyela ekhanda lami, Ayigubhe!* For the devil's sake Almighty blinking God—futsek out of my house.

NAL: Where to?

NJA: Back to Qwaqwa. On top of the mountains and ride those horses until your bum is red like a monkey. I'm going to sleep now—Good night!

ZWEL: You're not going anywhere wena uncle.

NAL: I don't care Zweli. *Hantle hantle* Njandini is not my brother. He's my half brother. His mother is a woman from Kwana Zululand and my mother is a woman from Kwana Witsishoek where I come from. *Gale motho asotleha man.* [I have suffered long enough.] Three years. Going up and down just because of a pass. I go to Qwaqwa the Commissioner doesn't know me. I come to Jo'burgh, the commissioner doesn't know me. Hanti, where do I come from? Do I come from the sand—like a tortoise. *Bataue bommae sebono* [They are crazy]—I was born right here in Jo'burgh in the kitchens in Bramley. My mother was a domestic servant—Sheila—and today they say they don't know me. What must I do Zweli? Must I join the Police Force?

ZWEL: No uncle. Just because of a pass?

NAL: *Lenna* I don't want to be a policeman, Zweli.

(Enter Njandini)

NJA: *Ya! niyangibhunga*—oh futhi you're laughing. It's nice —I'm a bioscope. Hey mfo—I said I'm sleeping in my house—askies lights off Qho!! (*mimes switching off the lights*)

LIGHTS LIGHTS!!

SCENE FOUR

Outside a factory in the city. Naledi is kneeling and singing to pass the time.

SONG: HELA! HELA! (Hey! Hey!)
    I say I want a job
    Where could my mother and father be
    My children are dying in the house
    And the dogs need some bones
    I say I want a job
    Truly Truly I swear
    I'll never ever go back home
    I'd rather be like Xhosas and Pondons
    And carry shit-buckets on my shoulders
    And be like flies in the toilet
    I say I want a job (repeat chorus)

NALEDI: (*Kneeling and singing. Enter employer.*) Good morning sir . . .

EMPLOYER: Ja! What do you want?

NAL: I want a job, sir.

EMP: You want a job, you're not looking for a job . . .

NAL: Looking, looking sir.

EMP: Let me see your pass. (*Hands over the pass*) What type of a job?

NAL: Anything

EMP: Anything? What type of a job is that? (*pause*) Look! No qualification.

NAL: They said I must come back next week sir.

EMP: Okay! Come back next week. I don't take people with no qualification no more! No more! You people are no good! No good! I give one a job, plus free accomodation tomorrow you tell the police. I get into serious trouble! I pay big money man. R30 R30 R30! (*Exits*)

NJA: *Hak! Wafika Unjandini kwakhal' abantwana kwasuk' amaphepha!* Hey let's see your pass mfo. (*Naledi turns to strike him. Stops*)

NAL: *Abuti,* [Brother] I'm sorry.

NJA: Sorry *yamasimba* [my arse]! What are you doing here?

NAL: I'm looking for a job.

NJA: Looking for a job . . . Hey I'm with the baas you're going to jail wena.

(*Enter Constable Dupe, played by Zwelakhe, wearing blue police cap*)

DUPE: *Eh! Njandini wat gaan aan hierso!* [What's going on here?]

NJA: *Die man is my broer baas* [The man is my brother, boss].

DUPE: *Is hom pass reg?* [Is his pass in order?]

NJA: *Hy is reg baas, maar as hy kan daar gaan . . .* [He is okay boss, but if he goes there . . .]

DUPE: *Laat ek sien jong* [Let me see].

NJA: (*To Naledi*) Hey pass!! (*Naledi submits the pass*) Woza la! [Come here!] You see now, doing things behind my back.

DUPE: Eh! Njandini, this man doesn't qualify to be here. *Is die jou broer?* [Is he your brother?]

NJA: *Hy is my broer, baas, maar hy is baie purmantag!* [He is my brother, boss, but he is very arrogant!]

DUPE: *Hoekom?* [Why?]

NJA: He doesn't want to work. [He lies]

SCENE FIVE

FIRST TRAINING COLLEGE ASSEMBLY!!

SONG AND DANCE AND PHYSICAL TRAINING

BUFFALO: Morning recruits—you're all recruits man. Suspects. Welcome to the SAP [South African Police] Training College. This is not Sun City where you dance with the naked women all night long. This is the SAP Training College. Here I cook a policeman all night long. 5 o'clock in the morning the recruit jump makes his bed and washes his ass. *Akukho recruit elizolala ilanga liphume engquza la.* And you must run recruit, you must run. You go to eat, you go to the toilet you drop your shit and run, do you understand?

STUDENT 1: Yes Serge.

BUFF: Do you understand?

STUDENT 2: Yes Serge.

BUFF: *Hela madoda*—did you see all those policemen in the passing out parade? They come from these hands. Do you know what they call me? BUFFALO—*inkuzi*— And on Sundays you go to church. NG *Nerde Duiste Gereformeerde Kerk.* Any questions?

NAL: Er—what about weekends Serge?

BUFF: Ha! Play boys—playboys. Hardly two weeks you think about women. I'm going to tighten recruiting. *Ngizoyibopha. Futhi ngathi uyadelela wena. Uyadelela wena.* [What is your name? You look like a hard-headed one.]

NAL: *Ke Naledi wa Moloi. Kemotlakapipi wamog . . .* [I am Naledi Moloi from . . .]

BUFF: Shut up recruit. *Uyisididi wena.* Where do you come from?

NAL: I come from Qwaqwa.

BUFF: Bullshit you can come from *e Qwaqwa noma e Nquthu noma emnqundu* I am baffalo la. You go to Fort Hare University you fail, you go to Turflop university you fail, you go to *Medunsa* you fail—you come to me you pass—first class distinction.

SONG

LECTURES
(The actors run for the chairs and sit)

BUFF: Let us revise our previous lesson. Influx control Imuumo. What do you do if you find a black man who does not have a permit to be in the Bantu Affairs Administration area in terms of section 10(1)a, b, c of act no. 25 of 1945?

STUDENT 1: I arrest him without a warrant Serge.

BUFF: Very good recruit.

NALEDI: Even white people?

BUFF: Naledi, the law says do not arrest a white man *finish and klaar*! [period!] *Uyadelela wena. Uyadelela strue's bob.* You are hard-headed.

NAL: Hayi Serg, every time I ask a question *warikiyadelela.* [You say that]

BUFF: Shut up—*uyadelela wena.* *(To students)* Class dismiss *Usididi wena.* [Follow me.]

NAL: I'm not a *sdididi.*

BUFF: *Usididi wena.* I'll show you what I can do with a recruit who's got his brains *emnqundu* [in his ass]. Haak!

TO THE MAJOR'S OFFICE

BUFF: Good morning Major.

MAJ: *(Zwelakhe is now the white major with a mustache)* Good morning Buffalo. Why so early in the morning?

BUFF: I've got a rebel in my class Major.

MAJ: A rebel? Who's that?

BUFF: Naledi Moloi. He's always bullshitting me Major. Today when I teach him about influx control he want to know if he can arrest white people.

MAJOR: Bring him in.

BUFF: Naledi Moloi.

NAL: Serg (*Enters*) Good morning Major.

MAJ: Listen here. We teach you what is written in those books *verstaan jy*? [Do you understand?]

BUFF: And when I tell him that a white peace officer is his senior irrespective of rank he said no, no, no.

MAJ: No, no, no what? *Jy's nie die baas nou.* [You are not the boss. What else Buffalo?.] *En wat nog Baffalo?*

BUFF: Even before immorality act was scrapped he said if he found a black man having carnal intercourse with a white woman he was going to leave them alone!

MAJ: Wat? *Jy's maal* [Now listen here]. *Nou luister hierso.* Immorality Act scrapped—let me catch you on top of a white woman *ek skiet gat dwaars deur*. I'm defaulting you. And do you know what that means? You're a criminal in the police force. Buffalo, strong physical training.

BUFF: Dankie Major. (*To Naledi*) *Ngiku tshelile but. Sakuni Baffalo mina ngihuma le a Giyane.* The law says if you find a black man who does not have qualification "*Bopha!*"

Lights

SCENE FIVE

LAST TRAINING COLLEGE

MAJOR: I am the willing. Led by the knowing, doing the impossible for the ungrateful, I've done so much, with so little, I'm now qualified at doing anything with nothing at all! And now remember . . .

A police officer is a public servant. He comes into contact with people of opposing views and opposing politics, but he does not take sides. He must be a minister, a social worker, a diplomat and a tough guy. A very tough guy, Rambo, Cobra.

And he must be a genius, *nie a houdkop nie!* Because out there in your townships, you are at once the most

needed and the most unwanted. You are just strange
nameless creatures. They call you an officer in your
face, and a bloody dog behind your back. They call
you Pig. P.I.G. And if only those knew what Pig stands
for in the Police Force, they wouldn't use that word.
Njandini P . . . ?

NJA: P is for the Power of the Police Force.

MAJ: I . . . ?

NJA: I is for the Intelligence of the Police Force.

MAJ: G . . . ?

NJA: G is for the Guts to be in the Police Force! Telele!!!

Blackout

SCENE SIX

POLICE STATION 1
(Song—Enter Naledi)

NAL: Abuti. [Brother]

NJA: *(chant)* Sit down mfo. How was it?

NAL: Fine

NJA: Did you die?

NAL: Suka!! [Go away!!]

NJA: How's Buffalo?

NAL: Fine. How's Zwelakhe?

NJA: He's worse. They are not going to school three
months. They've burnt a policeman. Necklace. I can't
even walk past Bekisizwe High School with this cap.
I'm afraid of my own son, u Zwelakhe.

(Enter the captain)

SALUTE!!

CAP: Constable Naledi Moloi! Welcome to Bekisizwe Police
Station. I'm the Station Commander here. Captain Van

Donder. This is your record file from the Training
College *en die bliksem se donder* [and the
motherfucker] has got one default already.

NJA: *Hayikhona* [No] baas, I smell a rat!

CAP: That is a very bad start, but we can clean up your
record if you prove yourself a very good policeman,
and remember you'll have to feed your family on a
policeman's salary. Welcome!

(Salute. Exit)

NJA: You heard for yourself, mfo, lets go home and have a
beer. And listen here, in this Police Station we speak
one language, BOPHA!

Fade

SCENE SEVEN

HOME 2
*At home, dressed in his school blazer, Zwelakhe is
practicing his speech.*

ZWEL: I will be standing like this . . . and there will be a
large crowd of students, and I will say "Comrades, we
want to be proud of our education. *Amandla!* Away
with white teachers who carry guns in our classrooms,
Amandla! Comrades, it is never too late to learn, age
limit must be scrapped. Aluta continua! Viva! Viva!
(Chant from Njandini. Enter with Naledi.)

NJA: *(After business)* Nanku! A whole policeman . . .
qualified . . . bright future . . . ! Naledi, I'm going to get
some beers. I want you to talk to this boy. You see
that book. *(points to a book under one of the chairs)*
Black power under the chair. *(Exit)*

NAL: *(Sits)* How are you doing at school, Zweli?

ZWEL: Bad uncle. We are not going to school anymore.
And fifteen of our school kids have been shot by the
police.

NAL: Fifteen Zweli! South Africa weh! And where's your friend Pule?

ZWEL: He's in jail. The police arrested him six months ago, and since then we don't know what happened to him.

NAL: You see, that's why I didn't want to be a policeman.

ZWEL: But you're a policeman now uncle—One of these days I'm going to see you on top of a hippo.

(Enter Njandini)

NJA: Naledi, the beers are getting hot. Mi! [Take this] get mealie meal, sugar, potatoes, roast beef, Omo, Sunlight Soap, Life Bouy. And keep the change. Naledi, this is my son, my only son. When he finishes school, I want him to become a policeman.

NAL: *Le Zweli hape?* [And him too?]

NJA: Why not?

NAL: Abuti, our grandfather was a policeman, our father was a policeman, you are a policeman, I'm a policeman, *Le Zweli hape*! [And Zweli too!]

NJA: This boy is educated man. One, two, three, Major!

Exit. Lights

SONG: We are going to Pretoria
        Watchout Botha
        Watchout Malan
        We are going to Pretoria

SCENE EIGHT

MPANTSULA

(Naledi on stage. Enter Njandini with Zwelakhe as Mpantsula)

NJA: Ngena Come! Do you think you can shit where you like hey. Naledi give me the keys.

NAL: I don't have the keys. Van Donder wants to see you.

NJA: *Bamba lenja* [Hold this dog]. I'm coming back! (*Exits*)

NAL: Hey what have you done?

MPANTSULA: You see grootman [big brother], I was walking down Victoria Street, so suddenly I got pressed, since I took some laxative tablets in the morning. *Uyazi mfowedhu, ngithi ngikhiph'inyongo!* So I looked around and I saw a lavatory, and I went in there to relieve myself. *Ganti neh*, I didn't check that this toilet is for Europeans only. So I was sitting there grand *ke kaka nice, skielik* the door opened *tla Njandini*, and he said I'm under arrest. I asked him *smoko* [problem], and he said don't I know where to shit. I said no man what do you mean, because I'm in the toilet. He didn't understand. He clapped me and wanted to drag me outside. I said, no wait, let me wipe myself. He didn't understand so I waved *haniyani* so that I could pull up my pants. Because he wanted to drag me outside being naked, man, plus *weer* [again] my madam is waiting for me outside. I mean like a man I must I must hide my body, that thing is public indecency and that's another charge *weer*! I tried to explain and he said I'm resisting arrest. Another charge *weer, weer*! He handcuffed me and beat me all the way in front of the people.

(*Enter Njandini*)

NAL: Abuti, can you really arrest a boy for shitting in the toilet.

NJA: Why not?

NAL: *Hinja—le!* [This little dog!]

NJA: Do you shit where you like wena! I'm charging him. Hey pass!

MPANTSULA: My pass fell in the toilet!

NJA: Bopha! (*Drags him to cell*) I'm charging you with Trespass, Resisting arrest, Failing to produce a pass!

Lights

SCENE NINE

DARKTAIL

(Enter Naledi pulling Zwelakhe as a white man)

NAL: Kenna. [Come in.]

NJA: Naledi, a white man. *Nansi mihlola!* [This is amazing!]

NAL: *Pis in die straat. Angeke ahamba abonisa umthondo wakhe obomyu yonke indawo.* [He was pissing in the street, he cannot expose his red penis all over the place.]

(Njandini offers a chair to the white man, Naledi pulls the chair and the white man falls.)

NAL: Ema [Stand up] *Leatella leboro lena.* I find him pissing against the wall. I try to talk to him nice, he calls me a kaffir police boy, I clapped him and I'm charging him.

NJA: Naledi, I am 25 years in the police force. I've never seen such a thing. Arresting a white man!

NAL: *Utlaebona.* [You will see it.]

D. TAIL (ZWE): *My ma hoor my* [I swear on my mother]. A kaffir police boy comes and hits me with a kaffir clap. I'm going to commit suicide. I'm going to commit suicide.

NJA: *(To Naledi) Uyamuzwake!* [Do you hear that!]

NAL: *Tsamonyela* [Go to hell] *(Dragging Darktail to the cells)*

D. TAIL: *Los my jou vokken kaffir. Ek gaan jou doodskiet as ek hier uitkom.* [Leave me you nigger. When I am released I will shoot you to death.]

(He locks him in.)

NAL: I'm charging him. *Ayatella maboro ana.* ["Your mother's. . . ."] [These Boers are obstinate.] They are just like their children. Hallo police boy, hallo police boy. *Nyoammao*

NJA: *Uyabonake mfo* [You see my brother], I don't want to be a witness.

(To audience) Uyabona mina, when I see a white man committing a crime, *ngenza ugathi angibomi*. I close one eye and dial 99 Squad car.

(To Naledi) Release the baas or I'm calling Van Tonder.

NAL: *Abuthi ule Italian, ule China ele Arab, ule Indian una Bopha!* [Whether you are Italian, Chinese, Arab, or Indian, I arrest!]

Lights

SCENE TEN

INTELLECTUAL

VAN DONDER: *(on the phone)* Bekisizwe Police Station. Captain Van Donder Speaking. Hello, Hey Katrina. What! Now listen here Katrina, go tell that Martins that his cattle are destroying my vegetables in my farm. Where is Kleinboy? Tell him that he must fix that falling fence. Yes! *(laughs)*

(Enter Styles)

Katrina, call me later. OK. I have a visitor here. *(laughs)*

(To Styles) Yes! What do you want.

STYLES: I want my brother!

CAP: *Wie is joy broer?* [Who is your brother?]

STYLES: Pule Rampa.

CAP: What has he done?

STYLES: I don't know.

CAP: Then how the fucking hell do you expect me to know him?

STYLES: You sent your policemen to come and arrest my brother six months ago, and you tell me you don't know what he has done. I'm flabbergasted.

CAP: Hey don't come and speak big English here.

STYLES: I want my brother!

CAP: Your brother is not here.

STYLES: I detest this. This is catastrophe!

CAP: Hey, you want to speak English. Right let's speak English. My friend, don't trouble trouble till trouble troubles you. *Ek gaan jou toe sluit.* [I will lock you up.]

STYLES: Constable Naledi told me he saw my brother's name in your occurrence book.

CAP: Right! Constable Naledi told you, so what. Your broer committed suicide. *Dood* [Dead]. So what Mr. English. I'm sitting in this office and I'm doing my job. I got a warrant to go and arrest some school kids in the location. Die Security Police die No charge, no trial, no doubt, no fucking case. I kept him here for two days and they came and took him away. And after two months, they come and tell me he took a blanket and hanged him himself. So what?

STYLES: Six months. Mr. Van Donder. You didn't even have the decency to notify his family about such an unfortunate arrest. I've been to Pretoria, Brakpan, and John Voster Square and you're sitting in this office, talking to Katrina, and you know what has happened to my brother. I'm getting my lawyer. And there will be no circumlocution, no double speaking diplomatic denials.

(*Exit*)

CAP: *Jou moer man!!!* [Fuck you] What do you think you're? Come and talk big English here. (*Notices the pipe. Runs to the phone. Dials.*) Hello explosive department. Ja! There's something like a bomb here, sitting nicely on a chair in my office. What do I mean a bomb sitting on a chair, what about the bomb that exploded in Captain Van Der Merwe's face . . . wasn't it sitting nicely on the table? I don't know . . . it looks like a pipe . . . Wait! How do I know what's inside there? Send me your people asseblief! [Please] (*Creeps out*) Die swart engelsman die bliksem! [The Black Englishman, the bastard!] (*Exit*)

(*Enter Njandini*)

NJA: Baas, your tea is getting cold. Baas! Baas! (*Sees the pipe. Picks it up. Examines it. Tries to open it*)

(*Enter Captain*)

CAP: Njandini! Do you know what you've got in your hands?

NJA: Ja, it's a pipe, Captain. There was a plumber here. That short man who came to fix your toilet.

CAP: Njandini, do you remember that explosion in John Voster Square?

NJA: Ja baas!

CAP: Then how the hell do you know if that's not a bomb!

(*Throws the pipe. Captain catches it*)

Lights

SCENE ELEVEN

MAGOGO AND VAN DONDER

MAG: Baas why do send your man to come and destroy my shack? *Nithi mandilalephi kwedini?* [Where do you think I will sleep?]

V.D.: *Wat sê jy?* [What did you say?]

MAG: I want my shack man.

V.D.: *Magogo moenie man sêby my.* [Don't say man to me!]

MAG: The mayor gave me the permission to build that shack in a piece of paper. Or maybe your pieces of paper are useless *kwedini?*

V.D.: That piece of paper is useless. We got orders from the major to go and clean up the ghetto. *Jy moenie kom geraas hier maak.* [Don't come here and make noise.]

MAG: Five years ago you sent your men to come and kick me out of my house because I don't have a husband. Ngoku I build myself a shack and you say it's a ghetto. *Undikwatisela ntoni kwedini.* [Why do you make me angry?]

V.D.: Magogo, go back to your mayor and tell him to give you another piece of paper.

MAG: Haai, baas there's no mayor. Our mayor has run away. Our councillors have resigned. What is left Ngoku in the area are these hippos.

V.D.: It's not your fucking business.

MAG: It is my business man, right now my grandson is lying in the hospital. *Kuyambulwa kuyambeswa ngaye* because of these hippos. I had to sit with a bucket of water right inside my house ready for action because this teargas ndini could come in any minute. Ndithi any minute. Where's the respect apho. *Ndixelele* [Tell me] baas? *Ndithi* where's the respect *apho.*

V.D.: Magogo, I said go back to your mayor.

MAG: I said there's no mayor.

V.D.: Now I must become a magician. Do you expect me to wave my stick in the air Magogo here's a shack, Magogo here's a house, *jy's maal* [you are mad].

MAG: *He hake baas*, I'm going nowhere. I'm going to sleep in this office tonight.

V.D.: *Wat sejy?* [What?]

MAG: I said I'm going to sleep in this office tonight.

(She sleeps.)

Lights

SCENE TWELVE

NALEDI AND THE CAPTAIN

(Naledi on stage)

NAL: Hak! Captain Van Donder. Room no. 6

(Enter Captain)

CAP: Constable Naledi!

NAL: *(Salutes)* Captain

CAP: *Captain sê gat!* Why do you keep sending people to my office?

NAL: Who's that Captain?

CAP: *Daardie magogo jong!* [That old woman!]

NAL: That magogo is my neighbour, Captain. I was trying to help.

CAP: I've been watching you. Since you came to this Police Station, *alles is onderste bo! Jy's net 'n "bubble bek."* [Everything is helter skelter. You are just a loud mouth.] Three months ago, Njandini arrested a kaffir boy for shitting in a white man's toilet, and you had too much to say. And you went outside and arrested a white man pissing in die *straat* [street]. What are you trying to do?
   Give me your pocketbook. I'm defaulting you. You told some *swart Engelsman* that his brother's name appeared in our occurrence book.

NAL: He was looking for his brother, Cap, I was trying to help.

CAP: Help him for what!!! *Kyk hier*, his brother committed suicide. Dood. *En jy maak net jou gaat oop!* I'm defaulting you. *(Books him)* *(Enter Njandini)* Njandini, your brother is trying to form a trade union in the police force! And even when he was hardly three months at this station, he called 7 policemen and they came to ask for an increase. *(To Naledi)* Hey kyk hier, the Government is doing you a favour by paying you.

You're volunteers, you should be living on rations . . . patriots!

NJA: What's wrong now mfo?

NAL: Magogo came here looking for her shack. I sent her to Captain!

NJA: Hey if you don't want to be a policeman forget it man.

NAL: *Leyatela leburu lena abuti man!* [This Boer is obstinate!]

CAP: *Hey wie's 'n boer?* [Who is a boer?] (*Fight*) *Njandini, polisieman of nie poliesieman, BOPHA!* [Policeman or no policeman, Arrest!]

SCENE THIRTEEN

FUNERAL SONG:

Why pack us all in one place
What have we done, oh government
Everytime we protest
We're always met with police armoured cars.

CHANT

We've all agreed, comrades
We've all agreed about this job
Our brothers are in jail
Our sisters are in jail
These policemen are our oppressors
These policemen are bloody bastards
These police trucks are our murderers
These machine guns are killing us
Run, run, run, comrades run.
But we are going to crush them again and again

Go tell Botha we're coming
Jump and dance comrades

STREET SCENE

ZWELAKHE: Policemen were advancing the fighting, the destruction, the shooting bullets breaking windows above you dogs barking, the running, the ducking, the falling, the screaming, the panic, the fear, and the dying, and this was only a funeral of our Comrade Pule Rampa, who died in detention held under the state of Emergency. Why don't people know when to stop. Ngudle died in Pretoria, suicide by hanging. Modipane died in Prison—slipped in the shower. Timol died in Johannesburg, fell from the tenth floor window during interrogation. Biko died in Pretoria, injured in a scuffle. Many unknown people died on unknown dates in unnamed prisons no details given. We take it easy and bury our dead, and I'm telling you gents, there is never any violence until the police come. These people are killing us. Many people lay scattered in the streets, many were injured, many were dying, and many were dead. I saw a black policeman kick a young boy in the face, a boy who was shot and almost bleeding to death, and he said we school children are giving them overtime. Another white policeman was laughing at a man who was rolling on the ground in terrible pains and he said he was doing break dance. People were hiding in their houses and in the back-yards waiting. Suddenly I heard voices singing from far-away. People were coming back, the whistling, the shouting, "*SIYAYI NYOVA.*" Everybody came out and charged into the streets. One two three the whole township was in flames—Putco busses, delivery trucks, company cars, hippos, police vans, houses, shops, and people. The township was also filled with smoke from burning people. Mayors, community councillors, informers and black policemen.

I saw a small boy pick up a stick, with it he shoved pieces of human flesh back into the fire, a policeman burning to ashes, with tears in his eyes said the police killed his mother. Policemen killing people and people killing policemen *wafa-wafa* [die-die]. Policemen were waiting outside the church with guns, and also waiting outside the church with a gun was my father. He knew I was inside the Church. And I was singing.

SCENE FOURTEEN

PIET AND VAN DONDER

V.D.: Piet, what is happening?

PIET: Captain, I was sitting on top of a hippo and all of a sudden a stone hit me on the chest and I fell off.

V.D.: And you don't know who hit you?

PIET: It was skiet rekker [slung] from somewhere inside the house.

V.D.: You panicked. And gave orders to shoot.

PIET: It was a matter of life or death Captain. Those kids they've got courage.

V.D.: Those kids in the hospital have wounds in the back. Piet, how can you shoot people in the back? A four-year-old baby?

PIET: *Verskoon* my Captain. [Forgive me.]

V.D.: *Moeni verskooning vra nie.* [Don't ask for forgiveness.] (*phone rings*) This telephone has been ringing for two hours. The minister, newspaper, TV, Helen Suzman. Suppose its Katrina calling there. My wife?

PIET: It was a matter of life or death Captain. Those kids are treating the situation like a carnival. Burning of our policemen and burning of innocent people is seen as some kind of fire works display. I thought that laughing must come to an end.

(*Telephone rings again*)

V.D.: Pick it up. Answer it.

PIET: What must I tell them Captain?

V.D.: Tell them you shot those kids in the back.

PIET: Hallo, Bhekizizwe Police Station. (*Nods*) It's Katrina Captain.

(They both laugh)

Lights

SCENE FIFTEEN

PIET AND NJANDINI AND ZWELAKHE

(Piet pacing in the Charge office)

PIET: Khotso Bogoloane, Boykie Motlamme, Mzwandile Kente—Zwelakhe Buthelezi—*Die vokon strout, hy's hierso.* [The bloody swine, he's here.]

NJA: Baas, it's bad. There's war out there. It's no longer school children. It's parents and *tsotsis* [hooligans/thugs]. Baas Duys is in hospital. *Khona manje.* [Right now.]

PIET: What happened?

NJA: He shot one of those tsotsis and they all attacked him with pangas sticks, bricks, stones . . .

PIET: And you ran away stupid. How can you leave the baas behind?

NJA: *Haai khona baas*, if I was not there he would be dead. *Nya, finish Khona manje* I've got 15 kids in the van and you say I ran away. I'm not a coward *mina ngingungqengelele mina* [I am very brave].

PIET: Okay Njandini, What must we do?

NJA: I'm worried about my son Zwelakhe. He's gone missing baas.

PIET: He's here. *Hy's hierso.* Call No. 9 Public violence, pamphlet distributor, arson looting, UDF T-shirt distributor.

NJA: *Haikona baas* [No! Boss]

PIET: Njandini you're hiding a small communist *in daardie huis* [in that house].

NJA: *Hai kona baas.* Captain Van Donder knows about him. He's just a small boy baas. He doesn't know what he's doing.

PIET: *Hy ken. Hy ken.* [He knows.] Njandini you know me. *Ek is Piet ek. Ek komvan Parys. Ek gaan hom wys.* [I am Piet, I come from Parys. I will show him.]

NJA: *Hayikhona baas.* Don't touch him, that's my son. I've worked in this Police force for so many years and I've always respected my superiors. Even you baas, a constable, and I a sergeant. I've been always out there in the township doing my job as a policeman and Khonamanje now you say my son is a communist.

PIET: Ja, why do they wave the communist flag in the funerals?

NJA: I don't know.

PIET: Ja, you know me. *Ek kom van Parsy af.* (*Exit*)

(*Piet and Zwelakhe enter*)

PIET: Sit (*to Zwelakhe*). *Jy gaan my sê wie het my met'n skiet rekker geskiet. Jy gaan my sê wiehet Sgt. Shabalala dood gemaak. Wie het ons Polisie wa gebrandt.* [You will tell me who hit me with a stone. You will tell me who it is that killed Sgt. Shabalala. Who burnt the police van.] What do you want from us? We give you schools, we give you education. What do you want from us? (pause) *Julle maak net kaak, net kaak, Njandini, praat met hierdie kaak.* [You are just fucking up, fucking up. Njandini talk to this piece of shit.]

NJA: (*to Zwelakhe*) Hey wena. Where's the Black Power *uma sekunje* [now]. Is this freedom? *Ngikhuluma nawe. Ngikufaka isicathulo khona manje.* Just tell the baas who hit him on the head and fuck off *uhambe uye ekhaya.* [I am talking to you. I will kick you right now.]

(*Zwelakhe slowly rises and clenches his fist and salutes.*

Njandini, extremely embarrassed, pulls the fist down.
He struggles with his son, who keeps the fist raised.)

Lights

SCENE SIXTEEN

VAN DONDER AND NJANDINI

VAN DONDER: I'm very sorry my friend, your house is on
fire, the famous petrol bomb. Kids and parents
surrounded your house with bricks and bottles carrying
placards, shouting Njandini release your son, he's
fighting for your freedom. The police found the house
in flames and dispersed the crowd. At least two people
died, a woman and a child and it is reported that your
ex-wife Rosie is seriously injured and admitted in
hospital. She was caught up by a stray rubber bullet
while she was running down the streets looking for
your son Zwelakhe. Njandini, the station commander
is talking to you.

(They salute)

Lights

SCENE SEVENTEEN

HOME 3

*(Zwelakhe finds Njandini on stage. Zwelakhe is
holding a wooden frame close to his face, as if behind
bars.)*

ZWEL: Baba! Baba!

NJA: Is that you Zwelakhe my son?

ZWEL: Yebo baba

NJA: *Sekonakele mfana wani.* [It is bad, my son.] You have
no home now. *Sebayothile* [They burnt it]. Your
mother is in hospital. Stray rubber bullet. Your uncle

Naledi has been fired from the Police Force. *Nawe awubheke* [and now look] where you come from.

ZWEL: I don't regret it baba. *Kade nginitshela.* Look now My mother is in the hospital because of a stray rubber bullet from the stray Police Force. Uncle is fired. And what about you? Can you see if they found you at home, you would have been roasted alive. Can you see your job has made you an enemy of your own family. Right now I don't have a home all because of your job.

NJA: It's your Black Power Kwedini!

ZWEL: It's your job baba!

NJA: It's your Black Power man!

ZWEL: It's your job baba!

NJA: Okay. Let's leave it right there.

ZWEL: What are you going to do now?

(Enter Naledi)

NAL: Zweli. It's bad wena. I'm no longer a policeman.

ZWEL: What happened?

NAL: Your father knows. Even right now he's still carrying a gun. *(To Njandini)* Abuti man. This is not your fight. People are dying in the townships. Even policemen are dying. Kere leafella, where's your house now? Finished! Where's Van Donder? Van Donder doesn't stay in the township. He's got his waterbed in the farm. Think abuti, think.

ZWEL: What are you going to do now Uncle?

NAL: Zweli, I'm going to get myself a job. I was locked up for seven days and the board of enquiry was called and I was fired. But I'm very very happy because my pass has come right. And I'm still saying it. I was born right here in the kitchen in Bramley. Whether they like it or not. My pass has come right. And what about yourself?

NJA: *Ningazodakwa la.* [Don't be crazy.] I'm left with only two years to go on pension.

ZWEL: Baba, a community councilor has resigned in Alexandra.

NAL: Because the police shot his son dead in the street.

ZWEL: Six policemen have resigned in Pretoria. Mayors are resigning.

NAL: Even teachers are resigning in Durban, Cape Town, Bloemfontien, Johannesburg.

ZWEL: Even Van Zyl Slabbert has resigned.

NAL: Dr. Boraine is joining the People.

ZWEL: People are afraid baba. They are fighting each other.

NAL: Policemen against school children

ZWEL: Botha versus Botha

NAL: About the Black President

ZWEL: Gatsha versus Botha

NAL: About the tape

ZWEL: Slabbert versus Botha

NAL: About the tape. Right now in Port Elizabeth they are fighting about the beach.

ZWEL: The army versus tourists

NAL: Not the terrorists this time

ZWEL: People are dying in the townships Baba.

NAL: Even policemen *Kere leafella*

ZWEL: After rubicorn two

NAL: Three Zweli

NJA: Zwelakhe, have you also killed a policeman?

ZWEL: (*happy*) My father is resigning.

NAL: (*chants*)

NJA: (*joins them in a song*)

—*SONQOBA SIMUNYE*—

GLOSSARY

TERMS

"Amandla Ngawethu!"—popular black radical slogan meaning "Power to the People" (literally, "Power is Ours")

baas, basie—subservient words for boss

baba—a Zulu word meaning father, a term of respect

bakkies—trucks or vans

bheshu—cowhide used by men as costume in traditional Zulu society

bra—brother

caspir—a riot control vehicle used since the 1976 uprisings

Cha!—No!, pronounced with a clicking sound

dignity bag—attache case

dwaals—daydreaming

gogo—old woman, "grandmother"

Hai!—No!

hippo—riot control vehicle

hostel—all male housing compound serving the mines and industrial areas

kaffir—nigger

knobkierrie—a fighting stick

kwela-kwela—a large police van used in raids

lekker—delicious, also beautiful, good, etc.

loafer-skap—vagrancy

melktart—delicacy similar to cheesecake

Morena—Sir, or Lord, term of respect

mtwanami—my child

ntate—a Sotho word meaning father, but also "sir" or address to old man

passbook—Every black man and woman over the age of sixteen is forced by law to carry at all times a passbook, also known as a dompass. It contains information about birth, family, background, employment, taxation, etc. If at any time the police discover a person without a passbook, immediate arrest follows. The passbook is the major symbol of oppression in South Africa

rand—South African unit of currency, about $.40.

rooinecks—rednecks

shebeen—place where liquor is sold and men gather after work, similar to a "speak-easy"

"Sonqoba Simunye"—United We Will Conquer

voetsek—a commonly used curse word which could be a lighthearted "go away" or a strong "fuck off" depending on the context

woza—rise up, come

NAMES

NEIL AGGETT—a political prisoner who died in detention, Aggett was the first white man to die at the hands of the security police.

ANC—African National Congress; the best known of the groups fighting for the overthrow of the South African government.

STEVE BIKO—Born in 1946, Steve Biko became the first president of the All-Black South African Students' Organization in 1968. The Organization and the Black Peoples' Convention, which Biko also helped form, were at the forefront of articulating the emerging philosophy of black consciousness. He was served with a five-year banning order in 1973. In 1975 he was arrested and held for 137 days without charge or trial. Following the Soweto riots of 1976, he was arrested and held in solitary confinement for 101 days. In 1977 he was again arrested and twenty-seven days later became the twentieth person to die in police custody over an eighteen month period. Despite numerous arrests, Biko was never convicted of a single crime.

COSAS—Congress of South African Students, a Black student body which was banned by the government in 1984.

MSIZI DUBE—was a member of the African National Congress who served ten years on Robben Island, a maximum security prison off the shores of Cape Town where many pioneers of the South African struggle are kept. When he came out of prison, he became a community councillor in Lamontville township in Durban. In 1983 he led a campaign against the government-imposed rent increase and was subsequently gunned down by government forces on April 25, 1983.

50's TREASON TRIAL—A trial where 156 persons, including Nelson Mandela, Robert Sobukwe and Albert Luthuli, were accused of treason in South Africa in 1956. They were all acquitted five years later, the longest political trial in history.

RUTH FIRST—Born into a politically radical family in Johannesburg, she studied social science. From the mid-forties she worked with African mine strikers, and with Nelson Mandela and others of the African National Congress. She was Johannesburg editor of radical journals, which were successively banned, and acting secretary of the Communist Party. Among the 156 accused and later acquitted in the Treason Trial in 1956, she was then banned and placed under house arrest. In 1963 she was held in solitary confinement for 117 days. A leading member of the ANC, while running a university department in Mozambique she was killed by a letter bomb on August 17, 1982.

BRAM FISCHER—Born into a prominent Afrikaner family in 1908, Bram Fischer was the son of a Judge President of the Orange Free State and grandson of a Prime Minister of the Orange River Colony. He became radicalized as a law student at Oxford. After becoming a lawyer, he led the defense in a number of political trials, including the Treason Trial of 1956–1960 and the Rivonia Trial of 1963–1964. In September 1964, he was arrested and charged under the Suppression of Communism Act, but fled underground to continue his political activism. Re-arrested within a year, he was sentenced to life imprisonment, and died in 1975.

JOE GQABI—was gunned down by a death squad in Harare on July 31, 1981, while serving as an ANC representative to Zimbabwe. Born in the Cape in 1929, he joined the ANC in the 1950s, and served twelve years in prison for his political activities. He left South Africa in 1978 and became a member of the National Executive of the ANC in exile.

THOZAMILE GQWETA is a prominent trade union leader who was born in the eastern Cape in 1952. Hated by the authorities for his unflinching commitment to the black struggle, Gqweta has been harassed, detained, and arrested continuously over the last eight years. While he was in detention in 1981–1982, his mother and grandfather were killed in a mysterious fire, and his fiance was shot dead by police in the Ciskei, a tribal "homeland" where Gqweta has enlisted many union members. Today Gqweta is on trial for treason with other trade unionists in Natal.

TREVOR HUDDLESTON was born in 1913 in Bedford, England, and became a member of the Anglican Community of the Resurrection, a monastic order. Between 1943 and 1956 he served as a priest in Johannesburg, and for six years was headmaster of St. Peter's School, known as the "black Eton" of South Africa. His support for the African National Congress was open and active, and the regime eventually declared him a prohibited immigrant. Today he is the president of the British Anti-Apartheid Movement.

ALBERT LUTHULI—Born in 1898, Albert Luthuli was a Zulu chief instrumental in organizing the 1952 Defiance Campaign—a civil rights crusade in which thousands of blacks demonstrated against apartheid. The same year, Luthuli became president-general of the African National Congress. Arrested in 1956, he was released after a year, but in 1959 was banished to his small farm under the Suppression of Communism Act, which prohibited him from attending meetings, from writing for publication, and from being quoted. He was awarded the Nobel Peace Prize in 1960, published his autobiography, *Let My People Go*, abroad in 1962, and died in 1967.

PHAKADE MAGWAZA—An actor who joined Mbongeni Ngema's Committed Artists in 1982, he was involved in the rent campaign in Lamontville township, and took part in *Asinamali* when it began. On February 15, 1984, he was sentenced to eight years imprisonment for his participation in the rent campaign.

SOLOMON MAHLANGU was the first ANC freedom fighter to be hanged by the South African regime. Mahlangu was a Pretoria youth who was caught up in the student revolt of 1976 and left the country to join the ANC. Returning as an armed cadre to South Africa in June 1977, he stumbled into an episode known as the Goch Street killings, in which two whites were accidentally murdered. Although the murders were committed by one of his companions and Mahlangu never fired a shot, he was convicted and executed on April 6, 1979.

NELSON MANDELA, the best-known leader of the African National Congress, has served twenty-four years of a life sentence for his resistance to apartheid. He was born on July 18, 1918, into the royal family of the Tembus of the Transkei, and in the 1940s became a Johannesburg attorney in partnership with Oliver Tambo. Banned from public life, harrassed, and eventually charged with treason by the government for his leadership role in the ANC, Mandela was acquitted with one hundred and fifty-five others in the marathon treason trial of 1956–1961. Defying the regime's efforts to silence him, Mandela went underground after the trial, and began to organize Umkonto we Sizwe, the ANC's military wing. To prepare himself for the coming struggle, he secretly left South Africa and traveled to London and Addis Ababa to meet leaders of independent African states. After seventeen months as a fugitive "black pimpernel," Mandela was apprehended in South Africa by the authorities and imprisoned in November 1962. In May 1964 he was sentenced to life with other leaders of the Umkonto High Command. Intense efforts over many years, both in South Africa and abroad, to achieve his release have thus far been unsuccessful.

WINNIE MANDELA was born in the Transkei in 1934, and became a medical social worker in Johannesburg in the 1950s. She married Nelson Mandela in 1958, and was drawn into the maelstrom of politics in the ANC and the Federation of South African Women. Persecuted relentlessly by the regime, she repeatedly has defied the restrictions placed upon her and over the course of twenty years has become a living symbol of black resistance. In 1969–1970 she was held in solitary confinement for seventeen months as a "detainee"—a prisoner who has not been charged with any crime. In 1976 she was detained for another six months, and in 1977 she was banished to the "Siberia" of a small town in the rural Orange Free State. When her house there was destroyed by a firebomb in 1985, world pressure mounted for her to be permitted to live in her own home in Soweto. "My private self doesn't exist," she has said. "Whatever they do to me, they do to the people of this country."

LUCAS MANGOPE/KAIZER MATANZIMA—two homeland leaders who accepted "nominal independence" from the government of South Africa. They are considered puppets by most blacks.

GOVAN MBEKI is serving a life sentence for his membership in the Umkonto High Command. He was born in the Transkei in 1910, and is the author of two books about the Transkei's political history. Mbeki's activism as an organizer and writer helped to make the eastern Cape area the stronghold of ANC support which it remains today.

OSCAR MPETHA was born in the Transkei in 1909, and became a trade union organizer in the Cape. At the time the ANC was declared an unlawful organization in 1960, Mpetha was serving as ANC Cape provincial president. After black unions won recognition in 1979 and the union movement gathered momentum, Mpetha reemerged as a militant leader of the African Food and Canning Workers. Hated by the regime for his loyalty to the ANC, Mpetha has repeatedly been charged with political "crimes," and is today, at age 76, serving a five year sentence for "terrorism."

GRIFFITHS MXENGE was another political activist who became the victim of a death squad murder. Born in 1935 in the eastern Cape, he served two years on Robben Island in the late 1960s and was detained for several long periods under South Africa's sweeping security laws. As a lawyer, Mxenge defended many other victims of state repression. On November 19, 1981, his body was found near a Durban stadium with multiple stab wounds.

VICTORIA MXENGE's murder followed four years later. A lawyer from the Cape like her husband, Griffiths Mxenge, she acted on behalf of blacks charged with political crimes. On August 1, 1985, she was shot and hacked to death by four never-identified assailants outside her Durban home while her three children looked on in horror.

NAT NAKASA was one of South Africa's most talented young writers of the early 1960s, and the first black journalist to write a column for the liberal *Rand Daily Mail*. In 1964 he was awarded a Nieman Fellowship to Harvard, but the South African government denied him a passport, so he left the country on a one-way exit permit. On July 14, 1965, he committed suicide by jumping from the seventh floor of a building on Central Park West in New York City.

LILIAN NGOYI—Within one year of joining the Women's League of the African National Congress in 1952, Lilian Ngoyi became its president. Her eloquence as a public speaker and energy as an organizer made her a target of the government. In 1956 she was arrested and became one of those prosecuted in the massive Treason Trial that did not end until 1960. Restricted for many years by various bans and forms of house arrest that confined her to her home and prohibited her from having visitors and from holding a job, she died in 1980.

NUSAS—The National Union of South African Students, the most representative body for white university students in the country.

PIET RIETIEF—One of the early settlers who, in the 19th century, was invited by the Zulu king Dingane to come with his soldiers to a feast—while they were feasting Zulu warriors attacked and killed them.

SARIE MARAIS—popular Afrikaans patriotic song.

LENNOX SEBE—One of the leaders of the nominally independent homelands, considered puppets by most blacks.

SECTION 29—One of South Africa's numerous security legislations under which people could be detained without being charged.

WALTER SISULU—Born in the Transkei in 1912, Walter Sisulu rose to become the secretary general of the ANC in 1949, and was sentenced to life imprisonment at the Rivonia trial of 1964 for his membership in the High Command of Umkonto we Sizwe. He is a largely self-educated leader whose dedication to the popular struggle brought him high esteem among blacks and vengeful repression from the ruling whites.

ROBERT SOBUKWE—Born in 1924, Robert Sobukwe was a militant college leader and one of the founders of the Pan Africanist Congress. He was elected its president in 1959. One of the leaders of the 1960 anti-pass laws protests, he was arrested and charged with inciting the destruction of passbooks. After being sentenced to three years' imprisonment, Sobukwe was released in 1963 but promptly detained through an act of parliament for an additional six years on Robben Island. This so-called "Sobukwe clause" permits indefinite detention of political prisoners after their sentences have been served. Finally released in 1969, Sobukwe was restricted by bans and confined to the Kimberley district until his death in 1978.

OLIVER TAMBO—President of the African National Congress, following the imprisonment of former president Nelson Mandela in 1962.

CAN THEMBA immortalized the vibrant life of Sophiatown, an African area of Johannesburg razed by the National Party government in the mid-1950s. A writer for the magazine *Drum*, and later for the *Golden City Post*, he helped to create a distinctive style of tragicomic expression in African fiction. Themba became a banned person in the 1960s—forbidden to publish or speak publicly—and he left South Africa and died in exile.

AHMED TIMOL was a young Muslim teacher who left South Africa in the late 1960s to train as a freedom fighter for the ANC. He was captured by the police after his return to the country and on October 17, 1971, he fell to his death from a tenth floor window at John Vorster Square police headquarters in Johannesburg.

ABRAHAM TIRO shocked the white establishment and galvanized black students by delivering a blistering attack on South Africa's education system in a speech to graduating students at the University of the North in 1972. His subsequent summary expulsion led to campus protests country wide. Tiro, who was a leader in the Black Consciousness movement, left South Africa, and on February 1, 1974, was brutally murdered by a parcel bomb in Botswana.

ANTHONY BOBBY TSOTSOBE was given a death sentence in late 1981 for his part in ANC attacks on a police station at Booysens and an oil plant at Sasolburg. Three days before the sentence was to be carried out in 1983, his sentence was commuted to life imprisonment, following world-wide appeals for clemency.

RICK TURNER died from a death squad bullet when he answered a knock at his door in January 1978 in Durban. As a lecturer at the University of Natal, he had openly supported black resistance and trade union organization. As in all death squad murders, police "investigations" uncovered no clues and led to no arrests.

UMKHONTO WE SIZWE—"Spear of the Nation," the military wing of the ANC, is a guerrilla group fighting for the overthrow of the South African government.

WITS—The University of Witwatersrand, located in Johannesburg. It is the most popular white university and has been called the home of white liberal thought.

ANDREW SIBUSISO ZONDO is presently on death row for planting a bomb in a shopping mall in Amanzimtoti in Natal in December 1985. Five people died in the blast.

PLACES

Albert Street—This Johannesburg street is the location of the Pass Office that controls the influx of black workers to and from the city. Workers often line up for days awaiting permits to seek work. A black born outside the city becomes an illegal immigrant if he loses his job and can be 'endorsed' out of the city back to a homeland. Black men, legal or otherwise, wait in Albert Street for whites driving by who are looking for labourers.

Crossroads—squatter camp

Diepkloof—a township in Soweto

Homelands—Also known as 'Bantustans' and 'Reserves,' the homelands are the tribal areas set aside for blacks. They are run by governments set up by the South African regime. Rather than being 'homes,' they are areas of great devastation and poverty that offer few opportunities for employment. Because young men are recruited away by white industries and mines, homelands such as Kwazulu, the Transkei and Bophutat-swana are populated largely by women, children and old people. Blacks employed in white areas may not bring their families with them. Consequently they often live in all-male hostels, and are able to see their families for only a few weeks at Christmas. Through the apartheid policy of homelands, only 13% of all South African territory is ceded to more than 20 million blacks. The rest of the land, which includes the richest agricultural and mineral areas, is reserved for five million whites.

Joubert Park—a white suburb of Johannesburg

King Williamstown—a black township in the Cape

Limpopo—river in South Africa that forms a significant border with Zimbabwe

Lusaka—capital of Zambia

Modderbee Prison—a maximum security prison outside of Johannesburg

Orange Free State—one of South Africa's four provinces (similar to a state)

Pollsmoor—a prison outside of Cape Town where Nelson Mandela was transferred after being removed from Robben Island.

Regina Mundi—a Roman Catholic Church in Soweto which is usually used for large gatherings of a political nature by the black residents

Robben Island—Surrounded by the icy Atlantic Ocean off Cape Town, Robben Island is the high security prison where black political prisoners are confined.

Sazonwoold—a suburb in Johannesburg

Sharpeville—a black township outside of Johannesburg where, in 1960, sixty-nine people who had been peacefully protesting the use of passes were shot to death by government forces

Sophiatown—a black township in the fifties before the creation of Soweto.

Soweto—This huge black ghetto outside Johannesburg was the scene of the Childrens' Uprising in 1976, which began as a protest against poor education, became a protest against all government policies and ended in riots and the massacre of at least 467 people.

Sun City—A huge pleasure resort and gambling casino in the heart of Bophutatswana. Here top entertainers like Frank Sinatra, Liza Minelli, Olivia Newton-John, Ann-Margaret perform for enormous fees. Here gambling, bare-breasted dancers, miscegenation—all illegal in South Africa—are permitted to South Africans. Sun City offers employment, but it is surrounded by terrible poverty.

Wintveld—squatter camp

Zola Park—park in the township of Zola

MATSEMELA MANAKA (Playwright/Director), poet, playwright and visual artist, was born and raised in Soweto and was inspired to write after the uprisings of June 1986. He has taught school since 1977 and currently serves as an arts administrator and educator at the Funda Arts Centre, where he is also the project director of the Soyikwa Institute of African Theatre. His art has been exhibited all over South Africa, as well as in England and Scandinavia. His plays include *Egoli—The City of Gold,* which won the Fringe Award at the Edinburgh Festival, *Imbumba, Vuka* and *Pula* which have been produced at international theater festivals in London, Edinburgh, Berlin and Copenhagen.

MAISHE MAPONYA (Playwright/Director) started writing plays in the mid-seventies, working with a number of township cultural organizations. *Umbongikazi, Hungry Earth, Dirty Work,* and *Gangsters* have been showcased in Great Britain, Germany, and the Edinburgh Theater Festival. Maponya is also a poet and award-winning actor and is the founder and director of the Bahumutsi Drama Group.

PERCY MTWA (Playwright/Director) was born in Watt-ville, Benoni. He studied as a poet and painter with Mafa Mgwenya and two of his paintings were selected as the best in the Youth Cultural Art Exhibition. He began singing and dancing at the age of 17 and formed a singing group called "Percy and the Maestros" while in high school. After leaving school he worked for Dunlop Industrial Products as a clerk. He continued to sing and dance and won two dance competitions in nightclubs. He also composed and arranged songs and developed choreography for many plays in Daveyton including *Destiny Calls* and *Umthakathi, The Witch*. He also assisted in directing Godfrey Dlamini's *Son of Africa*. In 1979 a successful audition for Gibson Kente resulted in a role as a singer and dancer in *Mama and the Load* which toured extensively throughout South Africa. It was during this tour that his friendship with Mbongeni Ngema began and that initial ideas for *Woza Albert!* were conceived. *Woza Albert!* went on to become a smash hit and took Mtwa to the Edinburgh Festival, London and Berlin, as well as on a long tour of the U.S.A. He and Ngema recently starred in the production in Australia.

Mtwa made his debut as a director with the popular and highly praised play *Bopha!*, which he also wrote. This year he has been a resident director at the Market Theatre, and his production of *Bopha!* appeared at the Traverse Theatre for the Edinburgh Festival, where it received the Fringe Award.

DUMA NDLOVU was born and raised in Soweto, Johannesburg. He worked for *The World* newspaper as a journalist until 1977, when it was banned by the government. After the 1976 uprisings he was one of the founders and later became the president of Medupe Writers' Association, an organization which grew throughout the country and became the voice of young poets and writers. It was banned by the government together with 17 other organizations on October 19, 1977.

He left the country in 1978 for Lesotho and subsequently came to the United States to pursue his studies.

Four years ago he started working with the Harlem based Roger Furman Theatre, where two years later he was to produce the world-acclaimed play *Woza Albert.* In April 1986 he co-produced *Asinamali!* when it made its world premier at the theater.

"In all I do, I pay tribute to the man who has inspired my life and touched it in more ways than one, Bantu Biko," Mr. Ndlovu says. "I hope these efforts will bring a new awareness of South African culture and thus fulfill Biko's vision of using culture and cultural expression to change the world."

MBONGENI NGEMA (Playwright/Director) was born in Verulam, near Durban. Growing up with the rhythms of township music in bars and in the streets, he became a guitarist, performing in many plays in Durban including Lucky Mavundla's *Isigcino* in which he made his acting debut. Later he worked at the Stable Theatre with Kessie Govender, after which he wrote and directed his first play, *The Last Generation.* In 1981 he collaborated with actor Percy Mtwa and Market Theatre Company director Barney Simon in writing and creating the internationally acclaimed *Woza Albert!* In 1982, after touring with *Woza Albert!* in the United States and inspired by the Mexican/American experimental theater company El Teatro Campesino, he started a theatrical group in Durban called the Committed Artists where he wrote and directed *Asinamali!*. In 1985, he won the A.A. Mutual Life Vita Award for Excellence in Direction, and shared the award for Most Promising South African playwright. In addition, *Asinamali!* won the award for Best Play of the Year. Mr. Ngema recently made his entrance into the music world as he wrote, arranged, produced and was lead vocalist for a record album with the African Mbaqanga group, the Soul Brothers, and the Music Unlimited Orchestra. The album is entitled *S'timela Sase-Zola* and has received critical acclaim since its debut last November.

BARNEY SIMON (Director) is three-time winner of the Breytenbach Epathlon. Johannesburg-born, he backstaged for

Joan Littlewood in the late 1950's. In 1961 he joined Athol Fugard in the Dorkay House Rehearsal Room where *Blood Knot* was first staged. He continued holding workshops for eight years and he directed Fugard in *Krapp's Last Tape* and *Hello and Goodbye.* Between 1968 and 1970 he directed plays in New York and Boston and worked as Associate Editor of "New American Review." On returning to South Africa he formed the theater group Mirror I, ". . . a reflecting surface in which we might find an image of ourselves," and three years later founded The Company with Mannie Manim. He directed the opening production of *Marat/Sade.* His many productions include *The Seagull, The Maids, Oedipus, Six Characters in Search of an Author, The Crucible, Lysistrata, Long Day's Journey Into Night, Mother Courage, Medea, People Are Living There, Antigone, Death of Bessie Smith, Trojan Women, Still Life* and *'Night Mother.* Scripts created with actors include *People, Storytime, Call Me Woman, Cincinnati, Outers* and *Woza Albert!* He wrote three scripts for the Nadine Gordimer *Six Feet of the Country* series and directed *City Lovers* which was shown at the New York Film Festival. His production of *Black Dog Inj'emnyama* was presented at the Traverse Theatre as part of the 1984 Edinburgh Festival and travelled to the Tricycle Theatre in London.

In 1985 Mr. Simon directed *Antigone* at the Haifa Municipal Theatre in Israel. This year, he has adapted and directed *The Dybbuk* at the Market Theatre, and has been invited to do a play-making project by the Massachusetts Arts Council which will be based at Brandeis University.